CALLED TO WITNESS

THE GOSPEL AND OUR CULTURE SERIES

A series to foster the missional encounter of the gospel
with North American culture

John R. Franke
General Editor

• •

Volumes Published to Date

Called to Witness

Doing Missional Theology

Darrell L. Guder

WILLIAM B. EERDMANS PUBLISHING COMPANY
GRAND RAPIDS, MICHIGAN / CAMBRIDGE, U.K.

Published 2015 by
Wm. B. Eerdmans Publishing Co.
2140 Oak Industrial Drive N.E., Grand Rapids, Michigan 49505 /
P.O. Box 163, Cambridge CB3 9PU U.K.

Printed in the United States of America

21 20 19 18 17 16 15   7 6 5 4 3 2 1

Library of Congress Cataloging-in-Publication Data

Guder, Darrell L., 1939-
    Called to witness: doing missional theology / Darrell L. Guder.
        pages   cm.   — (The Gospel and our culture series)
    Includes bibliographical references.
    ISBN 978-0-8028-7222-7 (pbk.: alk. paper)
    1. Mission of the church.   2. Church.
    3. Evangelistic work.   4. Missions.   I. Title.

    BV601.8.G785   2015
    266.001 — dc23

                                            2015014137

www.eerdmans.com

To my students at Princeton Theological Seminary from 2002 to 2015,
with whom and from whom I continue to learn
how to do missional theology

Contents

Foreword

In one sense, the use of the adjective "missional" in conjunction with the idea of theology should be seen as an unnecessary redundancy. In the history of the church, it is the missionary encounter with surrounding cultures and the effort to bear faithful witness to the gospel in the midst of these social settings that provides the context for all theological reflection. The New Testament itself is best understood as a collection of writings focused on missiological practice. Paul's letters were written in conjunction with his missionary activity and wrestle with the questions and challenges that arise from the missionary engagement of the church with the world. The Gospels are missional reflections on the life and ministry of Jesus that arise in the context of particular cultural settings and concerns. Indeed, the origins of all the New Testament documents are found in the missionary activity and witness of the earliest Christians who are telling the story of Jesus and reflecting on the implications of that story for themselves and the world around them in the common idioms of their day. The oft-repeated assertion that mission is the mother of theology arises directly from the New Testament. Christian theological reflection has its roots in a missionary praxis connected with the sending of the church to bear witness to the gospel among all the peoples of the earth.

In another sense, however, the adjectival use of "missional" to describe the nature, task, and purpose of theology has become a necessary modifier in the contemporary setting. With the advent of Christendom, the missionary impulse for theology was minimized and the substance of the Western Christian tradition took its distinctive shape "during the long period in which Western Christendom was an almost enclosed ghetto precluded

viii

from missionary advance."[1] In this context the intuitions and assumptions that governed the discourse of theology were increasingly those of Christendom rather than missionary encounter.

This shift had a profound effect on the discipline of theology and led to its virtual separation from the missionary witness of the church. Even as the West faces the eclipse of Christendom and the emergence of an increasingly virulent post-Christian culture most theology is still taught with primary reference to early modern debates and concerns rather than to those of mission. Courses in missiology are generally taught only in the practical theology department of seminaries and are often primarily for those heading overseas. Rarely are such courses taught in the systematics department, and the two disciplines, missiology and systematic theology, have generally evidenced little significant overlap or interaction.

The effort to repair this divide and restore the inherent relationship between mission and theology has resulted in the emergence of missional theology as a distinctive approach to the discipline. A missional approach to theology arises from the conviction that the triune God is, by God's very nature, a missionary God and that therefore the church of this God is missionary by its very nature. From this perspective mission defines the church as God's sent people and is therefore at the very core of the church's reason and purpose for being and should shape all that the church is and does. In the words of the authors of *Missional Church:* "Either we are defined by mission, or we reduce the scope of the gospel and the mandate of the church. Thus our challenge today is to move from church with mission to missional church."[2] Like the challenge facing the church in moving from church with mission to missional church, so the discipline of theology, if it is to serve the church and be faithful to its subject, must move from theology with a mission component to a truly missional conception of theology — that is, one in which mission is at the very core in both concept and method.

This task has captured the attention of commentators, teachers, researchers, practitioners, and consultants alike, and the notion of missional theology has become increasingly ubiquitous among the churches and schools of North America. It seems these days that everyone is mis-

1. Lesslie Newbigin, *The Open Secret: An Introduction to the Theology of Mission,* revised edition (Grand Rapids: Eerdmans, 1995), p. 4.

2. Darrell L. Guder, ed., *Missional Church: A Theological Vision for the Sending of the Church in North America* (Grand Rapids: Eerdmans, 1998), p. 6.

sional. Yet in spite of all this, as one recent observer has noted, "there really is no shared notion about what missional theology is — to this point there has been no substantive crosscurrent of conversation about the parameters and shape of missional theology."[3] The emergence of such a crosscurrent of conversation about the nature, task, and purpose of theology in missional perspective is a crucial phase in the process of its development.

It is precisely at this point that I believe the publication of this collection of essays by Dr. Darrell Guder to be of particular significance in the development of missional theology. For over two decades Guder has been one of the leading voices in conceptualizing and developing the themes of the missional church, missional hermeneutics, and missional theology. While he is perhaps best known as one of the authors and the editor of *Missional Church,* he has also been one of the leading voices in the Gospel and Our Culture Network (GOCN); the missional hermeneutics forum sponsored by the GOCN that has been meeting at the annual meeting of the Society of Biblical Literature; and the American Society of Missiology, serving as president in 2008. In addition, he has also written widely on these themes in books and articles and spoken on them in classrooms and at lecterns throughout the world in both academic and ecclesial settings.

The essays gathered in this volume cover a wide spectrum of concerns relating to the missional turn and its implications for theology, the church, hermeneutics, leadership, and ecumenism. Their breadth is indicative of the comprehensive and interdisciplinary scope of missional theology and its potential significance for all aspects of Christian witness in the world. Their integration of theory and practice admirably demonstrates that the end of missional theology is not simply a textbook or a manual of ideas but rather a way of life. In these ways, as well as others, this volume represents a benchmark in the development of missional theology, gathering together for the first time some of the most significant contributions to the subject from one of its leading exponents.

As such, I hope and believe this volume will have a catalytic effect on the development of missional theology in the years ahead. It provides important and needed definition to the conversation while also pointing to new and unexplored territory in what is still, in many ways, an emerging field of inquiry. Years from now, when the history of missional theology

---

3. Benjamin T. Connor, *Practicing Witness: A Missional Vision of Christian Practices* (Grand Rapids: Eerdmans, 2011), p. 11.

is written, Darrell Guder will be seen as one of its most seminal and influential figures and this volume will stand as one of his most important contributions.

JOHN R. FRANKE, *DPhil*
Professor of Religious Studies and Missiology,
  Evangelische Theologische Faculteit, Leuven
General Coordinator, The Gospel and Our Culture Network,
  North America

Preface

The phrase "missional church" became a theological commonplace after the publication in 1998 of the volume titled *Missional Church: A Theological Vision for the Sending of the Church in North America.*[1] The team of six missiologists who researched and wrote the book intended it as a catalyst for discussion of the challenge posed by Lesslie Newbigin. Since the early 1970s, he had confronted Western Christianity with the fact and its implications that "with the radical secularization of Western culture, the churches are in a missionary situation in what once was Christendom." The consequence is the growing awareness that "a church that is not 'the church in mission' is no church at all."[2] In his many publications, Newbigin pressed the case that the changed context of the West required a profound realignment of the church: this difficult mission field required a church that understood itself comprehensively as the servant and instrument of God's mission. The issues were profoundly theological and foundational, not merely matters of renewal, strategy, or innovation.

In North America, Newbigin's challenge was taken up by the Gospel and Our Culture Network, which began to meet regularly from 1987 on to explore the many ramifications of Newbigin's theological and missiological offensive. The published outcome of its first years of meetings and consultations was the appearance in 1996 of *The Church Between Gospel and Culture:*

1. Darrell L. Guder, ed., *Missional Church: A Theological Vision for the Sending of the Church in North America* (Grand Rapids: Eerdmans, 1998). The six missiologists were Lois Barrett, Inagrace Dieterrich, Darrell Guder, George Hunsberger, Alan Roxburgh, and Craig Van Gelder. Guder served as the project coordinator and edited the volume.

2. Lesslie Newbigin, *The Open Secret: An Introduction to the Theology of Mission*, revised edition (Grand Rapids: Eerdmans, 1995), p. 2.

The Emerging Mission in North America.[3] Its agenda was clearly laid out by George Hunsberger with his essay, "The Newbigin Gauntlet: Developing a Domestic Missiology for North America."[4] As a result of the growing resonance to the Network's work, a grant was given that made a research project possible. The stated purpose of that project was to raise the theological issues that needed to be addressed if the Western church was to be faithful to its missionary mandate. The result was the volume *Missional Church.* The "al" added to "mission" was intended to focus attention on the essentially "missionary nature" of the church, to use the Roman Catholic formulation emphasized by the Second Vatican Council. This constructive intent was connected with a polemic directed against the absence of mission as a major theological theme in the centuries of doctrinal work addressing the nature and purpose of the church in Western Christendom.

The book proved to have the catalytic impact envisioned by its project team. The discussion that ensued was energetic and diverse. Many responded that the authors of the book had found ways to name issues and describe challenges that were long since emerging and awaiting articulation. Since 1998, the term "missional" has become a basic concept in global missiological discourse. At the same time, the term took on a life of its own and soon became as much a cliché as a useful theological formulation. It began to appear in a vast range of publications, many of which had no connection with the basic claim, made by the project, that there were major theological issues that needed to be engaged if the church in the West was to be faithful to its calling.

For the six researchers and authors, the publication of the book has meant continuing involvement in many different aspects of the conversations stimulated by the initiative. It has certainly become a focal point of my work as a missiologist. When I was called to Princeton Theological Seminary at the end of 2001, I was appointed a professor of "missional and ecumenical theology," with the charge and the opportunity to attempt to develop this theme in the form of courses offered in both the theology and the history departments. To my knowledge, it is the first chair to have such a title and charge (but a few others have followed suit). Course development has been the primary focus of my work. It has been rewarding to explore how to teach

3. George Hunsberger and Craig Van Gelder, eds., *The Church Between Gospel and Culture: The Emerging Mission in North America* (Grand Rapids: Eerdmans, 1996).

4. Hunsberger and Van Gelder, eds., *The Church Between Gospel and Culture,* pp. 3-25. The essay appeared in 1991 in the journal *Missiology: An International Review* 29, no. 4 (1999): 391-408.

missional theology through engaging the work of missional thinkers and practitioners such as Lesslie Newbigin, David Bosch, John Mackay, and Karl Barth. Through co-teaching courses with a New Testament colleague, Dr. Ross Wagner, I have had the chance to explore just how "missional hermeneutics" can be taught in close connection to the discipline of Greek exegesis. It has been especially challenging and rewarding to work with a small and very gifted group of doctoral students whose research has already generated major contributions to the growing theological investigation of the missionary nature, purpose, and action of the church.

There has been, as well, a constant flow of invitations to go off campus and participate in diverse ways in the expanding missional theological conversation. This has taken place in conferences, retreats, guest lectures, workshops, and even media interviews. Although we were emphatic in our project that our attention was focused upon North America, there have been exciting opportunities to present lectures on missional theology in Canada, Korea, India, South Africa, Australia, New Zealand, Hungary, Switzerland, Germany, and Denmark. Several of these invitations have entailed the writing of a chapter or a lecture for ultimate publication. In 2010, as I was finishing a five-year term as Dean of Academic Affairs at Princeton Seminary, I reviewed the paper trail of these activities and realized that, without ever intending to do so, I had in fact generated a book of studies on various aspects of missional theology. I began to consider the possibility of publication, but I wanted to be sure that such a step was worth the sacrifice of trees it would entail.

Shortly after returning to the classroom fulltime (2011-2012), I became involved in a reorganization of the Gospel and Our Culture Network and was asked to serve as the Chair of its Board. Linked with the formation of that Board was the decision to ask Dr. John Franke to serve as the Coordinator of the Network. Among his first actions was to pursue with our colleagues at Wm. B. Eerdmans Publishing Company the possibility of resuming the publication of books under the umbrella of the Gospel and Our Culture Network. The first round of publications, from 1996 to 2005, had comprised six titles which had been well received and broadly discussed. Under Dr. Franke's leadership, a second series is now contracted, and this volume is one of the first to appear. I am deeply grateful for Dr. Franke's initiative, for his encouragement of me with this project, and for his willingness to write the foreword for this book.

All of the essays in this book deal with some aspect of "missional theology." They all seek to integrate theology and practice, out of the conviction that a truly missional church cannot function with a false division between thought and action, being and doing. Their themes are shaped by the questions and interests presented to me by my hosts. Sometimes the themes have actually been assigned. In these interactions, I have experienced the power of thoughtful questions. As I follow through on the issues raised about the missional implications of a particular doctrinal theme, I uncover theological insights that have proven, for me, to be instructive as well as stretching.

In preparing these chapters for publication, I am beginning to discover a certain theological centering taking shape. The process is very much formed by the interactions with diverse conversation partners, including those who have invited me to speak. The question-and-answer part of such endeavors has proven especially stimulating and formative. Of course, the classroom interactions and student discussions in class and over coffee have contributed significantly to this emerging sense of a theological center for missional theology. It is risky to give a name to the center that seems to be taking on concrete shape. But with that risk in mind, I offer for the consideration of my readers the possibility that the underlying theme of these diverse studies is "Trinitarian missiocentricity." I am very hopeful that the process of conversation and learning that has generated these chapters will continue the exploration through supportive as well as critical responses.

I would like to acknowledge the very capable editorial work done by two outstanding research assistants, Adam Eitel and Christopher Dela Cruz. I have already expressed my appreciation to John Franke for his encouragement, suggestions for improvement, and for his foreword. It was also very helpful to have the opportunity in January 2013 to teach an intensive D.Min. course on missional theology under the auspices of Pittsburgh Theological Seminary, for which the assigned readings were the essays in this volume. The insights of the pastoral colleagues in that course, half of them from Scotland, guided the final editing process substantially. Each chapter retains some reference to the particular context in which the presentation was originally made. In our editing we have sought to reduce the duplication of content, but given the nature of the "missional theological conversation," certain themes necessarily recur and are developed further.

Working with our colleagues at Eerdmans has always been a wonderful partnership, and I am grateful for their interest in and support of this work, and of the entire GOCN series.

There are many wonderful dimensions to the partnership that my wife and I enjoy together, including our work on the translation of German theology into English. Her contributions to this volume are many and diverse, but chief among them is the supportiveness she has shown in these last years as the missional conversation has required some increase in my travels. The best trips were the ones on which she joined me, and we look forward to more opportunities to do that as retirement approaches.

I would like to dedicate this book to my students and graduates, who have been and continue to be engaged conversation partners. It is a constant encouragement to discover how they are carrying on with the challenging task of translating missional theology into their congregations and ministries. They demonstrate what it means to be "called to witness" as they "do missional theology."

DARRELL L. GUDER
Princeton
Lent 2014

CHAPTER 1

From Mission and Theology to Missional Theology

Introduction: Mission at Princeton Seminary

Although the term "missional" is of recent coinage, the subject of mission has a long and honorable history at Princeton Seminary. The design of the Seminary, as it was drafted and adopted by the General Assembly in 1811, included the intention "to found a nursery for missionaries to the heathen . . . in which youth may receive that appropriate training which may lay a foundation for their ultimately becoming eminently qualified for missionary work."[1] In 1830, the General Assembly resolved to appoint a professor to the faculty "to bear the name and title of the 'Professor of Pastoral Theology and Missionary Instruction,'" arguing that "the spirit of the religion of Jesus Christ is essentially a spirit of Missions," and that the church should therefore "make all her establishment tributary to [this spirit's] advancement."[2] Speaking of the courses that were then offered, Olav Myklebust, the chronicler of

---

1. *Catalogue of Princeton Theological Seminary,* 1947, 11-12, cited in Olav Myklebust, *The Study of Missions in Theological Education,* 2 vols. (Oslo: Forlaget Land og Kirke, 1955), vol. 1, p. 146.

2. Excerpted from the Minutes of the General Assembly of 1830, cited in Myklebust, *Study of Missions,* vol. 1, pp. 147-48.

"From Mission and Theology to Missional Theology," *The Princeton Seminary Bulletin,* new series, 24, no. 1 (2003): 36-54. This essay was originally delivered as the inaugural lecture of the new Henry Winters Luce Professor of Missional and Ecumenical Theology at Princeton Theological Seminary in December 2002. The essay addresses the emergence of "theology of mission" and the transition to "missional theology" with an overview of what this newly named discipline will attempt to accomplish. It was dedicated to Prof. Dr. Eberhard Busch, friend and mentor of the author.

mission in theological education, noted, "So far as we know, these are the first courses on the subject given in a theological seminary or school in the U.S.A. and, in fact, anywhere."[3]

Mission disappeared in the Catalogue after 1855, but in the subsequent decades the theme was certainly present on the campus, judging especially from the way that faculty continued to lecture and write about it. It was a Princeton Seminary student who was the catalyst in 1880 for the formation of the Interseminary Missionary Alliance, which was the forerunner of the Student Volunteer Movement that came on the scene in 1886.[4] Robert Speer reported at the Seminary's centenary in 1912 that in its first century, 410 Princeton graduates had enlisted in foreign mission — that was one out of every thirteen alumni.[5]

Mission returned to the curriculum in 1895 with courses on mission-ary apologetics, mission history, missionary biography, and the biblical ba-sis of missions. Although ensconced in the area of Practical Theology, the Catalogue's description of mission studies indicated that the subject matter ranged across all the theological disciplines but focused on the formation of missionaries. In that same decade, the students at Princeton instituted and endowed the Students' Lectureship on Missions, for which the first lec-turer was James S. Dennis on the subject, "Foreign Missions after a Century." Among his successors in that lectureship in the next years were Robert E. Speer and John R. Mott.[6]

When J. Ross Stevenson became President of Princeton in 1914, he also became the first incumbent of a new Chair of History of Religions and Chris-tian Missions, signaling a shift of the study of mission from its location as a subtheme of Practical Theology to its own curricular area. Samuel M. Zwemer joined the faculty in History of Religions in 1930, bringing years of experience as a missionary in the world of Islam and a strong interest in comparative religions.

With the coming of John Mackay to the Seminary, the tradition of a missiologist-president continued. His experience in Latin America, where

3. Myklebust, *Study of Missions*, vol. 1, p. 149.

4. William Richey Hogg, *Ecumenical Foundations: A History of the International Mis-sionary Council and Its Nineteenth-Century Background* (New York: Harper & Row, 1952; repr. Eugene, OR: Wipf & Stock, 2002), p. 834; the student alluded to was Robert Mateer.

5. R. E. Speer, "Princeton on the Mission Field," in *The Centennial Celebration of the Theological Seminary of the Presbyterian Church in the U.S.A. at Princeton, New Jersey (1912)*, p. 419, cited in Myklebust, *Study of Missions*, vol. 1, p. 364; vol. 2, p. 88.

6. Myklebust, *Study of Missions*, vol. 1, p. 387.

he served with great distinction as an academic theologian and philosopher, was linked with his articulate commitment to the ecumenical movement, in which he was already an internationally recognized leader. He was appointed both President and Professor of Ecumenics, coining the term to define his interest and expertise. Within a year of his arrival, Ecumenics became a subdivision of the Department of History, and the separate area of History of Religions and Christian Missions disappeared from the curriculum. When the International Missionary Council convened in Whitby, Ontario, in 1948, he reported, "In Princeton we have established a new course for which we have minted a new name. We call it ecumenics. By ecumenics we mean 'The Science of the Church Universal,' conceived as a world missionary community; its nature, functions, relations and strategy."[7] This course title became the title of his classic book, published in 1964, a work that makes very clear that the study of mission is a theological and historical discipline. The role of mission studies at Princeton has continued to cross departmental borders in an interdisciplinary fashion. As a member of the Theology Department, Charles West played a major role in the formation of the present doctoral program in Mission, Ecumenics, and the History of Religion, which continues to be at home in the History Department. The establishment of the Luce Chair in Missional and Ecumenical Theology in the Theology Department honors this interdisciplinary tradition, and I am humbled by the cloud of witnesses, these theologians, historians, ethicists, and all of them ecumenists, who have built Princeton's tradition as a major center of mission studies: Stevenson, Zwemer, Christy Wilson, Mackay, West, Shaull, Moffatt, Neely, Jurji, and Ryerson.

Mission Studies as a Practical Discipline

As far as the general development of mission study is concerned, Princeton has been, since early in the twentieth century, out ahead of the larger and much slower process of developing mission's voice within the theological guild. Gerald Anderson, writing in 1961, bemoaned the fact that there was "surprisingly little creative theological endeavor available for guidance" when

---

7. John Mackay, "With Christ to the Frontier," in *Renewal and Advance: Christian Witness in a Revolutionary World*, ed. C. W. Ranson (London: Edinburgh House Press, 1948), p. 203; see also Myklebust, *Study of Missions*, vol. 2, p. 91. See also John Mackay, *Ecumenics: The Science of the Church Universal* (Englewood Cliffs, NJ: Prentice-Hall, 1964).

one turned to the "underlying principles and the theological presuppositions for the Christian mission."[8] In spite of the fact that the subject of mission had been included in a variety of ways in the curricula of theological education since the early nineteenth century, the relationship between theology and mission was mainly seen as a matter of theory and practice. This was the pattern established when the subject of mission first entered into the vocabulary of Western theological education early in the nineteenth century in Germany. Schleiermacher is credited with the invention of the discipline of Practical Theology in his *Brief Outline of the Study of Theology*. In its second edition, he expressly mentioned missions in his discussion of catechetics, noting that a "theory of missions" would be desirable inasmuch as there had not been such a thing up to then.[9]

The view that the study of mission was primarily a practical discipline, focusing on methods and practices and the theory that supports them, reflected the nature of the burgeoning world missionary movement in the nineteenth and early twentieth centuries. The missionary enterprise was a commitment and engagement of Western Christendom, emerging out of its modern revivals and awakenings on both sides of the North Atlantic, and imbued with the unquestioned assumption that the Western Christian tradition represented normative Christianity. David Bosch provocatively describes the modern missionary movement as "mission in the wake of the Enlightenment."[10] It was the enlightened obligation of the Western church to take the gospel, along with the benefits of Western civilization, to the rest of the unevangelized world, confident that the evident superiority of both the Christian faith and its accompanying culture would overcome all resistance and carry the day.

So, as far as the missionary enterprise was concerned, if theological scholarship took notice of it at all, then it did so to inspire enthusiasm for mission and to train students in the skills of mission. The relation of mission to theology was that of a subsidiary ministry practice, training missionaries next to the formation of local pastors.[11] With all of his commitment to

8. Gerald Anderson, ed., *The Theology of the Christian Mission* (New York: McGraw-Hill, 1961), p. 3.

9. Myklebust, *Study of Missions*, vol. 1, pp. 85-86; Johannes Verkuyl, *Contemporary Missiology: An Introduction* (Grand Rapids: Eerdmans, 1978), pp. 6-7.

10. David Bosch, *Transforming Mission: Paradigm Shifts in Theology of Mission* (Maryknoll, NY: Orbis, 2011), pp. 268-353.

11. Next to this emphasis upon missionary formation, the academic study of mission was, by the latter part of the nineteenth century, also generating major areas of scholarship

and support of mission, Charles Hodge never mentioned the subject in his *Systematic Theology*! For the theological guild at the turn of the twentieth century, mission was basically treated as one ministry activity among many in the division of Practical Theology. This reflected the impressive dynamism of the missionary movement, the self-assurance of the Western theological traditions, and the Enlightenment-influenced sense of optimism that global mission was a strategy to be laid out and then accomplished.

Missions and Theology in the Emerging Ecumenical Movement

The planners of the 1910 World Missionary Conference in Edinburgh agreed that there would be no discussion of questions of "doctrine or Church polity" in the program; it was only under these terms that the Anglicans agreed to participate.[12] At the founding meeting of the International Missionary Council at Lake Mohonk in 1921, one of the organizational principles was that "no decision should be sought from the Council and [no] statement should be issued by it 'on any matter involving an ecclesiastical or doctrinal question, on which the members of the Council or bodies constituting the Council may differ among themselves.'"[13] This policy reflected the Western consensus that the mission enterprise was really a matter of commitment to world evangelization and the strategy to do it, not of theology. There was certainly no sense that the hallowed theological traditions of Christendom might themselves be challenged or engaged by the church's missionary enterprise. The theological scholarship that the missionaries took into the non-Western world, wherever they established institutions for pastoral formation, was invariably the theology written and taught in their faculties back home. I well remember a student from Pakistan who told me one day that his theological education in his home seminary had consisted of memorizing the content of Louis Berkhof's *Systematic Theology* — and he was describing the curriculum in the 1980s.

This theological abstinence on the part of the mission discussion could not be maintained. Martin Kähler's much-quoted dictum, "The oldest mission became the mother of theology," from the year 1908, proved to be a valid

---

in anthropology, linguistics, and ethnology, much of which eventually made its way into the social science curricula of the university. See Verkuyl, *Contemporary Missiology,* pp. 10-11.

12. Hogg, *Ecumenical Foundations,* pp. 109, 112-13.

13. Hogg, *Ecumenical Foundations,* pp. 109, 112-13.

description of not only the early church's theological process but of emergent mission theology in the twentieth century.[14] In spite of its declared policy, the International Missionary Council found itself engaged in theological work as early as 1928 in Jerusalem, as it grappled with *The Christian Life and Message in Relation to Non-Christian Systems of Thought and Life*.[15] In order to discuss Christian mission in the encounter with other religions and especially with the emerging ideology of secularism, the participants had to reflect on the gospel itself, the calling of the church, and the meaning of the basic claims of the Christian confession in the changing world context. The theological challenges became more explicit and demanding in the 1930s, when Hendrik Kraemer's *The Christian Message in a Non-Christian World* laid out a compelling agenda for the global discussion of biblical authority, the confession of Jesus Christ as Savior and Lord, and Christian witness in the context of religious pluralism. A survey of the themes and discussions of global mission, as they crystallized in the regular gatherings of the International Missionary Council and later of the World Council of Churches' Commission on World Mission and Evangelism, reveals that a kind of theological discourse was emerging in which mission was clearly more than a method or a strategy. We can see the growing conviction that the study of mission required serious theological engagement with the fundamental loci of the tradition. Something like a "theology of mission" was beginning to take shape.

The Conversation Intensified

The emergence of mission as a theological discipline was a process that was defined, on the one hand, by the fact that the Christian church had become truly global — William Temple spoke of this "great new fact of our time" at his enthronement as Archbishop of Canterbury in 1942.[16] This new fact was, of course, the result of the modern missionary movement. On the other hand, after an extended period of gradual disintegration, it was becoming

14. Martin Kähler, *Schriften zu Christologie und Mission,* Theologische Bücherei, 42 (München: Chr. Kaiser Verlag, 1971), p. 190; see also his discussion of the locus of mission in dogmatics, pp. 105-7.

15. This was the title of volume 1 of the Jerusalem reports: *The Jerusalem Meeting of the International Missionary Council, March 24–April 8, 1928* (London & New York: International Missionary Council, 1928).

16. See Stephen Neill, *Christian Missions* The Pelican History of the Church, 6 (Harmondsworth, UK: Penguin, 1964), p. 15.

clear that the long and complex project defined as Western Christendom was over. Karl Barth wrote in 1935 that "Christendom in the form we have known it until now is at an end."[17] The mission activity generated by the last two centuries of the Christendom project ultimately produced a theological challenge to that project. The issue that intensified the discussion between mission and theology was the question of the church. It soon became clear that the formation of new churches on the mission field could not be simply an exercise in strategy and policy. Nor was it going to prove acceptable simply to transplant Western ecclesiologies into non-Western settings. The concerns that arose with the formation of so-called younger churches in non-Christendom settings raised questions that led, within a few decades, to a fundamental recasting of the theological understanding of the nature and task of the church and of its relationship with its cultural context. These theological issues were relevant not only for the new churches in the non-Western world, but they became a profound concern for the old churches of the West moving from Christendom to post-Christendom. The global Christian movement was confronted with the need to rethink and ultimately to rework the theology of the church. Once that process began to unfold, it became clear that it would not only be ecclesiology that would be challenged by the mission experience; virtually all of the traditional theological loci would, in some way, be called into question.

It is risky to assign specific dates to the chapters and phases of the theological process. As far as the development of the relationship between theology and mission is concerned, however, there can be little question that the theological revolution ignited by Karl Barth, as it interacted with the global discussion of mission, would eventually substantially reshape the theology of mission. Johannes Aagard, the Danish missiologist, spoke of him as "the decisive Protestant missiologist in this generation," and David Bosch described Barth's theology of the church as a "magnificent and consistent missionary ecclesiology."[18] Less than ten years after the appearance of the Romans commentary, Karl Hartenstein, the great German missiologist and strategist, published an essay titled "What Does the Theology of Karl Barth Have to Say to Mission?"[19] In 1932, Barth addressed the Brandenburg

17. Karl Barth, "Das Evangelium in der Gegenwart," *Theologische Existenz heute*, no. 25 (München: Chr. Kaiser Verlag, 1935), p. 33.

18. Johannes Aagard, "Some Main Trends in Modern Protestant Missiology," *Studia Theologica* 19 (1965): 238; see David Bosch, *Transforming Mission*, pp. 382, 399.

19. Karl Hartenstein, *Was hat die Theologie Karl Barths der Mission zu sagen?* (München: Chr. Kaiser Verlag, 1928).

Mission Conference in Berlin on the theme, "Theology and Mission in the Present Situation."[20] This address is frequently, but erroneously, cited as the actual initiation of the theological interpretation that later came to be known as the theology of the *missio Dei*.

In discussing the motive of mission, Barth reminded his hearers that the concept "mission" was used in the ancient church to describe the interrelations of the Trinity as a process of sending: the Father sending the Son, the Father and the Son sending the Spirit. This reference was for Barth a reason to be cautious about all human motives for mission; it has to be a matter of obedience to the "command of the Lord sounding here and now."[21] For, and this is the crux,

> The congregation, the so-called homeland church, the community of heathen Christians should recognize themselves and actively engage themselves as what they essentially are: a missionary community! They are not a mission association or society, not a group that formed itself with *the firm intention* to do mission, but a human community *called* to the act of mission.[22]

With this emphasis upon the missionary vocation of the church and its linkage with the mission or sending of God, Barth gave a profound and shaping impulse to the reorientation of Western ecclesiology that was already fermenting in the mission discussion. The focus was changing from a "church centered mission . . . to a mission centered church," as David Bosch described the process.[23] By the time of the Mission Conference at Willingen, Germany, in 1952, there was a strong, global consensus that the church must be understood as essentially missionary. At the Second Vatican Council, the Roman Catholic Church adopted this missiological ecclesiology in the first principle articulated in *Ad Gentes*: "The Church on earth is by its very nature missionary since, according to the plan of the Father, it has its origin in the mission of the Son and the Holy Spirit."[24]

20. Karl Barth, "Die Theologie und die Mission in der Gegenwart," in *Theologische Fragen und Antworten* (Zollikon: Theologischer Verlag Zürich, 1957), pp. 100-84; my citations are from my translation of this essay.

21. Barth, "Die Theologie und die Mission," p. 115.

22. Barth, "Die Theologie und die Mission," p. 115.

23. David Bosch, *Transforming Mission*, p. 379.

24. *Vatican Council II: The Conciliar and Post-Conciliar Documents*, ed. Austin Flannery, O.P. (Collegeville, MN: Liturgical Press, 1975), *Ad Gentes*, I, p. 814. It is of considerable interest

It is the widespread consensus that the "church is missionary by its very nature" that leads me to suggest that it is now appropriate to speak of "missional theology." I am very aware of the risks involved in proposing an adjectival theology; Helmut Thielicke never tired to warn us of the dangers and traps of such adjectival adventures. In view of the fact, however, that the Western theological tradition has for so long completely ignored the missionary character of the church, and that since the 1930s there has been a significant course correction going on that can best be described as the merging of missiology and ecclesiology, it seems to me that there is emerging a way of doing theology that is shaped by this consensus, and that it is helpful to think about it as "missional theology." Princeton Seminary's decision to introduce an emphasis on missional and ecumenical theology into the Theology Department in 2002 may be seen, I think, as a recognition of the larger process of rethinking and investigation promoted by the consensus of the missional character of the church.

The Case for "Missional Theology"

When Barth delivered his address to the Brandenburg Mission Conference in 1932, he used the phrase "mission *and* theology" to describe their relationship as he understood it. He affirmed that both endeavors shared common ground in that they were activities of the church, that they were forms of confession of Jesus Christ, and that they were acts of ecclesial obedience, doing Christ's will by communicating his message. As human activities, they were risked as acts of faith, totally dependent upon God's grace to justify them. But he saw important, complementary distinctions: mission was oriented to gospel communication to the unbeliever, both inside and outside the church. (Barth developed the provocative concept of the "heathen church" in this address!) For him, theology was that activity which does "reflection on the

---

that Thomas Stransky, the Roman Catholic ecumenist, reports that there was a meeting of leaders of the Commission on World Mission and Evangelism, led by Lesslie Newbigin, with Johannes Schütte and the other drafters of the Vatican II document on the missionary activity of the church *(Ad Gentes)* in April 1965 at Crêt-Bérard in Switzerland. The purpose of their meeting was to rework the first draft that had been rejected by the bishops. Newbigin felt that their meeting might have had some influence on the final missional thrust of the documents. Stransky is blunter: "Crêt-Bérard had just as much influence on the mission document as did the delegated observers to Vatican II on the Decree on Ecumenism." Thomas Stransky, "From Mexico City to San Antonio," *International Review of Mission* 79, no. 313 (January 1990): 44.

rightness of that communicative process." It was a "corrective," the church's necessary and ongoing process of self-critique, emerging constantly out of the encounter with the church's one criterion, "the revelation that founds the church and which confronts us in its prophetic and apostolic testimony."[25] He warned against false distinctions, such as the attempt to define mission as the representation of Christian love and theology as the representation of Christian faith, or claiming that mission is the work while theology is the word, or the former is life and the latter is thought.[26] Rather, they were differing forms of service, one directed toward the world into which the church is sent, and one directed toward the church as it seeks to understand its calling.

"Theology *and* mission" gradually evolved in the 1940s and 1950s into the language of "theology *of* mission" and "mission theology." In his presidential address to the Ghana Assembly of the International Missionary Council in 1958, John Mackay described the "apocalyptic hour" in which Christian mission found itself at the time, and made this appeal:

> In such a situation, and at such a time, the question takes on new meaning: "What is the Christian mission at this hour?" Let me attempt to answer the question. The time is clearly ripe to probe deeply into the theology of *mission;* it is no longer to raise questions regarding the policy of *missions.* The basic question confronts us: What does *mission — mission of any kind* — mean? What does it signify to have a sense of mission?[27]

Mackay's appeal was finding respondents, especially in the productive discussion that emerged from the Willingen meeting of the International Missionary Council in 1952. Many were asking, "What does mission mean?" There was a rapid expansion of literature in which the relationship between mission and theology was explored and a variety of terminological options was offered.[28] David Bosch described this evolving relationship between

25. Barth, "Theologie und Mission," pp. 102-3.

26. Barth, "Theologie und Mission," p. 106.

27. John Mackay, "The Christian Mission at This Hour," in *The Ghana Assembly of the International Missionary Council, 28th December 1957 to 8th January 1958,* ed. Ronald K. Orchard (London: Edinburgh House Press, 1958), p. 104.

28. See, for example, Wilhelm Anderson, *Towards a Theology of Mission: A Study of the Encounter between the Missionary Enterprise and the Church and Its Theology* (London: SCM, 1955); Georg Vicedom, *Missio Dei: Einführung in eine Theologie der Mission* (München: Chr. Kaiser Verlag, 1958); Gerald Anderson, ed., *The Theology of the Christian Mission* (New York: McGraw-Hill, 1961); Charles Van Engen, *Mission on the Way: Issues in Mission Theology*

mission and theology with the phrase, "From a Theology of Mission to a Missionary Theology."[29] When a research team of the Gospel and Our Culture Network set out to investigate the question, "If one were to do one's ecclesiology missiologically, what would it look like?," we decided to title our findings *Missional Church*, which we published in 1998. We did so, in part, because the other available adjectives such as "missiological" or "missionary" had their problems, and we wanted the freedom to define what we meant with this new term.[30]

There are several models to which we can turn if we want to see what a missional theology might look like. The entire theological production of Lesslie Newbigin and John Mackay can be aptly described with this term. Missiologists in general, as I mentioned already, look to Karl Barth as a major exponent of missional theology, even though he did not use the term and, in 1932, stated the relationship with an "and": "mission and theology." It is possible, however, to trace an intensification of the linkage between mission and theology in Barth's own process as he moved through the project of the *Church Dogmatics*. You will remember that he unfolds his ecclesiology under and in interaction with the doctrine of salvation, his soteriology. After expounding his understanding of soteriology as justification, he turns immediately to "The Holy Spirit and the Gathering of the Christian Community."[31] The understanding of the church that emerges is well summarized with the statement that the church's mission is not secondary to its being; "the church exists in being sent and in building up itself for the sake of its mission."[32] This is a succinct definition of the "missional church." The discussion of soteriology as sanctification is followed by the exposition of "The Holy Spirit and the Upbuilding of the Christian Community."[33] This leads on to his explication of soteriology as vocation, in which he lays out in detail the character of Christian being as the calling to witness. It is, then, followed by his treatment of "The Holy Spirit and the Sending of the Christian Community" — which

---

(Grand Rapids: Baker, 1996). He defines "mission theology" as multidisciplinary, integrative, definitional, analytical, and truthful (pp. 17-31).

29. David Bosch, *Transforming Mission*, pp. 504-8.

30. Darrell L. Guder, ed., *Missional Church: A Vision for the Sending of the Church in North America* (Grand Rapids: Eerdmans, 1998).

31. Karl Barth, *Church Dogmatics* (Edinburgh: T. & T. Clark, 1956; German: 1953), IV/1, ¶61, pp. 514-642; ¶62, pp. 643-749.

32. Karl Barth, *Church Dogmatics* IV/1, ¶62, p. 725 (David Bosch's translation in *Transforming Mission*, p. 381).

33. Karl Barth, *Church Dogmatics* IV/2, ¶66, pp. 499-613; ¶67, pp. 614-726.

could be translated as the "mission" of the Christian community.[34] In his treatment of the various dimensions of the ministry of this sent community, he addresses the task of theology again, now as one of the word ministries (following the praise of God, proclamation of the gospel, instruction, evangelization, and mission). It seems to me that, by this time in Barth's project, the distinction between theology *and* mission is less compelling, and the explanation of the role of theology for the missional church would justify describing it as "missional theology." He wrote:

> There would be no theology if there were not a community obligated in a special way to the witness of its word. Its central problem is posed for theology not in an empty space but by the community's [service], and this is the problem that constitutes theology as a science next to other sciences. If one disregards its origin in the [service] of the community, then all of its problems would lose their theological character, if they had not become ephemeral already, and they would be consigned to the area of general and especially historical arts and letters. . . . In the [service] of theology, the community tests all that it does on the basis of the criterion given by its commission, ultimately and finally in the light of the word of its Lord and Commissioner.[35]

The Motive, Matter, and Manner of Missional Theology

In his 1932 address, Barth focused on the way that theology *accompanied* mission in its work, raising questions about the motive, the appeal, the task, and the proclamation of mission. In the meantime, we have arrived at the broadly affirmed consensus that the church is missionary by its very nature, and we are exploring the theological implications of that consensus. If we assume that our task is aptly described as missional theology, then it seems to me that it is now appropriate to invert Barth's process and suggest that mission accompanies theology by asking questions about theology's motive, matter, and manner. Or, in slightly different terms, if the church is mission-

---

34. Karl Barth, *Church Dogmatics* IV/3, 2nd half, ¶71, pp. 481-680; ¶72, pp. 681-901. I am indebted to David Bosch for this insightful overview of the design of Barth's project in *Transforming Mission*, p. 382.

35. Karl Barth, *Kirchliche Dogmatik* IV/3, 2nd half, ¶72, p. 1007 (my translation; in the ET, see p. 879).

ary by its very nature, *why* do we do theology, *what* do we do when we do missional theology, and *how* do we do missional theology?

The motive of missional theology is derived from the church's missional vocation. That vocation is the will and command of the church's Lord, and the formation of this community for its missional vocation is the work of the Spirit promised and sent by the Lord of the church. This is the common and pervasive message of the apostolic kerygma and its scriptural record. "You shall be my witnesses"; "as my Father has sent me, so I send you"; "go into all the world and disciple the nations." You are "a chosen race, a royal priesthood, a holy nation, a people for God's own possession, so that you may proclaim the excellencies of Him who has called you out of darkness into His marvelous light" (1 Pet. 2:9).

When mission accompanies theology, when it defines the way theology works, then it becomes the task of such missional theology to accompany and support the church in its witness by testing all that the church says and does in terms of its calling to be Christ's witness. Now, if the criterion for that process of theological testing is the self-revelation of God, the Three in One, and if that self-revelation is preserved for the continuing life and work of the church in history in the Word of God written, and if that Word of God defines the people of God as a missionary people whose task is witness, then missional theology will serve the missional church by attending to the way in which that church is formed by the scriptural testimony for its vocation. There is a hermeneutical corollary to the understanding of the essentially missional nature of the church: The scriptural testimony is to be understood as the empowered testimony that God's Spirit uses for the continuing formation of the church for its missional calling. James Brownson put it succinctly in a recent public presentation: "Early Christianity is a missionary religion."[36] The congregations founded by the first missionaries had, as their purpose, the continuation of the witness that had led to their founding. The writings that became the canonic New Testament all functioned basically as instruments for the continuing formation of these communities for the faithful fulfillment of their missional vocation. The first theological work of the church is found in the epistles and gospels that focus on the concrete situations of missional congregations and their

36. James Brownson, Presentation at the Additional Meeting on "A Missional Approach to Teaching Bible and Theology: Breakfast Sponsored by Tyndale College (Toronto)," Sunday, November 24, 2002, AAR/SBL, Toronto; see also James Brownson, *Speaking the Truth in Love: New Testament Resources for a Missional Hermeneutic* (Harrisburg, PA: Trinity Press International, 1998).

witness — here we see the earliest instance of mission functioning as the mother of theology. This biblical formation of the church requires a missional hermeneutic that constantly asks, "How did this written testimony form and equip God's people for their missional vocation then, and how does it do so today?" All the resources of historical, critical, and literary research on the biblical testimony can and must contribute to the church's formation by illumining all the dimensions of this fundamental question.[37] The goal of the process is the continuing formation of the church so that it "leads its life worthy of the calling with which it has been called." (See e.g., Eph. 4:1-2; 1 Thess. 2:12; Phil. 1:27.)

Defining the motive of missional theology as I have done might sound like license to define in a very global way the matter, the what, of missional theology. There is a danger here, of course, of falling into the trap described by Stephen Neill's remark, "If everything is mission, then nothing is mission."[38] I frankly confess that, as far as the motive of our theological work is concerned, I would like to think as comprehensively and globally as possible. John Mackay was right when he observed at the Ghana meeting of the International Missionary Council in 1958, "The Church's structure and doctrine, her liturgy, and even her sacraments, fulfill their highest function when they prepare the people of God to be the servants of God."[39] The formation of the church for mission should be the motivating force that shapes and energizes our theological labors in all their diversity and distinctiveness. The matter of missional theology will necessarily be more limited and selective, since it must always relate to particular contexts within time and history. It would be presumptuous for a Western theologian to define the matter of missional theology for a colleague working in India, or Indonesia, or Korea, although one can and should have very stimulating conversations about our common themes of interest. Missional theology is not universal theology, but always and essentially "local," that is, working out of and in critical interaction with a particular strand of Christian tradition in a particular cultural context. For us in the North Atlantic world, the matter of missional theology has its own challenges and themes, shaped by our history and especially by the profound paradigm shift through which we are passing from Christendom into post-Christendom. The ecumenical process, at which level the consensus of the

37. For further discussion of "missional hermeneutics" see David Bosch, *Transforming Mission*, pp. 15-180, and the literature cited there; Darrell Guder, *The Continuing Conversion of the Church* (Grand Rapids: Eerdmans, 2000), pp. 49ff., esp. 52 notes 7-9.

38. Stephen Neill, *Creative Tension* (London: Edinburgh House, 1959), p. 81.

39. John Mackay, "The Christian Mission at This Hour," p. 121.

essentially missionary nature of the church is most clearly articulated and bearing fruit, constantly calls us to account and raises questions for us as we contend with our particular story in our part of the world. But we have our own tasks to address as heirs of the Christendom legacy and resident aliens in a post-Christendom context that has become, in a very short period of time, one of the world's most difficult mission fields.

This question of the matter of missional theology also refines our understanding of its motive. For the critical and evaluative motive for the doing of theology includes within its responsibility the formation of servant leaders for the church. When we describe theology as missional, then we do imply that the work of theology is not an end in itself but is related to God's mission in the world. We focus upon the church's theology *and* the church's theologians, its teaching elders, those who are called and gifted to equip the saints for the work of ministry as the apostolic, prophetic, evangelistic, pastoral, and pedagogical ministers of the Word (Eph. 4:11f.).

A consideration of the matter of missional theology in our context leads quite concretely to the curricular question. What are the theological content areas that this particular missional theologian might be expected to work on in the courses he proposes to his colleagues? How will this assumption that the church is missional by its very nature be reflected both in the area of theological research and in the classroom enterprise? As I project the work I hope to do in this area over the next years, I am compelled by the desire to be a good steward of the already well-developed and provocative process of missional theology that has coalesced in the last seven decades. There is much work to be done simply carrying forward the discussions and themes that are already on the agenda. Because it is an ecumenical process, part of the challenge is to engage the diverse missional theologies of the church around the world in ways that will benefit, challenge, and hold accountable our theological research and teaching in our particular North Atlantic context.

As I have already implied, the work of a missional theologian in our context will have to focus upon the Christendom project and its disintegration. We have to ask about the impact of the Christendom project upon the missional vocation of the church in the West. We have to investigate how this fascinating and complex *corpus Christianum* has shaped our understanding of the gospel and our ways of reading and interpreting Scripture. Barth argued that there are two ways to read this legacy, critically and positively, as both a sequence of accommodations to the world for the sake of acceptance and survival, and as a promising reflection of the incarnation, an anticipation of a world totally subject to God and his Christ.[40] It appears to me that one aspect of the critical investigation of our legacy will focus upon the compromises and reductionisms we have made in our theologies as a result of our accession to hegemonic power and privilege in Western civilization. The roots of the problem of cheap grace as Bonhoeffer defined it go back very far in our history to early accommodations: the reduction of salvation to individual savedness, the separation of the message of the kingdom of God from the proclamation of the gospel of salvation, the reduction of the church's mission to the maintenance of individuals' salvation, the reduction of general vocation to clericalism, the reduction of the sacraments to individual salvific rites.[41] We must also examine the ways in which we have lost sight of the missional vocation of the early Christian movement, reflected in the distinctive kind of communities they were called to be and actually were. Our biblical scholarship will be a constant challenge to us to hear Paul's admonition that "we are to be no longer conformed to this world" (Rom. 12:2).

All of the classical loci of theology are, in some way, engaged by the matter of missional theology. We have spoken of the complex interactions between soteriology and ecclesiology. Christological issues will also continue to claim the attention and discipline of the missional theologian and will motivate explorations in partnership with systematicians, historians of doctrine, and social ethicists. The confession of the lordship of Christ and of the universal scope of the work of salvation has led to more than one tense encounter among Christians, and between Christians and adherents of other religions. The issues raised by such episodes are not merely matters of tactics or tact, but of fundamental theology, the discussion of which must be marked by patient, sensitive conversation with people of enormously diverse convictions. The missional theologian, working always from and for the biblical formation of the witnessing community, will be particularly attentive to the various ways in which we sinful Christians attempt to dilute or evade the scandal and foolishness of the gospel of the crucified Jesus. We will also be both patient and supportive as we encounter Christian communities in non-Western cultures that have to make their way through their own version of the Christological heresies that dominated our history for

40. Karl Barth, "Das Evangelium in der Gegenwart," pp. 30ff.; see also Eberhard Busch, "Die Kirche am Ende ihrer Welt-geltung: zur Deutung der Ekklesiologie Karl Barths," unpublished lecture, 1999, p. 2.

41. Dietrich Bonheoffer, *The Cost of Discipleship*, trans. R. H. Fuller with I. Booth (New York: Macmillan, 1959), pp. 35-37. See, on reductionism, Guder, *Continuing Conversion*, chapters 5-6.

our first six centuries. Perhaps our history can be helpful to them; perhaps they can use our experience fruitfully as they come to their own confession of the humanity and deity of Christ. But we cannot preempt the necessary struggle with that scandal and foolishness wherever the question is rehearsed again, "Who do people say that I am?"

Also part of the Christological discussion is the current focus upon issues of gospel and culture, which emerged in the 1990s as a major theme for the global discussion of missional theology. Western theologians are particularly challenged by our common tendency to look upon the Christendom legacy as somehow normative Christianity and normative Christian theology. The global church, the "great new fact of our time," will constantly demonstrate the fundamental translatability of the gospel, its powerful destigmatization of all cultures, and its concomitant relativization of all cultures — themes to which Lamin Sanneh has made us sensitive.[42] From every such passage of gospel translation from one culture to another, the missional theologian learns and is obligated to find out how to pass that learning along in ways helpful to the church in one's own context. With the growing emphasis upon the cultural distinctiveness of the contextualized church, there is good theological reason to pay careful attention to the catholicity of the multicultural church. The task that particularly must occupy the missional theologian examines how we learn to articulate and celebrate the oneness of the gospel in the great diversity of its witness. Lesslie Newbigin, as a bicultural missional theologian, shaped as much by India as by his British roots, is an especially important mentor for missional theology in the West, as we try to sort out the differences and interactions between the gospel, the church, and our Western cultures.[43]

The rapid expansion of the Pentecostal and charismatic communions poses questions and themes for the missional theologian. How do we understand the work of the Holy Spirit in the formation of the church? What have the old churches of the West perhaps lost with regard to the power and work of the Holy Spirit, which was present in early Christianity and is being reclaimed in the contemporary flourishing of Pentecostal churches? These are particularly important and difficult challenges for a missional theologian shaped by the Reformed tradition who certainly is alert to the significance

42. Lamin Sanneh, *Translating the Message: The Missionary Impact on Culture* (Maryknoll, NY: Orbis, 1989).

43. The best introduction to this aspect of Newbigin's work is George R. Hunsberger, *Bearing the Witness of the Spirit: Lesslie Newbigin's Theology of Cultural Plurality* (Grand Rapids: Eerdmans, 1998).

of the internal testimony of the Holy Spirit but skeptical about certain gifts of the Spirit that are said to be requisite for sanctification! And yet there is real danger that our theological caution could lead us to miss what the Spirit is doing in the churches.

Another way to speak of the matter of missional theology in our setting would be to consider the particular conversation partners whose work is of formative importance for the church in North America. I have betrayed the names of my particular conversation partners in this enterprise in the course of this essay: Karl Barth, David Bosch, John Mackay, and Lesslie Newbigin. These are four missional theologians whose work will undoubtedly demand attention and discipline for many years. There are, of course, many more, especially when we look over our denominational fences and engage our Roman Catholic and Orthodox brothers and sisters. But it seems to me that there is still a great deal of work to be done in order for us to derive from the work of these missional theologians all that is there that could guide, challenge, and perhaps correct us in our attempts to be faithful to the church's vocation. The formation of leadership in the area of missional theology for the next generations will produce leaders who will develop its insights and skills in no small measure from the disciplined engagement with their work and issues.

I have spoken briefly about the motive and matter of missional theology. The term "missional" also speaks to the *manner* with which we do theology. There is an adverbial function as well as an adjectival function to the term. Here, I am thinking of the distinctive ways in which our theological work and life together share in the church's missional mandate as witness to the gospel. How do we lead our life as a theological community worthy of the calling with which we have been called?

The term "ecumenical" certainly addresses the manner of missional theology. The fact that the church is truly a global movement, multicultural, multilingual, and multistructural, should result in a theological manner that is modest, aware of its limitations, and open to learning through interaction with the ecumenical church. The real art of the missional theologian is to learn how to do theology modestly and yet with conviction. John Mackay serves us as a mentor in this regard. It is fascinating to see, for instance, in his treatment of *Ecumenics: The Science of the Church Universal,* how naturally and eloquently he moves back and forth from discussion of the "what" of our proclamation to an investigation of "how" we do it.[44] His longstanding

44. For one example see John Mackay, *Ecumenics,* pp. 172-86.

emphasis upon the incarnational character of Christian mission ultimately bore fruit in the worldwide attention to "mission in Jesus Christ's way" that became a theme of missional conversation in the 1980s.[45]

The ecumenical manner of doing missional theology will also insist on integrity in our work. It has to do with worthy living, with the character of our corporate life and the ways in which it provides evidence of the healing work of God's love, before a watching world. Another way to speak of this integrity is to emphasize the congruence of the message and the way it is communicated. Mackay spoke of this as "the incarnational principle," the enfleshing of the good news in the behavior of the community and its members. It evokes an understanding and practice of theological discipline that reflects that the gospel is about healing, shalom, reconciliation, forgiveness, and new beginnings.

Finally, it is an essential aspect of the manner of missional theology that we go about it both patiently and expectantly. It is not for us to know the *chronos* time or the *kairos* time that are solely under God's sovereignty (Acts 1:7), which is difficult for us as late moderns to accept. We are still quite sure that we are capable of organizing the kingdom, that we know the shape of heaven on earth and can bring it about with the right strategies, resources, and personnel. The manner of missional theology is one of confident waiting while carrying out the task assigned to us now: witness. One of the most urgently needed outcomes of our reclamation of the missional character of the New Testament witness is the gift of eschatological confidence: God will complete the good work God has begun in us (Phil. 1:6). Our task is to "gird up the loins of our mind, to be sober, and to set our hopes completely on the grace that will be brought to us at the revelation of Jesus Christ" (1 Pet. 1:13).

45. See especially the documentation of the World Council of Churches' World Conference on Mission and Evangelism at San Antonio in 1989, *International Review of Mission* 78, nos. 311-12 (July/October 1989).

CHAPTER 2

The *missio Dei*:
A Mission Theology for after Christendom

Mission within Christendom and the Emerging Critique

The thesis of this essay is that the theological consensus on the missional nature of the church that has emerged since the 1930s constitutes a major critique of the entire theological project of Western Christendom. The irony is that this critique has developed parallel to the obvious decline of that Western Christian tradition. To make this case, we examine first of all the emergence of the *missio Dei* consensus.

It is one of the major areas of consensus in the global missiological discussion today that authentic theology needs to be "contextual," "local," at home in and relevant to the particular setting within which a Christian community confesses and witnesses to its faith. This means, of course, that the theological discourse itself is by definition multicultural, and that no particular cultural articulation of Christian faith and practice may make the claim to be "normative." As Lamin Sanneh has argued, the necessarily multicultural and translatable character of the gospel has the effect of "destigmatizing" all cultures while precluding any particular claim to normativity.[1] For the long-established churches of Western Christendom, this

---

1. Lamin Sanneh, *Translating the Message: The Missionary Impact on Culture* (Maryknoll, NY: Orbis, 1989), pp. 28-34, 51-56.

This essay was presented in May 2004 to "The Consultation on 'Interrogating Mission Today,'" a joint research project of the Center of Theological Inquiry in Princeton and the United Theological College, Bangalore, India. The essay, together with all of the papers of this research project, were published in Max L. Stackhouse and Lalsangkima Pachuau, eds., *News of Boundless Riches: Interrogating, Comparing, and Reconstructing Mission in a Global Era*, vol. 1 (Delhi, India: ISPCK, 2007), pp. 3-25.

movement from normativity to theological and cultural pluralism has been a difficult readjustment; the attitudes of theological and cultural hegemony, of entitlement to the claim of representing definitive Christianity, die hard. It is ironic that Christendom's pretensions to special authority in the global theological conversation should continue at the very time that the internal state of Western Christianity must be described as "in decline," both numerically and in terms of cultural influence. The "next Christendom" is now the theme of growing attention,[2] and its centers of vitality are found increasingly in Africa, Latin America, parts of the Orient, and the South Pacific.

The waning of the traditional structures and privileges of established Christendom has been paralleled by an important shift in the theological approach to mission, especially in the West. It has been a complex process. As already discussed in the previous chapter, traditional Western theology has really had little or no interest in missions, except as a term to describe the internal dynamics of the triune godhead. But beginning with Karl Barth's lecture on "Theology and Mission" in 1932 (although actually anticipated by his theological work from the Romans commentaries onward),[3] this theological deficit was beginning to be challenged. Rather than seeing mission as a subdivision of practical theology, a consensus going back to Schleiermacher,[4] it now was defined within the larger understanding of the Trinity.

This emerging theology of mission, and ultimately, of the missional church, focuses on God's saving and healing purposefulness over against the creation both loved by him and in rebellion against him, and on his actions to bring about the healing of this creation. God's mission, testified to by the long story of Israel's call and pilgrimage, arrived at its climax in the life, ministry, death, and resurrection of Jesus the Christ. The Jesus event brought about the reconciliation of humanity with God, heralded the in-breaking reign of God in human history through the authority given the risen Jesus Christ "in heaven and on earth" (Matt. 28:18), and through the gift of the Holy Spirit empowered the formation of the witnessing community to

---

2. Philip Jenkins, *The Next Christendom: The Coming of Global Christianity* (Oxford: Oxford University Press, 2002).

3. Karl Barth, "Die Theologie und die Mission in der Gegenwart [1932]," *Theologische Fragen und Antworten* (Zollikon: Theologischer Verlag Zürich, 1957), pp. 100-126; see also Karl Hartenstein, *Was hat die Theologie Karl Barths der Mission zu sagen?* (München: Chr. Kaiser Verlag, 1928).

4. O. G. Myklebust, *The Study of Missions in Theological Education,* 2 vols. (Oslo: Egede Instituttet, 1955), vol. 1, pp. 85-86; see Johannes Verkuyl, *Contemporary Missiology: An Introduction* (Grand Rapids: Eerdmans, 1978), pp. 6-7.

continue making known this good news of God's action "to the ends of the earth" (Acts 1:8). The continuation of that mission, in the tension between the "already" of God's action in Christ and the "not yet" of the consummation of all that God has both promised and begun, focuses upon the witness of God's called-out people. That witness is now intended to reach out across all cultural, ethnic, and social boundaries in the expansion of the called and sent people of God as the "ecclesia." The biblical witness to God's action is thus interpreted as both the testimony to God's mission and its implementation through those whom God calls and equips to be the agents, signs, and foretastes of his desired restoration of all creation to wholeness (= salvation). David Bosch summarized the theology of *missio Dei* as essentially Trinitarian: "[T]he classical doctrine on the *missio Dei* as God the Father sending the Son, and God the Father and the Son sending the Spirit . . . expanded to include yet another 'movement': Father, Son, and Holy Spirit sending the church in the world."[5] Daniel Migliore builds on Bosch when he states that

> the nature and mission of the church are grounded in the nature and missionary activity of the triune God. The mission of the church is to participate in the reconciling love of the triune God who reaches out to a fallen world in Jesus Christ and by the power of the Holy Spirit brings strangers and enemies into God's new and abiding community.[6]

The polemic force of this missional consensus confronts Western Christendom in very telling ways. The first, Roman Catholic missionary program of the West defined mission as the "planting of the church" *(plantatio ecclesiae),* whereby the planted church was an extension of European Christendom. The more individualistic Protestant mission that first began to spread outward from the North Atlantic in the eighteenth century had a meager theology of the church (it was, after all, carried out primarily by missionary societies, many of them lay, with little actual support from the established churches of Christendom). The churches formed by this dynamic movement tended, at least initially, to function as the "receptacle for converts," while the missionary emphasis continued to be upon soul-winning. In either form, the church was understood largely as the extension of normative Christendom

---

5. David Bosch, *Transforming Mission: Paradigm Shifts in Theology of Mission* (Maryknoll, NY: Orbis, 1991), pp. 399-400.

6. Daniel Migliore, "The Missionary God and the Missionary Church," *The Princeton Seminary Bulletin,* new series, 19, no. 1 (1998): 14-15.

structures in their Western cultural forms. The enterprise was one of cultural, theological, and ecclesiastical "diffusion," to cite Sanneh's terminology.[7] By this is meant the spreading outward of Western Christianity as both the faith "once delivered" and the cultures that normatively express it. When carried out in partnership with colonialism, as was often although not always the case, this mission process was engaged in cultural imperialism and the oppression of alleged "primitive" cultures and their religions. In spite of the resistance and resentment often caused by such polluted strategies, this very ambiguous mission movement generated the formation and expansion of new churches that have, in the course of the twentieth century, become the majority of the world Christian population.

The enterprise became obviously even more problematic when the "sending churches" begin to show signs of decline within their own cultures. The traumatic impact of World War I in Europe upon the missionary enterprise around the world revealed the crisis of the Western hegemony in mission.[8] For at least some theologians and church leaders, the horrors of that war made it virtually impossible for Western cultures to continue to define themselves as "Christian nations." A theological process began that pointed towards a radical reorientation of the church to God's mission, beginning with the candid admission that the church of the West was as pagan as any so-called pagan mission field.[9] The Western church could make no claims to spiritual or theological preeminence; instead, the gospel challenged precisely Western Christendom to confess its distortions and reductionisms of the gospel and to be converted to a renewed commitment to its authentic mission. The various voices of such a call to conversion (Kierkegaard, Barth, Thurneysen, Bultmann, Bonhoeffer, Visser 't Hooft, Temple) were gradually becoming a choir. But the attitudes of Christendom hegemony proved and continue to be very resistant to that conversion, and the mindset of Christendom persists in congregations, church administrations, and seminary classrooms.

If, however, the Christian mission is God's mission, rooted in the very character and purposes of God, and if God's mission is directed towards the entire world ("God was in Christ reconciling the world . . ."), then a Euro-

---

7. Sanneh, *Translating the Message*, pp. 29-34, 54-69.

8. William Richey Hogg, *Ecumenical Foundations: A History of the International Missionary Council and Its Nineteenth-Century Background* (Eugene, OR: Wipf & Stock, 2002 [1952]), pp. 165-201.

9. Barth, "Die Theologie und die Mission," *passim*; Hartenstein, *Was hat die Theologie Karl Barths der Mission zu sagen?*

centered theology and practice of mission, as developed in Western Christendom, must necessarily be reductionistic. In its tendency to reduce the
gospel to individual salvation, it fails to confess the fullness of the message
of the inbreaking reign of God in Jesus Christ. In its tendency to make the
church into the institution that administers that individual salvation, it fails
to confess the fullness of the church's vocation to be, do, and say the witness
to that reign of God breaking in now in Jesus Christ.[10] In its bondage to
Western cultural expressions coupled with the unquestioned assumption
that these traditions represent "normative Christianity," this approach effectively reduces the essentially multicultural and multi-organizational character of the church catholic that was intended by Jesus and so founded by the
apostolic mission. Thus, the *missio Dei* consensus is, theologically, a massive
critique of the Christendom theology project, especially in its various defor-
mations into ideologies captive to other gods. As we stated at the beginning,
it is ironic that this consensus has been emerging precisely at the time that
Christendom's decline was becoming obvious.

The *missio Dei* Discussion and the Shift to a Post-Christendom Context

The theological reorientation stimulated by the focus upon the *missio Dei*
centers on a Trinitarian rereading of soteriology and ecclesiology, with implications across the classical *loci*. The process has generated a further major
critique and course correction for Christendom theology by its reformu-
lation of the theology of election. This theological *locus* has reflected the
individualistic reductionism of the gospel already mentioned, preoccupation
with who is saved, who is not, and how one knows or does not know. Coming
from different although complementary directions, Karl Barth and Lesslie
Newbigin redefined election as "calling to witness" or "calling to God's service," thus making it an aspect of God's initiative in carrying out the *missio
Dei.*[11] God's healing purpose embraces all of creation, and God's electing
action in Israel and the engrafted church serves the accomplishment of that
purpose. Lesslie Newbigin put it very succinctly in his impassioned plea at

10. See Darrell L. Guder, *The Continuing Conversion of the Church* (Grand Rapids: Eerdmans, 2000), pp. 97-141.

11. Karl Barth, *Church Dogmatics* IV/3.2, ed. G. W. Bromiley and T. F. Torrance, trans.
G. W. Bromiley (Edinburgh: T. & T. Clark, 1962), pp. 561-73; Lesslie Newbigin, *The Open Secret: An Introduction to the Theology of Mission* (Grand Rapids: Eerdmans), pp. 30-34, 66-90.

the 1996 World Conference on Mission and Evangelism in Salvador/Bahia, Brazil (one of his last public appearances):

> ... I plead that we stop arguing about whether or not other people are going to be saved. I do not believe that this is our business. I do not believe that we have a mandate to settle those questions. We know from the teaching of Jesus that one thing is sure — that at the end there will be surprises; that those who thought they were in will be out, and those who thought they were out will be in. The Bible as a whole and the teaching of Jesus give to us both immensely universalistic visions of the all-embracing power of God to save and to heal, but also and especially in the teaching of Jesus very, very harsh warnings about the possibility of losing the way, about the possibility of being lost, about the broad and inclusive way that leads to destruction and the narrow way, the hard way, that leads to life.[12]

The effect, then, of this recasting of the understanding of election, at least in the Christendom traditions, is to place all the emphasis upon the witness of the believing community, upon its integrity, transparency, and faithfulness — while forswearing every form of judgment, all speculation about the outcomes of God's mission, any attempt to sort out the sheep from the goats. It engenders great modesty with regard to the claims that the Christian community makes about itself, but at the same time deep conviction about the utter reliability of God's mighty acts and certain promises. At the same time, there has been a growing interest in the concrete nature of the missional community that is elect for witness and service. One can discern in the areas of both New Testament studies and social ethics, for instance, a turning to questions of the character and conduct of the called and sent community, a kind of "missional ethics" of the particular congregation. These explorations are also linked with a more or less bluntly articulated criticism of mindsets inherited from Christendom, exemplified for the Western discussion in the recent work of theologians such as Hauerwas and Hays.[13]

---

12. Lesslie Newbigin, *Signs Amid the Rubble: The Purposes of God in Human History*, ed. Geoffrey Wainwright (Grand Rapids: Eerdmans, 2003), p. 120.

13. See, e.g., Stanley Hauerwas, *A Community of Character: Toward a Constructive Christian Social Ethic* (Notre Dame: University of Notre Dame Press, 1981); Richard Hays, *The Moral Vision of the New Testament: Community, Cross, New Creation; A Contemporary Introduction to New Testament Ethics* (San Francisco: HarperSanFrancisco, 1996). The focus upon the *missio Dei* and the emerging discussion of the missional church is having an integrative effect upon

The consensus around the *missio Dei* has, of course, not meant unanimity in its interpretation. The conference of the International Missionary Council at Willingen in 1952 is usually regarded as the public event in which the theology of the *missio Dei* began to form into an integrating consensus for mission theology, although not without considerable controversy.[14] The term itself entered the missiological discourse after Vicedom published his basic work on the subject, *Mission of God: An Introduction to a Theology of Mission.*[15] It has, for instance, been interpreted in ways that ultimately render the visible and organized church marginal, if not a questionable deviation from God's actual mission in the world (notably in the influential work of Hoekendijk and the World Council's study on "the missionary structure of the congregation" in the 1960s).[16] These continuing discussions do not reject the reality of God's mission but raise hard and important questions about the place of the (very human and fallible) church in the realization of that mission.

Arguments in rejection of the *missio Dei* consensus can be much more foundational in character. For many Christian thinkers grappling with the hard questions of Christian confession in contexts of religious pluralism, the *missio Dei* consensus is problematic precisely in its central conviction, its claims of the uniqueness of Jesus as Savior and Lord. The continuing debate appears ultimately to center on the conviction that God's self-revelation in Israel and Jesus is definitive for all of creation, and that humanity is dependent upon God's gracious action in this particular history for its salvation. Central to this consensus is an explicit emphasis upon human sinfulness as an irreparable breach, upon God's grace as unmerited favor enfleshed in particular events, upon witness to these events as the divinely ordained way to bring about healing, and thus upon the Scriptures as the authoritative source and instrument of that witness. The "particularity" of these events is understood as "having universal intent," thus necessitating mission, "so that you might proclaim the mighty acts of him who called you out of darkness into his marvelous light" (1 Pet. 2:10).

---

the contemporary theological process, one example of which is the publications of the Gospel and Our Culture Network (see www.gocn.org); see also the first chapter above.

14. Wolfgang Günther, *Von Edinburgh nach Mexiko City: Der Beitrag der Mission zu ihrer Erneuerung* (Stuttgart: Evang. Verlagsanstalt, 1970), pp. 103-5; Lesslie Newbigin, *Unfinished Agenda: An Autobiography* (Grand Rapids: Eerdmans, 1985), pp. 137-38.

15. Georg F. Vicedom, *Missio Dei: Einführung in eine Theologie der Mission* (München: C. Kaiser, 1965); English translation: *Mission of God: An Introduction to a Theology of Mission,* trans. G. A. Thiele and D. Hilgendorf (St. Louis: Concordia, 1965).

16. See Bosch, *Transforming* Mission, pp. 401-2.

The alternative cluster of approaches seeks to soften that claim to uniqueness with a wide range of interpretations that, in some way or other, assign to human initiative and experience an active role in the resolution of the human crisis, be it through the diversity of religions with their various "salvations," through an enlightened view of the educability of the rational human to virtue, or through any number of modern renderings of the idea that the many good roads lead to the same mountaintop. For the proponents of this cluster of approaches, "mission [is] a work of God that is common to all religions," and thus "the church no longer has the explicit role of mediator of the Christian faith to humanity beyond itself."[17] These approaches appropriate the *missio Dei* tradition in very different ways from those who espouse the universal and unique missionary vocation of the church to witness to the entire world. This is generating today creative and serious criticisms of the *missio Dei* consensus, all of which in some way alter or soften the classic claims of the Christian movement that in Israel's history and the events of Jesus Christ God has acted decisively and comprehensively to bring about the "healing of the nations."[18]

For the proponent of the *missio Dei* consensus, these proposals are important for many reasons, but especially because they throw the spotlight on the meaning of the claim of the lordship of Christ. If "all power has been given to Jesus Christ in heaven and on earth" (Matt. 28:18), how then is that power present and evident in the great diversity of human cultural experience, including religious experience? In his exposition of God's missionary purposes (he never uses the phrase *missio Dei*), Karl Barth addresses the "extraordinary self-manifestations of Jesus Christ in the realm of the cos-

---

17. Wilhelm Richebächer, "*Missio Dei:* The Basis of Mission Theology or a Wrong Path?" *International Review of Mission* 92, no. 367 (2003): 588-89. Dr. Richebächer cites S. J. Samartha, "Mission in a Religiously Plural World: Looking Beyond Tambaram 1938," *International Review of Mission* 78, no. 307 (1988): 311-25, esp. 322.

18. Such theological strategies are reflected in some of the other essays that appear in the volumes that report on the joint project: Max L. Stackhouse and Lalsangkima Pachuau, eds., *News of Boundless Riches: Interrogating, Comparing, and Reconstructing Mission in a Global Era*, 2 vols. (Delhi, India: ISPCK, 2007). For example, J. Jayakiran Sebastian, in his essay titled "Interrogating *missio Dei:* From the mission of God towards appreciating our mission to God in India today," proposes that the question should be reversed into a "mission to God," rendering *missio Dei* into *missio Deo*. His project is a particularly stimulating appeal to the co-authority of human experience in the exposition of gospel and mission. Mark Heim, in an essay titled "The Trinity and Buddhism: A Perspective on Christian Mission and Buddhist Mission," recasts Trinitarian theology in a way that "finds room for, indeed requires, concrete truth in other religions."

mos,"[19] showing one way to affirm the Christocentricity of God's mission while recognizing the divine sovereignty that is accomplishing that mission beyond the limits of Christian witness. Crucial to the *missio Dei* project is its expressly anti-ideological thrust, as it refuses to prioritize any particular cultural narrative, either positively or negatively. In every cultural expression of the gospel, as it is embodied in the life and witness of the emerging churches, the focus upon the person and work of Jesus Christ makes the Trinity explicit, disclosing, as it were, the eternal triunity of God in God's purposeful action to bring about new creation as well as the healing of the world.

The triune God who lives eternally in mutual self-giving love wills to include creatures in that community of love. The welcoming of the other that marks the life of the Trinity in all eternity is extended toward us. Through the divine missions of Word and Spirit, God welcomes creatures to share the triune life of love and community. In the mission of Jesus Christ God forgives sinners and opens the way to their reconciliation with God and others, and in the mission of the Holy Spirit God empowers our participation in the triune God's life of outgoing, self-giving love to others. The mission of the church has its basis and model in this reaching out to the world by God, this *missio Dei* or divine missionary activity.[20]

As serious as the many critical responses to the theology of the *missio Dei* have been and continue to be, they have not resulted in the dissolution of the consensus in missiological discourse. This is evidenced not only by the continuing recourse to this theological approach in the missiological discussion but also by major statements on mission such as the World Council's well-received paper, "Mission and Evangelism: An Ecumenical Affirmation" (1982). The discussion of mission theology has continued to work with both the emphases and the opportunities opened up by the central claim that God's mission defines the purpose, the process, and the character of Christian witness in the world. In the words of the Vatican Council: "The Church on earth is by its very nature missionary."[21] Thus the discussion about the

19. Dieter Manecke, *Mission als Zeugendienst: Karl Barths theologische Begründung der Mission im Gegenüber zu den Entwürfen von Walter Holsten, Walter Freytag, und Joh. Christiaan Hoekendijk* (Wuppertal: Theologischer Verlag Rolf Brockhaus, 1972), pp. 222-24.

20. Migliore, "The Missionary God," p. 18.

21. Austin Flannery, O.P., ed., *Vatican Council II: The Conciliar and Post-Conciliar Documents* (Collegeville, MN: Liturgical Press, 1975), *Ad Gentes*, 1, p. 813; see *Lumen Gentium*, 1, p. 350.

interpretation and adequacy of the *missio Dei* continues, especially as the issues raised by "contextual theologies of mission" receive more focused attention. But the references to and applications of this consensus do not appear to abate in the missiological literature.[22]

The *missio Dei* Consensus and the Global Interrogation of Mission

What then might be the relationship of the *missio Dei* consensus in theology of mission to the project of "interrogating mission" that is currently going on around the globe? For a missiologist whose work focuses on the missional challenges of the end of Christendom in the North Atlantic cultures, it would be presumptuous to propose an interpretation of the role of *missio Dei* thought for, say, the discussion in India, or Africa, or Southern Asia. It might, however, be helpful to explore the contemporary importance of this discussion within the Western post-Christendom context, with a view to offering this exploration as a modest ecumenical contribution to the global discussion. It appears to me that, with the fundamental paradigm shift to the "next Christendom" now going on, there are aspects of this discussion now surfacing that might contribute constructively to the conversations within non-Western cultures and between them and the North Atlantic discourse. In our contemporary "global village," what happens to the church in one part of the world can and does affect churches in many other parts of the world. The challenge before us now is to conduct this conversation as partners, moving beyond the imbalanced relationships of the missionary era with its ranking of "sending" and "receiving" churches and cultures.

It is, for instance, of some importance that the development of missional theology in what was once Christendom must now take seriously the implications of the decline already mentioned. It is not merely a matter of numbers. In Europe, the actual proportion of the population seriously involved in the Christian church is notoriously very small. There, the Christian community has become truly marginal and a minority, in spite of the vestiges of Christendom that still provide some privileges. In North America, Canada is one of the most thoroughly secularized countries in the West. The marginalization of the Christian movement is a more contested phe-

---

22. See especially the *International Review of Mission* 92, no. 367 (October 2003), for the papers resulting from the consultation devoted to the significance of the Willingen Conference of 1952 on its fiftieth anniversary.

nomenon in the United States. Of all the Western developed nations, the United States is probably the most religiously active: higher church attendance than in other Western nations, public attention to religion especially in politics, obvious practices of "civil religion" (prayers at public events, the singing of "God Bless America"), and enormous interest in diverse forms of religiosity as evidenced in the publication and sale of books on all kinds of religion. At the same time, mainline denominations are, across the board, losing members and income. The cultural and legal privileging of churches is rapidly disappearing (e.g., repeal of blue laws, increasingly restrictive zoning regulation of churches, loss of the "protected Sunday morning"). The interpretation of the Christendom history and legacy in public educational institutions is, when addressed at all, allegedly neutral but often negative. Biblical illiteracy is rampant inside the churches and endemic in the society at large. The separation of facts (scientific truth) and values (including religious convictions) has become dogma, with the public marketplace and the public conversation largely devoid of religious interaction, while religious activity in congregations is viewed as private, voluntaristic, and thus insular, inward, and member-oriented. The proportion of the population that is truly non-Christian, not just post-Christian, is rapidly growing, although with regional variations. The picture is complicated by a vocal conservative movement in the U.S. that is often trying to restore Christendom; by the emergence of indigenous forms of Christian churches with few links to the Christendom legacy, which are rapidly growing in some areas; by the megachurch phenomenon; and by the popularity of the electronic church.

The growing significance of so-called "evangelical" Christianity in the United States, and especially of its political influence, complicates the discussion of the "end of Christendom." Even if the legal forms of establishment are history, the attitudes and assumptions of a cultural Christian hegemony continue to assert themselves. Theologically, this recast Christendom continues the reductionistic gospel that focuses on individual salvation, personal morality, and the church as the privileged enclave of the saved. It tends to preserve the neglect of the kingdom of God as the core of the gospel message, a neglect that has characterized revivalist Christianity in the last three hundred years. Thus this evangelicalism is highly selective in its reading and reception of the biblical witness. This is evidenced by the continuing distinction made between "evangelism" and "social justice," which are seen as opposing interpretations of the gospel. The consequence is a piety that can be intense and yet lacking in any sense of the comprehensive scope of the rule of Christ and the challenge of that rule to the "principalities and powers" that dominate American culture. The biblical ambiguities and dissonances that obviously result reflect centuries of conditioning by a reduced gospel, a domesticated and tamed recasting of the rule of Christ, and a church that has adapted to the roles that its context assigns to it.

This massive cultural and social shift in North America has made the development of a missional theology of the church all the more relevant, if not urgent. The context has become a mission field, while many of the inherited church forms and attitudes remain captive to Christendom assumptions that are no longer valid. What appears to be of particular importance is the growing awareness that the Christian movement in the United States must come to terms with the mixed legacy of Christendom. We need to face the challenges of cultural captivity, of gospel reductionism, of ecclesial compromise with the surrounding culture. We need to recognize that we are "conformed to this world," so that we "may be transformed by the renewing of our minds to recognize what is the good, and perfect, and acceptable will of God" (Rom. 12:2). It is not an exaggeration to speak of the need for the "continuing conversion of North American Christianity," especially in light of the cultural captivity that still characterizes the movement along its entire spectrum from left to right.[23] Out of this painful but necessary engagement with our history, we may have insights and learnings that might be of use to ecumenical partners who contend with at least some of the same challenges we face. There are, for instance, some sections of the Indian church where something like a Christendom challenge is emerging, that is, where there is a critical mass of Christians that now become a factor in the formation and development of a cultural context (e.g., in Assam among the Naga and Miso peoples). Colonialism also often operated with attitudes and structures influenced by Christendom, so that there are at least points of contact between the Western post-Christendom passage and India's postcolonial process. Indian society is also grappling with the issues of public religiosity, religious pluralism, and the clashes between technological and scientific modernity and religious traditions. The human tendency to reduce the gospel in order to make it controllable is a constant challenge in every process of contextualization.

It is intriguing that the Christian movements in both the post-Christendom West and in many regions beyond the boundaries of the North Atlantic are, in many ways, closer to the situation of the earliest Christian communities in the first and second centuries: minorities, marginalized,

23. See, on this, my *Continuing Conversion of the Church.*

often powerless, and confronted with religious pluralism that is sometimes virulent and threatening. The gospel of the crucified Jesus Christ is again, in both our contexts, truly "a scandal" and "foolishness." The "cosmic" claims and scope of the Christian message — "God so loved the *world*," "God was in Christ reconciling the *world*," "at the name of Jesus *every* knee should bend . . . and *every tongue* should confess that Jesus Christ is Lord, to the glory of God the Father" — are, for both our contexts, a radical challenge that, in the encounter with other religions, can be problematic. Certainly the challenge convicts our Christian communities of their (often inherited) compromises with our cultures, whether it be in the Western failure to come to terms with our anti-evangelical forms of racism, sexism, and classism, or in the Indian struggle with the caste system, or Asian forms of patriarchalism. For us both, Miroslav Volf's reclamation of the essential gospel of reconciliation, especially in situations of deep-seated ethnic and cultural division, is a call to receive the transforming freedom of the gospel.[24]

In both our settings, it is possible today to be engaged by the biblical word in ways not really possible when Christendom held sway. We can read the New Testament documents as they were originally intended, addressed to small, struggling communities seeking to discern what it meant to "lead their life worthy of the calling with which they are called." For centuries, the citizens of Christendom have not really known what Peter meant when he addressed his first epistle to "strangers and aliens." Today, in the post-Christendom world, we are coming to know what that means. For centuries, Christendom has done its theology as an erudite attempt to show how the Sermon on the Mount does not apply to us — Bonhoeffer's work *The Cost of Discipleship* and his exposition of "cheap grace" have revealed those compromises and made plain our need as Western churches for continuing conversion.

The Relevance of the *missio Dei* Consensus in the Post-Christendom Setting

It can, thus, perhaps be instructive in our ecumenical interaction to examine how, in the post-Christendom setting, the theology of the *missio Dei* may be a potent and formative interpretation of the biblical mandate for the church's

24. Miroslav Volf, *Exclusion and Embrace: A Theological Exploration of Identity, Otherness and Reconciliation* (Nashville: Abingdon, 1996).

mission. Of particular concern is its capacity to focus the way that Western Christianity must approach the Christendom legacy with the combination of critique and receptiveness that is appropriately modest. The ecumenical interrogation of mission can assist the Western churches in this endeavor, particularly as it uncovers common themes and challenges. In this process, all of us may be helped to be faithful in this time of paradigm shift, whether it be to the West's post-Christendom reality or the increasingly complex postcolonial reality of religious pluralism in the so-called two-thirds world.

The contemporary significance of the theology of the *missio Dei* was addressed in a variety of ways at the 2002 Willingen symposium commemorating the 1952 conference of the International Missionary Council in that same venue. Prof. Theo Sundermeier addressed the question of its ongoing significance as he explored how the *missio Dei* defines the identity of Christian mission theologically. His analysis raises issues that might prove to be fruitful in our endeavor to "interrogate mission today" for both the Christendom and non-Christendom streams of the church.[25]

The strength and the difficulty of the *missio Dei* consensus are its radical centering of the entire work of salvation in the missional purpose and action of God, which necessarily unfolds in the missional calling and sending of God's people. The Trinitarian theology of this calling and sending must also address the ecclesial reality of divided churches and polarized theological pluralism. Sundermeier acknowledges that the mission theology discussion is in a cul-de-sac characterized by the tension between "evangelization" and "social action," "evangelical" and "ecumenical," "pluralist theologies of religion" and "exclusivist Christian claims." Structurally, the tension might be seen in the parallel movements of the World Council of Churches and the Lausanne Movement. My superficial impression is that these polarizations are not unknown within the current situation of Christian churches beyond the boundaries of the North Atlantic. The divisions of Korean Presbyterians come to mind. Thus, it may prove a useful exploration to see if there are resources in the *missio Dei* process emerging from Willingen that might address this situation — it is certainly germane for the post-Christendom context of North America.

25. Theo Sundermeier, "Missio Dei heute: Zur Identität christlicher Mission," *Theologische Literaturzeitung* 127, no. 12 (2002): 1244-62; English translation: "*Missio Dei* Today: On the Identity of Christian Mission," *International Review of Mission* 92, no. 367 (October 2003): 560-78. Citations in the text list the page in the German original followed by the page in the English translation in the *IRM*; the citations themselves are based on the *IRM* version with some editing for the sake of accurate rendering of the German.

Sundermeier proposes that the theology of the *missio Dei* expounds Christian mission in terms of its mystery, its freedom, its pluralism, and its "thick hope." These four dimensions correspond to recent anthropological analysis that interprets the human person not as something static but as a process made up of a "four-dimensional network." This network consists of that which is inward and universal (= mystery), that which is external and connectional (= freedom), the "ways and spaces" that make up the context of one's passage (= pluralism), and the character of the times that both condition a person and are conditioned by a person (= thick hope) (1246 = 561).

The inward and universal character of God's mission is defined as the [*mystery* or *secret* of God] which in many religious traditions is the protected, unknowable, arcane, and sacred domain open to no one or only a few (1245f. = 561-63). But for biblical faith, this mystery has become accessible in God's Word, God's self-disclosure. "The mystery remains a mystery, but it is no longer a 'secret'; it is interpreted and espoused" (1246 = 562). For Christianity, the incarnation of Jesus the Christ means that the mystery has become a person, has differentiated itself, in that God has sent the Son (John's Gospel). "This sending allows us to look into the mystery of God and allows God to be understood as the triune one who is defined solely by love" (1246 = 562). This results in the entry of the mystery into history, the possibility of telling the story and joining the history — "As my Father has sent me, so I send you" (John 20:21). The death and resurrection of Jesus Christ make the story totally open, totally universal, and totally accessible, because through this event God has made himself totally accessible to all humanity. "The open secret of God, the mission, in which, dogmatically speaking, the immanent and economic relations of the three persons flow together, evokes from inner necessity the *missio hominum*. The Christian faith cannot but involve mission. The Christian religion is essentially a missionary religion" (1246 = 563).

For our interrogation of mission, both in the Western world and in the global church, it is clear that the *mystery* of the *missio Dei* requires a profoundly critical encounter with the theological traditions of Christendom that still look upon themselves as normative for world Christianity. This critical encounter must be undertaken with care, however. The revelation of the mystery, which creates the church as its witness, does not imply that the human community that knows and confesses this distinctive history can also control it. With all the problems of the inherited theological traditions, their insistence upon the divine initiative in revelation, upon human dependence on God's gracious action in Christ, upon the giftedness of faith and the reality of justification and reconciliation as God's actions, is essential to the gospel's true mystery. It was a very problematic reaction to that gospel theology when the assumption of the human ability both to define and control the divine became an operative principle of Western Enlightened thought. In effect, Enlightened modernity has ascribed more mystery to the human person than to God! The axiom of this human capacity (whether defined as the rational or the spiritual) now forms the common ground that makes it possible to interpret all human religious expressions as various valid versions of the one universal truth. Thus, the late Christendom theological process in the West has been characterized by the tension outlined above between the traditional and classic emphasis upon the unique and divine initiative of God in Christ — with the reductionisms and the arrogant assertions of normativity as part of the mix — and the Enlightened emphasis upon the self-saving capacity of the rational human. In the theological work of our Indian colleagues we experience a concerted, disciplined, and critical engagement with both the traditional claims of the unique gospel and with the Enlightened critique of that tradition. The debate is complicated by the dynamics of the missionary movement in partnership with colonialism, whereby the classic theological traditions are handicapped by the ways in which they have been imposed upon emerging Indian churches — we return to that problem in the next paragraph. The postcolonial challenge energizes and informs this critical encounter with such problematic expressions of Christendom normativity. When, however, in the process of reaction the anthropocentric assumptions of Enlightened Western modernity have been adopted, there is a genuine threat to the essential mystery of the gospel.

This revealed mystery, culminating in Jesus Christ and continuing in the ministry of the Spirit, results in *freedom* as the second dimension of the identity of Christian mission (1247-49 = 563-65). It is precisely this aspect of Sundermeier's analysis that addresses helpfully, I believe, the tension between Theo- and Christocentric approaches on the one hand and the anthropocentric cluster of approaches on the other. Sundermeier candidly admits that freedom might be a surprising concept to link with mission in light of the "prejudice that [mission] disseminates religious coercion, fetters the conscience and paved the way for colonial dependencies" (1247 = 563). For Christian mission to violate this freedom, which it irrefutably has done in the history of Western Christendom, must be regarded today as "distortions and abuses" of the "actual meaning and context of mission" (1247 = 563). Those violations scarcely need to be enumerated. The repentance and conversion of the Christian movement shaped by Christendom will be necessary to enable it to reclaim this compromised freedom. Because the gospel mission is

35

about God's coming as the loving one to humanity, it must be characterized by freedom. Love does not coerce; it woos. It depends upon the decisional response of the beloved; it requires freedom in order to exist.

This is the only possible way to understand the idea that mission is to be fundamentally shaped by the fact and character of the once-and-for-all incarnation. It emulates the sending and coming of Jesus himself, who comes in love, comes to embrace, to touch, but always to heal and to transform. The church is discipled by Jesus in order to be sent out by him; discipleship always leads to apostolate. "The way of the *missio Jesu* is also the way of the *missio hominum*. Its characteristic is the sensibility of a lover, inwardly preparing to meet the other, and seeking and accompanying this special person. It is the posture of 'kenosis' (Phil. 2)" (1247 = 563). Thus mission respects the freedom of the other, which Jesus demonstrated in his discourse on friendship with his disciples (John 15). Friendship can only function on the basis of freedom, and can only flourish where trust is granted and received. Friendship unites freedom and faithfulness. "If Jesus' mission is to make the relation between God and Moses apply now to all human beings, and call them into this relationship with God, then our mission can have no other goal than to spread God's friendship, and that means, at the same time, to extend an invitation to freedom" (1247f. = 564).

Obviously this understanding of the freedom of mission will shape the methods of mission. It will require that we move beyond the problematic definitions of mission partnership to mission friendship, which will truly delight in our differences as well as focus on our commonality (1248 = 564). Bishop Azariah's passionate appeal, "Give us friends," called out at Edinburgh in 1910, gains new power in light of this understanding of the freedom of mission. The freedom of mission becomes thus an essential concept for the definition of the appropriate process of contextualization.

As freedom rooted in the practice of Jesus, however, this aspect of mission does not have to create a diversity within the Christian movement that has no common ground, no centering point. The problem of that diversity is clearly a major theme in our common interrogation of mission. The freedom modeled on Christ will shape practices that, in their diversity, express the common witness of the church. In infinitely varying ways, the common core of practices that distinguish the company of Jesus' followers and apostolic witnesses will become more and more a profound focus of cross-cultural witness and a source of encouragement for the Christian movement. These practices, while culturally distinctive, will demonstrate their catholicity as the worship of the triune God, sacramental celebration, prayer in the name of Jesus Christ, praise, gospel proclamation, scriptural formation of the community, hospitality as the overcoming of human boundaries, invitation to discipleship, concrete acts of mercy, grace and healing, discernment of God's work in human history, and prophetic witness over against the powers that hurt, divide, and demean. To live and act in such a way is to claim the freedom for which Christ has set us free (John 8:36)!

In the United States, this focus upon the necessary freedom of mission, evidenced in friendship, trust, noncoercion, and transparency, calls into question the whole spectrum of evangelistic practices shaped by consumerism. The "marketing" of the Christian faith has emerged as perhaps the dominant reaction to the end of Christendom and the perceived need to regain lost territory. The partnership of church and state has effectively been replaced by the partnership of church and marketplace. Some of the most "successful" forms of church (which are also some of the most exportable!) are unabashedly entrepreneurial, stressing the benefits gained by the convert, the prosperity God will surely bring the believer, and the blessedness of Christian confession — with neither mention of one's bearing of one's cross nor reference to the call to enter into God's service as part of his witnessing people. If a society dominated by modern advertising shapes the church and its proclamation, then we must ask if our witness can be characterized by the freedom of the gospel and the unconditional love practiced by Jesus in his earthly ministry. In terms of Lalsangkima Pachuau's exposition of salvation as the transformation of relationships under the power of evangelical reconciliation, these reductionisms of a marketed gospel are revealed to be subscriptural and as reductionistic as the Christendom legacy out of which they have emerged.[26]

In its testimony that its message is for all people, Christianity, like other world religions, is claiming that its truth is not restricted to any particular culture, tribe, caste, ethnicity, geography, or language. This ultimately implies the equal value of all people: all are loved, all are created for the wholeness of God's creation design, all can hear the good news in one's own language (Pentecost!), all can participate in the healing of God's salvation. This is essential to the *missio* that belongs to God! All are free to decide for or against the witness of this message and its invitation. Thus, Christian mission must actively engage in the struggle for human freedom, for the right to decide, for the right to differ, and the right to be different. To oppose or even dis-

---

26. L. Pachuau, "Christian Mission amidst Ethnic Pandemonium," in Stackhouse and Pachuau, eds., *News of Boundless Riches,* pp. 15-17.

allow the freedom of witness and the freedom of response to that witness is to violate fundamental human rights. The right to mission is an evidence of the upholding of human worth (1248f. = 564f.). This ultimately means that whoever opposes mission is really against freedom.

Understanding the *freedom* of God's mission in this way also provides us some needed criteria to reread and interpret the history of mission critically, globally, and from many cultural perspectives.[27] This global approach to history requires that we learn how to do our historical analysis dialectically and modestly. It might also become possible for Christian theological traditions emerging in non-Christendom contexts to work productively with the Christendom legacy, not as a model to be copied but as a set of case studies with complex negative and positive learnings to offer.

Christian mission is further characterized by *pluralism,* by which Sundermeier means the human reality of a multiplicity of cultures and ethnicities, and their interactions that necessarily influence one another and precipitate processes of change (1250-52 = 565-68). Because of the mystery and the freedom of God's mission, cultural pluralism means intercultural encounter, crossing boundaries, changing and being changed. "Mission means that dynamic that propels us towards the unknown person, to the religiously alienated person whom God wants to welcome back again" (1250 = 566). The changes that occur in this interaction affect all that are engaged, but certainly they affect the missionary, the witness. She will experience alienation and threat, but also new horizons and enriching new opportunities. "Anyone

who does not change is domineering and only tries to change the others they meet. That has nothing to do with mission" (1250 = 566). The sending of the Son is the supreme example of this pluralistic pathway. He did not accept the cultural and cultic boundaries imposed upon the pious Jew of his day. He allowed himself to be affected and to be changed by those whom he encountered. His way to the cross and grave was the supreme path to profound change, a total redefinition of what it means to be human, and what it means for God to love! Jesus' own "way into the strange land did not result in self-alienation, did not lead him away from God; death and resurrection opened up his, and thereby God's reality, in an unprecedented way. There is no going back on this. It is the belief of all Christian mission" (1250 = 566).

27. Dale T. Irvin and Scott W. Sunquist, *History of the World Christian Movement* (Maryknoll, NY: Orbis, 2001); Wilbert Shenk, ed., *Enlarging the Story: Perspectives on Writing World Christian History* (Maryknoll, NY: Orbis, 2002), especially his Introduction, pp. xi-xvii; Andrew F. Walls, "Eusebius Tries Again: The Task of Reconceiving and Re-visioning the Study of Christian History," in Shenk, ed., *Enlarging the Story,* pp. 1-21.

The way of the Son has immediate implications for the way of his called and sent community: "As it was Jesus' way to bring the lost sheep of Israel back to the fold (Mt. 15:24), the way of apostolic mission leads into the world of the nations, in order to call them back to God" (1250 = 566). The outcome is not intended to be either cultural or even organizational unity. Human processes of unification divide as much as they unite. The intentional cultural pluralism of the *missio Dei* is, instead, a source of blessing. It means, as Lamin Sanneh has emphasized, that all cultures may receive and enflesh the gospel, but no cultural formation of evangelical faith is normative for all others. The Holy Spirit gives everyone, young and old, male and female, the power to believe, to witness, and to serve. "The differences are not as such removed, but no one will now be given priority, and all claim to domination will lose its justification" (1251 = 567). "The Holy Spirit strengthens creaturely, social, and individual pluralism, but in such a way that differences are no longer felt to be divisive and fuelling hostility" (1251 = 567).

This intentional pluralism has always been a reality for mission, which has dealt with it under the rubrics of indigenization, inculturation, and more recently, contextualization. Our theology of mission today needs to attend to the fact that "unity cannot be pitted against pluralism" since this "diversity is a working of the Spirit." Such a theology cannot, of course, be idealistic about unity in plurality. It must also address the sinfully divided character of the church in its diversity. The ecumenical movement is an open admission of the global church's need to be converted to true pluralist unity, or in New Testament terms, to "live its life worthy of the calling with which it has been called" (Eph. 4:1). This can only be expressed in the Spirit-empowered obedience that enables the church to "make every effort to maintain the unity of the Spirit in the bond of peace" (Eph. 4:3). Christian unity will, therefore, be defined not in terms of organizational uniformity or some super-cultural commonality, but in terms of the unified witness made by the pluralist church to an often-hostile world. How, in fact, does the world God loves actually encounter that love that breaks down walls other than through the distinctive community disciplines of the churches?

The final dimension of Christian mission, as unpacked by the theology of the *missio Dei,* has to do with the role and reality of time for witness and is characterized by Sundermeier as *thick hope.* The central theme of the kingdom of God presents itself here — it has been a much-contested emphasis in the discussion since Willingen. Sundermeier's argument is itself "thick" and requires more exploration than possible here. For our purposes, it should be noted that mission takes place in space and time, which raises the question of history and our understanding of God's rule "before, during, and after" history as we temporally conceive of it. The contextualization of the gospel in Western, Greco-Roman thought patterns, shaped linguistically by the Indo-European verbal structure of tenses (present, imperfect, perfect, past perfect, future, future perfect) creates problems for Christian witness to God's rule already here, breaking in, and yet to reach consummation.

Only the scholar really recognizes the difficulties, even today, of the task of translating the Old Testament with its very different linguistic patterns into Western Indo-European languages. Lineal thinking is ultimately reductionistic when applied to the radical news that the "kingdom of God has drawn near" so that Jesus' disciples may learn to pray "thy kingdom come." In the encounter with Christian witness shaped in profoundly different linguistic patterns, the Western tradition can and should learn much about its own limitations in conceptualizing the eschatological character of Christian hope. "The future is coming in such a fashion that it explodes upon us as totally present! It comes in such a fashion that it interrupts time and disaster, and salvation becomes present in a 'nuclear' sense: as the forgiveness of sins, healing of disease, new incorporation into community, as the experience of righteousness, as the call to discipleship, as freedom from the bonds of wealth, rescue from death, liberation from demonic powers, as the meal of friends with Jesus, as re-birth, celebration" (1257 = 571). Humans, even the most faithful disciples, neither build nor bring about this kingdom. That is what God is already doing; into this inbreaking reign he invites his witnesses as the firstfruits of this certain future. The anticipation of God's completion of what God has begun transforms the present in such a way that obedience, endurance, and joy are possible.

The reclamation of the central New Testament theme of "the reign of God" and the "thick hope" of the church shaped by that reign, both present and coming, is the most powerful force to confront the many-faceted reductionism of the Christendom legacy. Nothing less sweeping than "conversion" will reorient the Western church to hear and respond to the unexpected fullness of the gospel.[28] The Holy Spirit could use ecumenical encounter as one way to bring about such conversion, as together we interrogate our missional calling and help each other to confront the cultural captivities that subtly but powerfully control our reception and formulation of the gospel.

It will prove unhelpful to try to distinguish between the message of Jesus and the person of Jesus, especially as we approach the meaning of

---

28. See Guder, *Continuing Conversion*, on this theme.

the proclamation of the kingdom of God in the pluralism of contemporary Christianity. At the core of the reclamation of earliest Christianity will necessarily be the investigation of what it truly means to confess that Jesus the Christ is the Lord *(kyrios)*. This is also part of the scandal and foolishness that we cannot evade, regardless of how our theological exploration articulates and informs faith in particular contexts. The careful movement to post-Christendom missional theology gives us the freedom also to reengage the earliest Christian history as our common ground. To do this, we will need to develop approaches to scriptural interpretation shaped by the missional vocation of the church. To interrogate mission fruitfully, we must give attention to the urgent need for a missional hermeneutic that will enable the church to encounter Scripture as the testimony God uses to form his people for their missional calling.[29] All Christian traditions, in the vast range of cultural contexts in which they are being formed, will constantly have to ask, "What was and is the church that Jesus intended?"[30]

This multilayered understanding of the *missio Dei* presents us with challenging insights for the task of interrogating mission today. In view of the "great new fact of our time," the global Christian movement, the theological process must learn how to work multiculturally and multilingually and with a new discernment for both the blessing of difference and the confessional strength of common faith and practice. This is a particularly hard challenge for the churches shaped by Christendom; it calls for rather significant retooling of our theological instincts and strategies. Rather than the static process of theological propositions assumed to possess eternal validity, we will have to learn how to do our theologies in conversation with the challenge to witness faithfully in very diverse contexts. Subtle claims to normativity on the part of some theological traditions will have to be contested, while all voices, past and present, will also be accorded a responsible place at the discussion table. There are many implications for the task of investigating mission today, at least for the North Atlantic partners at the theological round table.

The theology of the *missio Dei* focuses us upon the reengagement with apostolic Christian witness. When we engage that witness, we are confronted anew by the scandal and foolishness of the gospel of the cross and the empty

---

29. James V. Brownson, *Speaking the Truth in Love: New Testament Resources for a Missional Hermeneutic* (Harrisburg, PA: Trinity Press International, 1998); Richard Bauckham, *The Bible and Mission* (Grand Rapids: Baker, 2003).

30. Gerhard Lohfink, *Wie hat Jesus Gemeinde gewollt?* (Freiburg/Basel/Vienna: Herder Verlag, 1982); English translation: *Jesus and Community: The Social Dimension of Christian Faith,* trans. J. P. Galvin (Philadelphia: Fortress Press, 1984).

grave. The translation problems will not decrease, but increase, as the distinctive Christian calling reveals the radical differentness of the Christian faith and hope. Contextualization, as an essential aspect of the freedom and pluralism of mission, will grapple with the problems of new cultural captivities as well as with the gospel's claims that call for the conversion of cultures. One of the widely advocated approaches to global religious pluralism is the proposal that all religions function in some way as part of God's work of salvation. If we accept the ecumenical consensus since the International Missionary Council meeting in Jerusalem in 1928 that "secularism" is itself now one of the world's major religions,[31] and if we further concede that the practices of global secularism today are largely influenced by the market-driven consumerist systems of the West, then are we to accept this "religious tradition" as one viable expression among many of God's salvific activity? The heirs of Western Christendom, at least, will have to ask whether we, in our context, are then obligated to look upon our religiously defined secularism, our commitment to our style of democracy as somehow normative for all, the self-indulgence of our consumerism, and our moral relativism as aspects of God's mission, comparable to the tenets of any other religious tradition.

To be about this kind of theological investigation, missional theology in its diverse cultural expressions will constantly have to learn how to do its work both modestly and with conviction. This is especially true of the heirs of Christendom. The "thick hope" that unites all Christians gives us permission to experiment, to err, to repent, to re-form, and to move ahead as Christ leads us. It is because the mystery is now an "open secret" (Newbigin) that we have the freedom to confess Christ as witnesses who do not need to and do not want to become anyone's judges. The goal of the *missio Dei* as expounded by Sundermeier is the gracious gift of the friendship of God. "Mission is the invitation to open up to this divine mystery and entrust oneself to it. It is the invitation to become friends with God, and because it is an invitation, there is no obligation to accept" (1258 = 573). In practice, this will mean the freedom of pluralism and common hope. "There is a norm by which we are measured, namely the relation to the first dimension, i.e. the link to the inner-trinitarian mystery of God, from which *missio* springs. Yet this norm does not call for homogeneous structures and a homogenizing unity;

31. Rufus M. Jones, "Secular Civilization and the Christian Task," *The Jerusalem Meeting of the International Missionary Council, March 24–April 8, 1928*, vol. 1 (New York and London: International Missionary Council, 1928), pp. 230-73.

it expects of us that we make room for a 'creative complexity' (M. Welker)" (1259 = 574). We are not responsible for the making of the future, nor are we qualified to do so. That future is coming toward us and is already among us. "... the future of the kingdom of God precedes us. We can completely devote ourselves to the tasks God puts before us every day. This means that the nearer we are to Christ, the nearer we are to our neighbor" (1260 = 574).

The *missio Dei* as expounded in terms of its mystery, freedom, pluralism, and thick hope generates not one mission theology, but many, with all these theologies serving to equip the saints in all their cultural settings for the common missionary vocation. It is, in fact, a way of doing theology, better conveyed perhaps by the term 'missional theology.' By definition, such missional theology cannot claim normativity for any particular expression but must claim confessional authenticity as it witnesses to the gospel and equips the church to carry out its missionary vocation. Its common source is the event of Jesus Christ; its common goal is the certainty that "he who began a good work in you will bring it to completion at the day of Jesus Christ" (Phil. 1:6); its common witness is the practices that demonstrate before a watching world that God loves it and invites all into friendship and the service of his healing purposes.

CHAPTER 3

The Christological Formation of Missional Practice

Missiology and the Emergence of Global Christianity

In an essay titled "'But you, who do people say that I am?': Christological Perspectives from Africa," Christine Lienemann-Perrin demonstrates both the intellectual wealth and the challenges that confront the theological conversation in the globalized Christian movement.[1] The possible responses to Jesus' question to his disciples, "Who do you say that I am?," increase in number and complexity in a world church that, in a relatively short period of time, has become truly multicultural, multiracial, multilingual, and multistructural. In terms of the classic Nicene definition of the church, it is the catholicity of the church that is being redefined in our historical experience.[2] The ways in which the church is formed and functions *kat' holon*, in relationship to and in expression of that which is the *holon*, the essential center and common ground of the Christian faith, are incredibly diverse. That *holon* is, however, in all the diversity of its interpretation and witness, still Jesus who is asking the question, "Who do you say that I am?"

1. Christine Lienemann-Perrin, "'But you, who do you say that I am?': Christological Perspectives from Africa," in *Jesus Christ Today: Studies of Christology in Various Contexts*, ed. Stuart George Hall (Berlin and New York: Walter de Gruyter, 2009), pp. 299-316.
2. See below, chapters 5 and 10 on the Nicene marks.

This essay was presented at a meeting of the Académie Internationale des Sciences Religieuses that took place at Princeton in August 2007. The Académie's work was centered on Christology, and its papers were subsequently published in Stuart George Hall, ed., *Jesus Christ Today: Studies of Christology in Various Contexts: Proceedings of the Académie Internationale des Sciences Religieuses* (Berlin: Walter de Gruyter GmbH & Co., 2009). This essay is found on pp. 316-35.

Because of the central role of Bible translation in the emergence of global Christianity, it is still the Christian Scriptures with which this debate in all its cultural settings necessarily engages. In all this diversity, the global Christianity that has resulted from the modern missionary movement is still fundamentally defined by the event, the person, and the work of Christ. It should be by now abundantly clear, however, that the ancient doctrinal traditions of Western Christianity, which have looked upon themselves as normative Christian thought for a very long time, are to be seen as one culturally defined cluster of theologies interacting with other growing clusters of culturally diverse ways of doing theology. In that process, these allegedly normative theological traditions in the West are often confronted with hard and even threatening questions from Christian colleagues in the non-Western world. Such questions have become a major area of endeavor for missiologists and other scholars whose work relates to the academic discipline of Missiology.

Missiology as an academic discipline emerged in Germany and Scotland in the nineteenth century in response to the modern missionary movement — although the earliest documentation of the teaching of the subject matter is at Princeton Seminary in 1830.[3] From its inception, it has been an integrative and often interdisciplinary theological enterprise, reflecting the incredible complexity of the modern mission movement itself. Going back to William Carey, missiologists deal with the biblical foundations and understandings of mission, including everything that Bible translation entails. While church history has tended to be a Eurocentric enterprise, missiologists address the history of the Christian movement in terms of the essentially missionary nature of the church catholic. Missiologists grapple with the issues of cultural translation and what used to be called enculturation and is discussed today under rubrics such as "the encounter between gospel and culture" and "contextualization." Although Western missiologists are obviously shaped by their location in European Christendom where Christians still claim to be in the majority, they track the doctrinal and confessional formation of Christian communities whose identity is shaped by the fact that they are minorities in their contexts. Missiology has thus sought to articulate the spectrum of questions that surface as the Christian movement entered into and contextualized itself in non-European settings. Many of these questions have turned out to be, as I have already suggested, hard and

---

3. The standard reference work is Olav Myklebust, *The Study of Missions in Theological Education*, 2 vols. (Oslo: Forlaget Land og Kirke, 1955), especially vol. 1, p. 146. See chapter 1.

threatening, especially for the old Western churches that sent out so many generations of missionaries.

The modern missionary movement has not only generated a discipline called "missiology"; it has stimulated a whole spectrum of theological and ecclesial issues that moved onto the agenda of the ecumenical church, often shepherded by missiologists. It was on the mission field that the scandal of the divisions of Western Christendom became such an obvious problem that the energies that resulted in the Ecumenical Movement emerged. It was on the mission field that the compromises of centuries-old Western partnerships of church and state began to be questioned as reductionisms of the gospel — although, to be fair, we must acknowledge that the radical Reformation had been challenging these compromises before the onset of the modern missionary movement. It was on the mission field that unexamined and powerful forms of Western racism, classism, and sexism became shockingly visible. The notorious intertwining of mission and colonialism reveals in profoundly disturbing ways the *Lebenskrise* in which Western Christendom found itself at the end of the millennium, but which had been building for at least four centuries. And it has been our colleagues in our sister churches, in what Philip Jenkins calls "the next Christendom,"[4] who have raised especially pointed questions about the problematic ways that Western theologies have answered the question, "Who do you say that I am?" Prof. Lienemann's essay shows how that process is unfolding as the ecumenical discussion engages contributions of contemporary African theologians. In this paper, I would like to examine some aspects of the possible interaction between Christology and Missiology, the doctrine of Christ and the doctrine of the church's mission, in light of the impact of the modern missionary movement, both real and potential, upon theological discourse. Two important clarifications are needed before I proceed further, and they will draw together some themes already discussed in different contexts above.

Modern Mission, the Critique of Mission, and Emerging Secularism

It is, firstly, a commonplace of late-modern secular intellectuals in the West to deplore the foreign missionary movement of the last three centuries. If the students I encounter at Princeton Seminary have learned anything at

4. Philip Jenkins, *The Next Christendom: The Coming of Global Christianity* (Oxford and New York: Oxford University Press, 2011).

all in their secular universities and colleges about the modern missionary movement before arriving here, then generally they have learned that it was an enormous enterprise of cultural and economic domination, cultural ar- rogance, and ideological intolerance. The stereotypes of the culturally insen- sitive, supremacist Western missionary are legion — and they are frequently propagated by Christian scholars! It is important that Western Christians face the many negative aspects of this chapter in our history honestly. There is no gainsaying the hard and critical issues that arose out of the enterprise — the missiologist deals constantly with this very ambiguous history. But there is also a great need for enough intellectual honesty to see that the pic- ture is a very mixed one. Missionaries cannot be forced into one negative stereotype. Often the commercial and military interests of the colonializers were opposed by the missionaries because of the injustices they were wreak- ing upon the indigenous populations. As Lamin Sanneh has pointed out,[5] it was often the dedicated work of missionaries in West Africa that saved threatened cultures and preserved languages from disappearing. It was, over and over again, the efforts of Western missions that developed educational, medical, and agricultural infrastructures essential for the survival of many colonies as they moved into independence after World War II. A fair reading of this history must avoid sweeping generalizations that either demonize or heroize the missionary movement.

And secondly, when we deal with the fact and the outcome of the Western missionary movement, we have to confirm that, in spite of all its ambiguities and problems, it worked! The majority of the world Christian population is now located in those churches that resulted from the Western mission. This is the astounding and much-commented-on demographic shift that took place in the course of the twentieth century. Prof. Lienemann's nu- merous African conversation partners illustrate this new reality. The irony is plain to see: while the Western cultures that sent out those missionaries have experienced the rapid decline of their Christian institutions and constituen- cies, the missions they fostered overseas have generated churches and move- ments that continue to prosper and grow. Some are comparing this dramatic shift in the demographics of the global church with the loss of North African Christendom to Islam, linked with the spread of Christianity northward throughout Europe. Be that as it may, the "end of Western Christendom" is now upon us, as alert observers have been pointing out for most of the past

---

5. Lamin Sanneh, *Translating the Message: The Missionary Impact on Culture* (Maryknoll, NY: Orbis, 1989), pp. 88-125, and *West African Christianity* (Maryknoll, NY: Orbis, 1983).

century. Karl Barth wrote, looking back in 1935, that "Christendom in the form we have known it until now is at an end." The idea of Christendom itself had been profoundly discredited at least since the outbreak of the First World War, when so-called Christian states unleashed the most horrendous war in human history against each other, and the churches on both sides blessed the weapons and sanctioned the violence. What began, at least in America, as the *The Christian Century* in 1900 turned out to be its very opposite — the journal took that title in 1900 as one sign of the ill-founded optimism that still reigned just fourteen years before the war.

The Reclamation of Mission

In spite of the ambiguity of the modern missionary movement, its theological impact would ultimately be very great, especially with regard to our theological understanding of the purpose and activity of the church. The changes were very slow in coming, but they were signaled early on by some shifts in vocabulary. The term "mission" had virtually disappeared from the church's conversation about itself; for many centuries, it did not appear in the majority of treatises dealing with the doctrine of the church. This was a result of the Constantinian project. David Bosch summarized the process: "[A]s Europe became christianized and Christianity became the established religion in the Roman Empire and beyond, theology lost its missionary dimension." The disappearance of mission from the formal theologies of Western churches undoubtedly had to do with the intellectual hegemony created by the establishment of Christianity as the privileged religion of late classical and medieval Europe. Given the *corpus Christianum,* mission was not needed, and the church's major task was reconstrued to focus upon the administration of salvation and the maintenance of the churchly institutions and rites that carried out that task. This meant that, theologically, established Western Christendom could understand itself with virtually no sense of the missionary vocation that had characterized the church in the first centuries of its history.

Beginning in the eighteenth century, however, North Atlantic Christians were engaging in mission overseas and finding that their Bibles did,

---

6. Karl Barth, "Das Evangelium in der Gegenwart," *Theologische Existenz heute,* no. 25 (München: Chr. Kaiser Verlag, 1935), p. 33.

7. David Bosch, *Transforming Mission: Paradigm Shifts in Theology of Mission* (Maryknoll, NY: Orbis, 2011), p. 501.

in fact, define the very nature of the church as missionary. They began to discover that "apostolicity" had to do with missionary vocation long before it became an institutional mark of the church. One of the most important signals of this change in perspective was William Carey's *An Enquiry into the Obligations of Christians to Use Means for the Conversion of the Heathen* (1792), in which he interpreted the Great Commission of Matthew 28:18-20 as a binding mandate upon Western Christians. In the preceding centuries, it was virtually never applied to the contemporary church but always interpreted as applying only to the original apostolic generation. In actual practice, it was on the foreign mission fields that the gradual reclamation of the essentially missional nature of the church began. And it was in the theological interactions of the International Missionary Council in the first half of the twentieth century that these insights began to be articulated.[8] John Mackay summarized the growing consensus in his address to the Council's Willingen Conference on World Mission in 1952: "It is part of the mandate of Jesus Christ to Christians and to the Christian Church that all that He said and stood for shall be taken seriously and, not least, the observance of the missionary injunction to go into all the world with all that it involves. The church simply cannot be the Church in any worthy sense if it is not loyal to its apostolate. A truly apostolic Church can never be satisfied with merely sponsoring missionary interest or in giving birth to 'mission.' It must itself become the mission. Let the Church be the Mission."[9]

The Christian vocabulary related to the internal life of established Christendom also began to change. In the eighteenth century, the terms "evangelism" and "evangelize" reappeared. The terms were needed because it was becoming clear that not everyone in Christendom was Christian . . . anymore. While not going so far (yet!) as to declare Europe to be a mission field, it became clear that there was a need to evangelize those who might be cultural Christians but were not, in any definitive way, actual believers. Evidences of this aspect of missional reclamation included the vibrant organized expressions of Pietism, the recurring revivals and awakenings on both sides of the North Atlantic, and the formation of mission societies and countless

8. William Richey Hogg, *Ecumenical Foundations: A History of the International Missionary Council and Its Nineteenth-Century Background* (New York: Harper & Row, 1952, repr. Eugene, OR: Wipf & Stock, 2002), *passim*.

9. John Mackay, "The Great Commission and the Church Today," in *Missions Under the Cross: Addresses Delivered at the Enlarged Meeting of the Committee of the International Missionary Council at Willingen, in Germany, 1952*, ed. Norman Goodall (London: Edinburgh House, 1953), p. 141.

other volunteer organizations devoted to Christian causes. It is still possible to find reference works that define "mission" as Christian outreach beyond the boundaries of Western Christendom, and "evangelism" as a necessary aspect of the church's task within secularizing Christendom. The theological reclamation of mission, especially as the essential definition of the church's being and purpose, proceeded much more slowly in the formal development of doctrine. As I have emphasized several times, it had been absent from Western ecclesiologies for centuries. The theme "mission" plays no role in the great confessions of the Reformation, whether Lutheran or Reformed. We recall that Charles Hodge, the great teacher of Reformed theology at Princeton Seminary from 1851 to 1878, was devoted to foreign mission, preached on the subject frequently, sent his sons into the mission field, but never mentioned the theme in his monumental *Systematic Theology*.[10] We would find this lack in the majority of works in systematic theology published over the last century. Alister McGrath's widely used textbook for the study of systematic theology, published in 2001, does not address mission thematically.[11] The major exception is Karl Barth, and along with him, a small band of dogmaticians including Hendrikus Berkhof and Jürgen Moltmann. But we will return to that subject a little later. As we turn to the question of the interaction between Christology and Missiology, we should bear in mind that the church's missionary vocation is not a part of the legacy of Western Christendom's ecclesiologies.

Christology and Mission

That dichotomy between church and mission in Western theology is paralleled by a similar dichotomy in the development of Christology. It goes beyond the scope of this essay to survey the history of Christology in order to document that separation in detail. Aware of the inherent danger in generalizations, I would suggest that classical Christologies have, on the whole, paid little attention to the mission of Jesus as it informs the earthly ministry

10. Charles Hodge, *Systematic Theology*, 3 vols. (New York: Charles Scribner's Sons, 1893).

11. Alister E. McGrath, *Christian Theology: An Introduction*, 3rd ed. (Oxford: Blackwell, 2001). The index has no references for "mission," "vocation," or "witness," but in his discussion of "apostolicity" he does mention on p. 504 "the continuing evangelistic and missionary tasks of the church." Seeing mission as a "task of the church" rather than of the essence of the church is precisely the theological problem I am discussing.

documented by the New Testament. The tacit consensus appears to be that
there is little doctrinal significance in the earthly ministry of Jesus, especially
as it demonstrates his sense of his sentness. This is not to say that the person
of Jesus has not been a dominant theme in Christian thought, in liturgy and
hymnody, in architecture and art, in the disciplines of spiritual formation
and the practices of the Christian life. We are thinking here, however, of the
classical doctrinal development of Christology with the emphases upon the
two natures of Christ, the inter-Trinitarian relationships, the deity of Christ,
the titles of Christ, and the saving work of Christ (which blends into soteriology). Hendrikus Berkhof describes this very large picture in this way: "We
face the strange fact that, while innumerable people through the centuries
have first of all been fascinated and gripped by the picture which the evangelists draw of the earthly Jesus, the study of the faith has for centuries hardly
shown any interest in the life of Jesus. . . . As a rule, dogmatics has based
itself on the proclamation structure of the epistles, not the story structure of
the gospels."[12] This observation builds upon his analysis of the approaches
to Christology, which he describes as "Christ from above," "Christ from
behind," and "Christ from below." He comments that "in the history of the
church [the Christ from above approach] . . . has been one-sidedly followed.
This had to lead to a minimization of Jesus as a man living in a particular
historical context."[13]

While in the broad view Berkhof's critique can be upheld, there is also
merit in Alister McGrath's different perspective in his discussion of "the
place of Jesus Christ in Christian theology," where he notes that "Jesus Christ
defines the shape of the redeemed life." It becomes clear in his exposition,
however, that by the "redeemed life," he is referring primarily to "Christian
spirituality and ethics." He says, quite rightly, that "the New Testament itself
is strongly *Christomorphic* in its view of the redeemed life — that is to say,
it affirms that Jesus Christ not only makes that life possible; he also determines its shape. The New Testament image of being conformed to Christ
expresses this notion well."[14] He further observes that "narrative theology"
has underlined this emphasis, stating that "it is the narrative of Jesus Christ
which exercises controlling influence over the Christian community. Christian belief, and especially Christian ethics, are shaped by the narrative of

12. Hendrikus Berkhof, *Christian Faith: An Introduction to the Study of Faith* (Grand
Rapids: Eerdmans, 1979), p. 293.

13. Berkhof, *Christian Faith*, p. 268.

14. McGrath, *Christian Theology*, p. 350.

Jesus Christ, which gives flesh and substance to otherwise abstract ideas of values and virtues."[15]

It is clear, however, that this emphasis upon the church's ethics based upon the pattern of Jesus lacks the concomitant emphasis upon the mission of Jesus, and, as I will argue below, upon the specifically missional thrust of Jesus' calling, formation, and sending of the disciples. It appears to be a fair conclusion that McGrath is not thinking of the "redeemed life" in explicitly missional terms. "Christomorphism" is something other than the dominical role of the Rabbi Jesus in his formation of his disciples for their approaching apostolate. The "redeemed life" does not appear to center upon the Christian vocation to witness, as expounded by Karl Barth, for example.[16]

Rather, this emphasis in McGrath's Christology follows James Denney in his critique of two widespread and "deficient understandings of the place of Christ in the Christian life," the one focusing upon Christ as a moral example, and the other upon Christ as the basis of salvation.[17] We see here, in the Western development of doctrine, evidence of a continuing pattern of separating the theologically inseparable: separating the church and its mission, separating ethics and witness, separating the gospel of personal salvation from the gospel of the inbreaking reign of God in Christ, separating Christ our example from Christ our redeemer, separating Christ as moral example from Christ as the basis of salvation. Such dichotomies are a deeply engrained problem in Western Christendom. I have described this as a pattern of reductionism exemplified by the separation of the benefits of the gospel from the missional mandate of the gospel. This has resulted in a highly individualized understanding of the gospel of salvation that finds its very questionable expression in North America in the consumerist reduction of the gospel to the question, What do I get out of it? What does Jesus do for me?[18]

When we look back upon the course of theological development in the twentieth century, however, we can see that these false dichotomies, especially the separation of Christology and Missiology, were challenged from at

---

15. McGrath, *Christian Theology,* p. 350.

16. See his exposition of "The Christian as Witness," which is the "Goal of Vocation," in *Church Dogmatics* IV/3.2, trans. G. W. Bromiley (Edinburgh: T. & T. Clark, 1962), pp. 554-614.

17. McGrath, *Christian Theology,* p. 350. He references James Denney's *The Christian Doctrine of Reconciliation* (1917) without further citation details.

18. See Darrell Guder, *Be My Witnesses: The Church's Mission, Message, and Messengers* (Grand Rapids: Eerdmans, 1973), *passim,* and *The Continuing Conversion of the Church* (Grand Rapids: Eerdmans, 2000), especially pp. 97-119.

least two directions. One major challenge arose out of the critical reflection about the modern missionary movement that began to emerge after the 1910 Edinburgh Conference. Among the factors that fostered that critique was the disintegration of Western Christendom signaled by the outbreak of World War I, to which I have already referred. The loss of credibility on the part of the West was intensified by a growing awareness among church leaders and theologians both in the West and in the emerging so-called "younger churches" that the transplantation of the gospel as a Western colonial project was flawed. From the 1920s on there was a growing chorus of questions about the mission enterprise. Did the call to follow Jesus Christ have to mean that one had to become a proto-European or North American? Were the confessional formulations and liturgical traditions of the Western churches the universal norm that all emerging churches should adopt? Did Western patterns of governance and hierarchy necessarily have to be incorporated into the newly forming churches in non-Western cultures? Did church buildings have to be Gothic or baroque in order to house properly the people of God? Were Western prejudices about race, class, and gender an unavoidable adjunct of the gospel? Was Jesus to be encountered as a European male?

When one surveys the discussion from this distance, it becomes clear that a great deal of its energy was directed at the disparity between the person and work of Jesus Christ who was being proclaimed, and the way in which the missionary method implemented this gospel in the institutional development of the church. As more and more cultures received direct access to the Scriptures in their own languages, they discovered for themselves that there was much more to the gospel than they had received from their missionaries. They began to build bridges between Missiology and Christology by asking very direct, very blunt questions about the connection of message and method in the missionary movement. This was a different skepticism about Western mission from that secular and disdainful dismissal of the entire movement about which my students report when they reflect on what they have learned about the missionary movement before they arrive at Princeton. This was a critical engagement of mission informed by the person and work of Christ as he was encountered and responded to in the growing churches of the non-Western world. It was the Jesus of Scripture who raised questions about the Christ of Western missions.

This Christological questioning of missionary tactics and assumptions found its articulate expression in the World Council of Churches' World Conference on Mission and Evangelism that took place in San Antonio,

Texas, in 1989. Its theme was "Your Will Be Done: Mission in Christ's Way." Lesslie Newbigin wrote the Bible studies in preparation for that meeting, and he based them on Bible studies on the theme "Mission in Christ's Way" that he had conducted at the meeting of the synod of the church of South India in January of 1986.[19] He starts his exposition by referring to John's great commission, "As the Father sent me, so I send you" (John 20:21), and states his thesis: "This must determine the way we think about and carry out the mission; it must be founded and modeled upon his. We are not authorized to do it in any other way. What was, and is, the way? *How* did the Father send the Son?"[20] The exploration of that "how" question leads him then to investigate Jesus' earthly mission as the demonstration and proclamation of the kingdom of God. This emphasis must necessarily critique well-engrained dualisms and tensions in both Christian theology and practice. He implores his readers, "So, for God's sake, let us not fall into this game of setting words and deeds against each other, preaching against action for justice and action for justice against preaching. Do not let us set 'kingdom' against 'church' and 'church' against 'kingdom.' The church is not an end in itself. 'Church growth' is not an end in itself. The church is only true to its calling when it is a sign, an instrument and a foretaste of the kingdom."[21] Much of the problem of Western Christendom can be summarized by Newbigin's statement, "The church is not an end in itself." Rather, the church's very being and task are to be derived from the person and work of Jesus Christ, whom God has sent and who sends the apostolic church. And if Jesus is both the message and the model for its witness, if he is both the proclaimer and the embodiment of the kingdom, then there must be much more to how we teach the doctrine of Jesus we call Christology — it must engage his missionary calling and action, what he proclaimed and how he demonstrated it.

In 1991 the Presbyterian Church U.S.A. adopted a statement titled "Turn to the Living God: A Call to Evangelism in Christ's Way." Drawing on the ecumenical and missiological discussion of the preceding decades, it developed a "missional Christology" that is classically Trinitarian in its structure but interprets the church's missional vocation in terms of the ministry of Jesus. Newbigin's influence can be seen in statements like these: "As God sent Jesus to announce the promised kingdom and to urge everyone to repent

19. Lesslie Newbigin, *Mission in Christ's Way: A Gift, a Command, an Assurance* (New York: Friendship Press, 1987), p. vii.

20. Newbigin, *Mission in Christ's Way*, p. 1.

21. Newbigin, *Mission in Christ's Way*, p. 12.

and believe the good news, so the church is sent into the world to continue Christ's work. As the Body of Christ, the church is charged not only to make the deeds of Christ visible, but also to make the word of Christ audible."[22]

"Evangelism in Christ's Way" is explored by reference to how Jesus identified with the people of his time and place and evangelized with inclusive love, servant love, healing, through prayer, with urgency, through shared ministry, through proclamation, by living and calling people to a holy life. One might summarize the significance of this major emphasis upon mission in Jesus Christ's way as, first of all, a reaction to the many aspects of the mission process that contradicted the way of Jesus. At the same time, this approach signaled that both the theology and practice of mission must be shaped by the person and work of Christ, who he is and what he did, is doing, and will do. Christology defines mission, and Christologically defined mission that takes the earthly ministry of Jesus seriously will necessarily reshape the character and action of the church. As Lesslie Newbigin never tired of emphasizing, the church is not an end in itself, but a "sign, foretaste and instrument of the kingdom." The Jesus who is the Christ and the Lord embodies that kingdom. His message and how it is to be communicated are inextricably linked in the biblical witness.

The Christological Formation of Missional Practice

If classical expositions of the doctrine of the person and work of Christ tend to neglect the earthly ministry of Jesus, that is certainly not the case when we look at the work of New Testament scholars. Here I will proceed modestly because I am not a New Testament scholar. There is certainly, however, a rich range of New Testament studies that unpack the theological importance of Jesus' earthly ministry for the future formation of the church, beginning with the original disciples. I was privileged to study New Testament under Leonhard Goppelt in Hamburg, before he moved to Munich. To the first volume of his *Theology of the New Testament,* he gave the title *The Ministry of Jesus in Its Theological Significance.*[23] Guided by the conviction that "normative . . .

22. "Turn to the Living God: A Call to Evangelism in Christ's Way," in *Selected Theological Statements of the Presbyterian Church (U.S.A.) General Assemblies (1956-1998)* (Louisville: Office of Theology and Worship [Presbyterian Church U.S.A.], 1998), pp. 617-34, especially p. 620.

23. Leonhard Goppelt, *Theology of the New Testament: The Ministry of Jesus in Its Theological Significance,* trans. John Alsup, ed. Jürgen Roloff (Grand Rapids: Eerdmans, 1981).

is that which is to be addressed to the community from the life and ministry of Jesus," he worked out how that ministry shaped the emerging church in the second volume, *The Variety and Unity of the Apostolic Witness to Christ.*[24] His work was preceded and followed by an amazing diversity of investigations of the life and ministry of Jesus in their theological significance for the church's life and ministry, both in topical studies and in commentaries on various New Testament books. For the purposes of missiological scholarship, this focus upon Jesus' formation of the disciples for the continuation of his ministry has emerged as especially important. There has been a catalytic convergence of New Testament studies of "how Jesus intended the community," to use the original German title of Gerhard Lohfink's seminal work, with the missiological concern to "do mission in Jesus Christ's way."[25]

Rudolf Pesch's analysis of the "theological accomplishment" *(die theologische Leistung)* of Mark may be cited as a persuasive example of the interpretation of the biblical witness to Jesus' earthly ministry as the Christological formation of the apostolic communities that the disciples, as his witnesses, will found.[26] "With the placing of the calling stories in 1:16-20 at the beginning of the presentation, the witnesses of Jesus' work, in the sense of the narrative pragmatic, and the mediators of the Jesus tradition, in the sense of historical reflection, both of whom are those very witnesses who are the original ecclesial authorities, are present in the history of Jesus from the very beginning."[27] The verbal and written witness provided by these original ecclesial authorities is intended to serve the emerging communities in their new calling to be witnesses to Jesus Christ.

> In Mark the pre-Easter history of Jesus is made into the subject of the presentation, but this recourse to that report arises out of the [early church's] proclamation and stands in its service. What happened once in the history of Jesus is to be investigated in relation to its significance for what is happening now and what will happen hereafter in the future of God. The

---

24. Leonhard Goppelt, *Theology of the New Testament: The Variety and Unity of the Apostolic Witness to Christ,* trans. John Alsup, ed. Jürgen Roloff (Grand Rapids: Eerdmans, 1982). See p. 3.

25. Gerhard Lohfink, *Jesus and Community: The Social Dimension of Christian Faith* (Philadelphia: Fortress Press, 1984). The English translation is a pallid rendering of the German title, *Wie hat Jesus Gemeinde gewollt?* — How did Jesus intend the community?

26. Rudolf Pesch, *Das Markusevangelium: Erster Teil, Einleitung und Kommentar zu Kap. 1,1–8,26* (Freiburg/Basel/Wien: Herder, 1977).

27. Pesch, *Markusevangelium,* p. 50.

guiding interest of Mark is . . . the awakening and strengthening of faith. The words and stories of Jesus are collected and passed on in the form of simple narratives, in order to show ancient Christian communities the ground of their faith and to provide their mission the strong foundations needed for preaching, instruction and argument with their opponents.[28]

Especially important in this missional reading of the gospel witness is the calling of the Twelve in Mark 3. Pesch comments that at this point in the narrative "a new, missionally accentuated section begins which emphasizes the decisive function of Christian mission. As followers of Jesus, the Twelve are the bearers of Christian mission, the bearers of ecclesial continuity. At the same time, they represent the people of God to be gathered, the true family of Jesus . . . , the recipients of the mysteries of the kingdom of God. . . . They are the core of the new salvation community called and created by Jesus, which is a missional community, and which the evangelist serves with his missionally intended gospel report."[29] The call to discipleship will issue forth into the apostolate, whose purpose is to form witnessing communities that are prepared to live out the good news of the gospel.

There is in Mark 3:14 that ancient variant that wanders back and forth in various translations between the text and the footnotes. It is the text that re-counts Jesus' calling of the Twelve "whom he desired." The Revised Standard Version translates verse 14, "And he appointed twelve to be with him, and to be sent out to preach." The New Revised Standard Version renders it, "And he appointed twelve, whom he also named apostles, to be with him, and to be sent out to proclaim the message." Prof. Pesch explains that the variant, "whom he also named apostles," was borrowed from and dependent upon Luke 6:13.[30] I wish that I had asked the late Bruce Metzger why the NRSV restored the variant to the main text. Whether original or very old, it appears to underline the apostolic purpose of Jesus' calling, not only of the original twelve, but of the church he intended. Those drawn into the relationship of discipleship will graduate into his apostolate. Including the variant in the main text of the translation seems to confirm Prof. Pesch's emphatic claim that "the entire book of Mark is a mission book."[31]

28. S. Schulz, *Die Stunde der Botschaft: Einfuhrung in die Theologie der vier Evangelisten*, 2nd ed. (Hamburg: Furche Verlag, 1970), pp. 9-46, 35-36, 38, cited in Pesch, *Markusevangelium*, p. 53.

29. Pesch, *Markusevangelium*, p. 209.

30. Pesch, *Markusevangelium*, p. 203.

31. Pesch, *Markusevangelium*, p. 61.

There is a growing conversation among biblical and missiological scholars today around the theme we have come to call "missional hermeneutics."[33] One might describe its basic presupposition in an adaptation of Prof. Pesch's statement: "[T]he entire New Testament is a mission book." The New Testament documents are addressed to communities of believers. They are living in the light of the resurrection and confessing that Jesus Christ is Lord. The diverse testimonies written to and for them serve their continuing formation for their distinctive vocation, which is to be witnesses to Jesus Christ. The Gospels, in particular, are not merely passion stories with long introductions. The narratives of the earthly ministry of Jesus focus primarily upon the calling and formation of the disciples. The communities for which they were written have responded to the gospel of God's love made concrete in the suffering, death, and raising of Christ. Now, as they carry out their own missional vocation, they join the original disciples in the process of formation for that vocation. They "go to school with Jesus," in order to be sent out by him. Discipleship leads to apostolate, just as the gathered church must become the scattered, sent-out church. And apostolate is nourished and enabled by the continuing discipling of the Christian community that is primarily the work of the scriptural witness in its midst. Speaking of the writers of the New Testament, N. T. Wright makes the bold claim that "they were conscious of a unique vocation to write Jesus-shaped, Spirit-led, church-shaping books, as part of their strange first-generation calling."[33]

This way of reading the New Testament documents might be described as the Christological formation of missional practice. It is a crucial meeting and interaction of Christology and Missiology. The texts, in their diverse ways, tell of Jesus Christ. As empowered by the Holy Spirit, they enable every witnessing community to encounter Jesus, to be called and claimed by him, and to be formed to be his witnesses "in Jerusalem, Judea, Samaria, and to the ends of the earth" (Acts 1:8). As their engagement with Christ through the biblical word grows and deepens, they recognize how they are conformed to their world so that they might be transformed by the renew-

32. See David Bosch, *Transforming Mission,* pp. 15-181, and the literature he cites; James V. Brownson, *Speaking the Truth in Love: New Testament Resources for a Missional Hermeneutic* (Harrisburg, PA: Trinity Press International, 1998); Michael Barram, *Mission and Moral Reflection in Paul* (New York: Peter Lang, 2005). In chapter 6 and 7 below we return to a more detailed exposition of "missional hermeneutics."

33. N. T. Wright, *The Last Word: Scripture and the Authority of God — Getting Beyond the Bible Wars* (San Francisco: HarperSanFrancisco, 2005), p. 52.

ing of their minds (Rom. 12:2). Their own evangelization continues as the apostolic formation continues through these written testimonies.[34] They are to be equipped for the work of ministry and the upbuilding of the body of Christ as the Word of God works in their midst apostolically, prophetically, evangelistically, pastorally, and instructionally (Eph. 4:11f.).

The focus upon a missional hermeneutic appears to open up ways of understanding and engaging Scripture not burdened by some of the controversies that have polarized Christians for so long. If we read both the Pauline epistles and the four Gospels through the lenses of a missional hermeneutic, there does not seem to be compelling reason to pit them against each other. In their distinctive and complementary ways, they are forming witnessing communities to be faithful to the same Christ in the living out of the same calling. Paul's letter to the Philippians may be taken as a case in point. It is an epistle sent by Paul to a community that he had founded, and whose formation for continuing witness he had conducted while in their midst. In his epistle, he continues that formation, taking up particular themes that are important for his friends in Philippi. They have been his partners in the gospel "from the first day until now" (Phil. 1:5). They share with Paul in the "defense and confirmation of the gospel" (Phil. 1:7). Under his continuing tutelage, they are learning "the mind of Christ" as they are discipled in Jesus for their apostolate as his witnesses.

To reiterate an argument made more than once in these chapters, the missional purpose of the epistle is summarized in 1:27, "Only let your manner of life be worthy of the gospel of Christ." It is the gospel of Christ which is their first priority. But this gospel is not simply a story that stands in a vacuum surrounded by the acceptance of faith. It is an event that generates a different way of living, a public way of living. Of the several passages in Paul that speak of "worthy living," this one has a distinctive verb. While all the others[35] relate that worthiness to the way believers walk the Christian life, the Philippians text stresses the public and political character of believers' vocation. Stephen Fowl proposes this rendering: "Do this one thing: Order your public life in a manner worthy of the gospel of Christ."[36] The admonition is addressed to the entire community. It has to do with how their public conduct provides a credible demonstration of who Jesus Christ is and what

34. See Darrell Guder, *The Continuing Conversion of the Church*, passim.
35. See 1 Thess. 2:11f.; 2 Thess. 1:11f.; Col. 1:9f.; Eph. 4:1.
36. Stephen E. Fowl, *Philippians*, The Two Horizons New Testament Commentary (Grand Rapids: Eerdmans, 2005), p. 59.

Phil 2

his gospel now concretely means. The presenting issue for the exposition of this text is then, what constitutes this worthiness?

In the context of Philippians, it would appear that all of the imperatives directed at the community fill out and define what is worthy of the gospel of Christ. Stephen Fowl comments that "walking worthily entails that the members of the body display certain types of habits, dispositions, and practices toward one another (several of which are also noted in Phil. 2:1-4)."[37] There, Paul enjoins them to "be of the same mind, having the same love, being in full accord and of one mind" (2:2). They should "do nothing from selfishness or conceit, but in humility count others better than [them]selves" (2:3). Each one should look "not to [one's] own interests but to the interests of others" (2:4). Such corporate conduct before a watching world is worthy of the gospel of Christ. It makes visible and tangible the fact that "encouragement in Christ, incentive of love, participation in the Spirit, affection and sympathy" (2:1) are now possible because of the enabling call of Jesus Christ through his Spirit.

The summarizing appeal defining worthiness comes in verse 2:5, introducing the celebrated Christ Song of verses 5 to 11. The community is to have the "mind among [them]selves that was in Christ Jesus" (2:5). We are challenged here by the difficult concept of *phronesis* with which translators into English constantly struggle. The term is anticipated in the injunction with which Paul concludes his sequence of rhetorical questions at the beginning of the chapter. There, the RSV translates *phronein* as "being of the same mind." Fowl proposes "manifesting a common pattern of thinking and acting."[38] For verse 5, he suggests, "Let this be your pattern of thinking, acting, and feeling, which was also displayed in Christ Jesus."[39] What then follows is, of course, one of the most important Christological passages in the New Testament, which figures largely in the history of the development of doctrine, especially in relation to the interpretation of the *kenosis* of Christ.

It is not my purpose to deal with the theology of the so-called *Carmen Christi*. I want to remain with the question of what constitutes conduct worthy of the gospel of Christ. After all, this passage serves the apostle's argument regarding the "patterns of thinking, acting, and feeling" that should characterize the public witness of the missional community. *Phronesis* is about the way in which the gospel is lived out, about how such conduct is engendered, what faithful witness looks like. The person and work of Jesus,

37. Fowl, *Philippians*, p. 63.
38. Fowl, *Philippians*, p. 77.
39. Fowl, *Philippians*, p. 88.

especially in his incarnation as one "in the form of a servant, born in the likeness of men, humbled, obedient unto death, even death on a cross" (2:6-7), serve here as the pattern to be followed. It should be noted that all through Philippians, the emphasis upon *phronesis,* mindedness, is linked with *mimesis,* imitation or modeling. This is Christological formation for missional practice rooted in the transformation of the "thinking, acting, and feeling" of the witness community, which comes about by following and imitating Jesus. What Paul advocates here as crucial to the continuing formation of the church for its calling is what the Marcan community experiences as it is joined with the original disciples, learning what it means to follow Jesus, to become "fishers of people" (Mark 1:17). If the gospel of Christ is the criterion for worthy living and walking, then this gospel is not to be understood as merely an abstract set of doctrines about Christ. It is as much the encounter with the lived reality of Jesus Christ as he calls people to be his disciples and sends them as his apostolic witnesses. Certainly the doctrinal grappling with the person and work of Christ is essential to the *phronesis* that guides Christian conduct. But the doctrinal grappling needs to be expanded in such a way that what we know and can teach about Jesus Christ is also demonstrated in our common life as his witnesses. To do a Christology that does not attend to the missional formation of the witnessing community by the encounter with Jesus in his earthly ministry, that does not engage the dynamic movement from discipleship to apostolate, is to maintain those dichotomies in theology that are so problematic a part of our theological legacy.

We return to the point already made in chapter 1 regarding the importance of Karl Barth's work for missional theology. There I made the claim that Karl Barth is one of the very few dogmaticians who counters that theological legacy by making mission, missional purpose, and missional vocation a pervasive and shaping theme of his theological project. One of the most powerful implications of this missional priority is his insistence that vocation to witness is an essential aspect of the gospel of reconciliation. Justification and sanctification are not adequately understood and confessed apart from their outworking in the vocation of the individual Christian as witness and the sending of the community of the Holy Spirit to be and do that witness in the world. This is the overarching energy of volume IV of the *Church Dogmatics.*[40]

40. For a comprehensive analysis of Barth's Trinitarian theology of the mission of God, culminating in the vocation to witness and the sending of the community of the Holy Spirit, see John Flett, *The Witness of God: The Trinity, Missio Dei, Karl Barth, and the Nature of Christian Community* (Grand Rapids: Eerdmans, 2010).

Toward the end of this comprehensive exposition, he discusses the role and function of theology, including the academic pursuit of theology, as one aspect of the "service" of the sent community of the Holy Spirit. He emphasizes the vocation to witness as the presupposition for his argument. His bold statement about the essentially missional character of the service of theology, already cited above, merits repeating: "There would be no theology if there were no community obligated in a particular way to the witness of the word. . . . Conversely, the community, both with regard to the witness of its word and, after careful consideration of everything involved, with regard to its *entire* service in all its forms, could never do without theology."[41] His description, toward the end of the last full volume of the *Church Dogmatics*, of the actual task of theology, picks up his reference to the church's "internal and external mission" on the first page of §1:

> In its theology the community renders critical accountability to itself and to the listening world about the appropriateness or lack of appropriateness of its praise of God, its preaching, its instruction, its evangelization and mission, and also of its action, which can never be separated from all of these, and of its witness in the broad and comprehensive sense of that concept, in its relationship to its origin, subject, and content. By means of theology's service, the community examines all that it does in terms of the standard of its *commission*, ultimately in light of the word of its Lord and Commissioner.[42]

The worthiness of the church's public witness is determined in terms of its appropriateness to its calling, and the standard for that determination is the commission set out by Jesus Christ, who is its "origin, subject, and content." It is the totality of who he was and is and shall be that defines who and what his witnessing people are and shall be. The Christology we teach is ultimately validated by the way in which it forms the disciple community for the practice of its apostolic vocation. What we confess about Christ must merge with how we confess Christ. We answer the question, Who do you say that I am? with doctrine that expresses the truth and equips for the living of that truth.

41. Karl Barth, *Kirchliche Dogmatik* (Zürich: Theologischer Verlag Zürich, 1959), IV.3.2, §72, p. 1007 (my translation; see in the English version p. 879).

42. Karl Barth, *Church Dogmatics* I/1, *The Doctrine of the Word of God*, trans. G. W. Bromiley, ed. T. F. Torrance (Edinburgh: T. & T. Clark, 1956), p. 3.

CHAPTER 4

The Church as Missional Community

Why the Term "Missional"?

The research project that generated the book *Missional Church*, published in 1998, must be held accountable, it appears, for the rapid spread of the term "missional" in many circles of discussion dealing with the situation of the church in North America.[1] The research team chose the term precisely because it was a relatively unknown word. We wanted to stimulate a theological conversation about the church that took seriously the premise that, to use the language of Vatican II, "the church is missionary by its very nature."[2] Within the Gospel and Our Culture Network, which sponsored that particular project, this was our working consensus.[3] We needed, somehow, to find a way to talk about the fundamentally missional nature of the church without using terms freighted with all kinds of baggage. By proposing the term "missional" we wanted to claim the right to define what it means. Of course, since then the word has taken on so many meanings that any discussion must always

1. The term is not a neologism (the *Oxford English Dictionary* records its first usage in English in 1907), but has been rarely used until the last few years. See Darrell L. Guder, ed., *Missional Church: A Vision for the Sending of the Church in North America* (Grand Rapids: Eerdmans, 1998).

2. See *Vatican Council II: The Conciliar and Post-Conciliar Documents,* ed. Austin Flannery, O.P. (Collegeville, MN: Liturgical Press, 1975); *Ad Gentes,* 1, p. 814.

3. See www.gocn.org.

This lecture was delivered at the 13th Annual Wheaton Theology Conference, whose thematic focus was "evangelical ecclesiology." It took place April 15-17, 2004, at Wheaton College, Illinois. This lecture was published in M. Husbands and D. Treier, eds. *The Community of the Word: Toward an Evangelical Ecclesiology* (Downers Grove, IL: InterVarsity, 2005), pp. 114-28.

begin with yet another clarification of terms! It is almost comparable to the terminological confusion that always surrounds the term "evangelical," for perhaps many of the same reasons.

That proliferation of possible meanings for the word "missional" complicates the terminological challenge we face when we approach the task of doing an "evangelical ecclesiology." The modern missionary movement of the last three centuries has generated a lot of vocabulary. It has restored the term "mission" to Western theological discourse, along with "missionary" and "missioner," "mission society," "mission field," and that problematic plural term, "missions." And it fostered that more intimidating neologism, "missiology." Here in the West, in the old territories of established Christianity whose history and complexities we lump together under the term "Christendom," the emergence of the term "evangelism" parallels the growth of mission language. For centuries, Western Christendom rarely spoke of "mission," except as a technical term used by medieval theologians to discuss the internal dynamics of the Trinity. We had no need for a verb such as "to evangelize," if we could assume that everyone was a Christian by virtue of birth, baptism, social conditioning, and geography. One still finds lexical definitions that speak of "mission" as that activity done by agents of Western Christendom when they are planting churches in non-Western cultures, and "evangelism" as that activity within Christendom which strives to make people who are culturally Christian into active and practicing Christians.[4] In either instance, the language of mission and evangelism refers to one of the several programs that Christian communities may be involved in, perhaps even to one of several primary emphases of the church. We often find "mission" listed next to things like "worship" and "service" in contemporary discussions of the church's purpose and practice. Rarely, however, would either "mission" or "evangelism" appear in any classical discussion of the doctrine of the church emerging from the Christendom tradition.

There is, of course, a very different attitude out there in our late-modern society with regard to the language of mission and evangelism. We don't have to go far to find wholesale condemnation of the entire vocabulary and practice of mission. Both the secularized intellectual establishment of the West and significant groupings within the theological guild pretty well agree that the Western missionary movement must be roundly criticized as a major misadventure — and not without some justification. As the sometime

---

4. For a more detailed discussion of mission terminology, see Darrell L. Guder, *The Continuing Conversion of the Church* (Grand Rapids: Eerdmans, 2000), pp. 9-15, and the literature cited there.

partner of colonialism, it is supposed to be regretted as the insensitive impo-
sition of Western religious cultures on captive populations, motivated by the
misguided assumption that the benefits of both the gospel and Western civilization were what the world outside Christendom desperately needed. The
decline of Western Christendom in the last century has thus been welcomed
not only as just deserts but as the only thing that enlightened societies could
do after centuries of what Kant called "self-incurred tutelage,"[5] the tutor
being the authoritarian tradition of Christianity embodied in the powerful
organization of the established churches. It has come as a great shock to this
secularized intellectual establishment that Christendom is not disappearing,
but has shifted, as Philip Jenkins documents in his important study titled *The
Next Christendom.*[6] While Christianity continues to recede in the territories
of its former domination, Prof. Jenkins chronicles the enormous growth and
vitality of the "next Christendom" in Africa, Southern and Eastern Asia,
and Latin America. That much-maligned Western missionary movement,
to everyone's surprise, worked, and the former "daughter churches" are now
our "sister churches," many of which are sending missionaries to the now
post-Christian societies that, not long ago, sent missionaries to them.

The term "missional" is an attempt to move the discussion beyond too-
narrow definitions of mission as merely one among the various programs of
the church, and to find ways to think about the church's calling and practice
today in light of the fact of the multicultural global church, what Archbishop
Temple famously called "the great new fact of our time." To describe the
church as "missional" is to make a basic theological claim, to articulate a
widely held but also widely ignored consensus regarding the fundamental
purpose of the Christian church. Rather than seeing mission as, at best, one
of the necessary prongs of the church's calling, and at worst as a misguided
adventure, it must be seen as the fundamental, the essential, the centering
understanding of the church's purpose and action. The church that Jesus
intended, to use Gerhard Lohfink's provocative book title, is missional by its
very nature.[7] The church that the triune God gathers, upbuilds, and sends, to

---

5. Immanuel Kant, "What Is Enlightenment?," in *Kant: Selections,* ed. L. W. Beck (New
York and London: Macmillan, 1988), p. 462.

6. Philip Jenkins, *The Next Christendom: The Coming of Global Christianity* (Oxford:
Oxford University Press, 2002).

7. The original of Gerhard Lohfink, *Jesus and Community: The Social Dimension of Christian Faith,* trans. J. P. Galvin (Philadelphia: Fortress Press, 1984), has the much more evocative
title, *Wie hat Jesus Gemeinde gewollt* (Freiburg/Basel/Vienna: Herder Verlag, 1982) = "How
Did Jesus Intend the Community?"

use the profoundly missional outline of Karl Barth's ecclesiology in volume IV of the *Church Dogmatics,* exists to continue the service of witness.[8]

The church whose planting is witnessed to in the New Testament is properly understood in terms of its missional calling.[9] That was the purpose of the apostolic mission: to found missional communities to continue the witness that had brought them into being. The interpretation of the New Testament Scriptures finds its interpretive key in that purpose. The apostolic witness preceded the writing of the scriptural documents. The communities were already missional when Gospel authors and epistle writers tackled the task of their continuing formation through these written testimonies. Thus, the Scriptures' collective purpose, we contend, was the continuing formation of already-missional communities for faithful and obedient witness. This formation took place in the Synoptic Gospels and John by incorporating young missional communities into the discipling process of Jesus, the outcome of which must always be apostolate, "being sent out." The formation took place in the epistles as the apostolic authors affirmed, prayed for, corrected, argued with, and continued to evangelize the missional churches to which they wrote. Their problems became the curriculum of continuing conversion to missional calling and its practice for the benefit of the church catholic.

Defining "missional" in such a way has broad implications for the entire theological task, starting with ecclesiology but not stopping there. It certainly bears upon our understanding of what it means to be "evangelical." There is virtually no attempt to define "evangelical" that does not emphasize, in some way, the priority of mission and the essential importance of evangelism — however problematically either may be understood in these definitions. In what follows, I would like to suggest, in broad strokes, some aspects of the task of formulating a missional ecclesiology that may contribute to a clearer understanding of what we mean by "evangelical."

---

8. Karl Barth, *Church Dogmatics,* ed. G. W. Bromiley and T. F. Torrance, trans. G. W. Bromiley (Edinburgh: T. & T. Clark, 1956: IV/1; 1958: IV/2; 1961: IV/3, 1st half; 1962: IV/3, 2nd half); see also David Bosch, *Transforming Mission: Paradigm Shifts in Mission Theology* (Maryknoll, NY: Orbis, 2011), pp. 381-82.

9. The subject under discussion is "missional hermeneutics," for which a small but important literature is beginning to appear. See, e.g., David Bosch, *Transforming Mission,* pp. 15-56; James V. Brownson, *Speaking the Truth in Love: New Testament Resources for a Missional Hermeneutic* (Harrisburg, PA: Trinity Press International, 1998); Richard Bauckham, *The Bible and Mission* (Grand Rapids: Baker, 2003); Christopher Wright, *The Mission of God: Unlocking the Bible's Grand Narrative* (Downers Grove, IL: InterVarsity, 2006). The "GOCN Forum on Missional Hermeneutics," meeting annually under the umbrella of the Society of Biblical Literature, has broadened the discussion since its inception in 2002. See chapters 6 and 7 below.

The Reductionism of Mission in Western Theologies

Wilbert Shenk defines "historical Christendom" as "the powerful religio-political synthesis that resulted when Christianity won recognition as the religion of state in the fourth century," with the result that "the church now took its place alongside the other powers controlling society but was thus itself redefined by its new role."[10] One outcome of the process by which the Constantinian project reshaped Christianity into Christendom was, as Shenk succinctly puts it, "Christianity without mission." As helpful as his general analysis is, this is an oversimplification. It discounts such important movements as the Celtic mission of St. Patrick and the Iro-Scottish mission that it fostered, or the Slavic mission of Saints Methodius and Cyril, or even the missional ministry within European Christendom of the Franciscan and Dominican movements. But it makes a valid point with regard to the formation of Christian *theology* within Christendom. It is not an oversimplification to say that the fundamentally missional nature of the church gradually disappears from the formulations of Western ecclesiology. We can only suggest some of the major reasons for that shift.

Certainly the reduction of mission in Western theology has to do with the so-called Christianization of Western cultures. Once the Christian religion had become the only allowed religion within the boundaries of Christendom, mission was not seen as the central task of the church. Rather, her theological definition gradually came to focus upon the care and tending of the salvation of her members, who were simultaneously citizens of Christendom. This centering on the savedness of the saved reflected another profoundly important shift in thought and practice, relating directly to the gospel itself. The biblical message of salvation underwent a reductionism that resulted in emphasis upon individual salvation, how it was attained and how it was maintained. The classic definition of Christian existence focused on the benefits the person receives from the gospel, to the neglect of the vocation of witness for which the benefits prepare the Christian.[11] The institutional church was thus construed as essential for individual blessedness, providing the rites that initiated salvation and baptism, and that tended and

10. Wilbert Shenk, *Write the Vision: The Church Renewed* (Valley Forge, PA: Trinity Press International, 1995), p. 33.

11. This is the focus of Karl Barth's critique of the "classic definition of a Christian," *Church Dogmatics* IV/3, 2nd half, pp. 561-73; see also Darrell Guder, *Be My Witnesses: The Church's Mission, Message, and Messengers* (Grand Rapids: Eerdmans, 1985); Darrell Guder, *The Continuing Conversion of the Church.*

maintained it, from eucharist through penance to unction. Diminished or distorted in the process was the biblical understanding of the corporate and cosmic scope of salvation as the healing of all creation, the restoration of all things to the sovereign and gracious rule of God. Together with that loss there was the diminishing of the church's understanding of how it did the minimal mission that remained. Ultimately, only the clergy did that mission — which consisted primarily of the administration of personal salvation — and the members simply received the benefits distributed by the church on behalf of God.

Further, the eschatological shaping of the gospel of salvation, so central to the New Testament, was distorted and reduced. Jesus' message was the inbreaking reign of God, and the early church confessed him as the one who is and brings that reign into human reality. He is enthroned and rules as Savior and Lord, witnessed to by his church through the empowering of the Holy Spirit. The church's empowered witness has, in the New Testament, a dynamic sense of God's work begun, God's work promised, and God's work being carried out now in the pilgrimage of faith and healing. The evidence of that inbreaking reign takes shape within the "community of the word" in the reality of continuing conversion and healing, and in the empowering of the community to live publicly in ways that point to God's rule. God's future, to be sure, will bring the end of history, the judgment of humanity, the abolition of all opposition to God's rule, and the "new heavens and new earth." But the community's common witness is so energized and focused by its confidence in God's future that its life now is already transformed and informed by the "living hope" established by "the resurrection of Jesus Christ from the dead." It looks forward to "an inheritance which is imperishable, undefiled, and unfading, kept in heaven" for God's children. Now, in this time of testing, God's power guards the community through the gift of faith "for a salvation ready to be revealed in the last time" (1 Pet. 1:3-5). And during this passage through time, the community experiences the healing power of the gospel and witnesses to this new reality as it looks forward confidently.

That sense of radical and transforming anticipation, of living hope that profoundly shapes the "now" of the corporate Christian witness, was gradually reoriented to an individualistic emphasis upon the Second Coming at the end of time with its threatening Judgment that determines where each soul will spend eternity. The biblical emphasis upon the "resurrection of the body" is replaced by the Hellenistic concept of the "immortality of the soul," which changes the nature of Christian eschatology and diminishes the strong biblical emphasis upon the integrated wholeness of the human person as body, spirit, and soul. Life now was understood not so much as faithful witness in hope but as wearisome and often anxious preparation in this vale of tears for what must come hereafter. Salvation is a question of "where one spends eternity" rather than the larger biblical witness to the restorative and salvific reign of God breaking in now, whose consummation is yet to come.

As heirs of the Christendom legacy, we inherit these tendencies towards reductionism both of the gospel of salvation (soteriological reductionism) and of the church's purpose and practices (ecclesiological reductionism). We struggle with the compromises made in the name of the gospel over the centuries that have gradually domesticated the gospel and produced what Dietrich Bonhoeffer so aptly called a gospel of "cheap grace."[12] The individualism of such a reductionist soteriology has only intensified in the self-centered and consumerist culture of present-day North America. The church's focus upon the tending and maintenance of the savedness of the saved is well attested today in churches that advertise themselves as "full-service" congregations and function as purveyors of the religious programs and products their member-consumers want. The partnership of church and state has, after the end of Christendom, effectively been replaced with the partnership of church and marketplace.

It is, however, an act of theological dishonesty to present the reductionist legacy of Christendom in monotonously somber tones. God has not been absent from Christendom — any more than God was absent from the long and unedifying history of Israel's kings — but has been graciously and powerfully present through our long history. We are heirs of both our human reductionisms and of divinely empowered resistance to such disobedience. One of the pressing requirements for the development of a missional ecclesiology today is the task of learning how to read and interpret our history dialectically. We need to discern how God has been faithful in and through the lives and activities of both the known and anonymous mentors of witness and obedience, those "special individuals" whom Karl Barth describes as "models and examples" for the church in their "special calling and endowments."[13] We trace God's formation of his people in the prayers and liturgies, the neighborly love and innovative charity, the theological scholarship, the gifts for music and architecture, and the courage of public witness of so many members of the cloud of witnesses that surrounds and supports us. That dialectical realism allows us and constrains us to speak without hesitation of the

---

12. Dietrich Bonhoeffer, *The Cost of Discipleship* (New York: Macmillan, 1959), pp. 35-37.
13. Karl Barth, *Church Dogmatics* IV/3, 2nd half, p. 888.

missional vocation and purpose of the church, in spite of the unquestioned fact that so much of our modern mission history is a very mixed and even questionable story. We did, in fact, confuse the message of the gospel with our own inflated sense of the normativity of our enlightened Western civilization. A reductionist soteriology did generate a reductionist vision of mission and a highly compromised understanding of the purpose of the church. But God has graciously overruled those shortcomings and allowed the message to be planted and the missional church to be formed in every major cultural area of the world. We are comforted by the wise word of the pastor from Malawi who told my class one day about all the changes the gospel had brought when the missionaries came to his tribe. "And," he concluded, "you must realize that we could always tell the difference between Jesus and the missionaries."

The Western Shift to Post-Christendom
and the Emergence of the Theology of the *missio Dei*

Now, however, we are coming to terms with the obvious fact that Christendom has ended — although, in some places it is more accurate to say that it is ending (there is a significant difference in the "state of Christendom" between Atlanta and Seattle!). Historians and social scientists must date and analyze the complex process of its ending and the character of the paradigm shift in which we find ourselves. Pastors must accompany their congregations through the painful recognition that we as the Christian church have indeed lost much, and that we are truly in a situation like that of Israel in exile, as Walter Brueggemann frequently has said.[14] Counselors must help parents deal with the challenge and the sadness of living with the decisions made by their adult children and their grandchildren to leave their faith behind and embrace our modern secularism or the growing variety of New Age religions. Students of culture must help us learn and understand the changes, the new languages, the values and goals of our rapidly changing society in all its subcultures. And theologians must recognize anew that, as Martin Kähler said over a century ago, "mission is the mother of theology."[15] We find ourselves as heirs of Christendom in a radically changed territory,

14. See, e.g., Walter Brueggemann, *Cadences of Home: Preaching Among Exiles* (Louisville: Westminster John Knox, 1997).

15. Martin Kähler, *Schriften zur Christologie und Mission* (Munich: Chr. Kaiser Verlag, 1971 [1908]), p. 190.

the Western mission field, which by any standards is one of the world's most difficult and complex arenas for Christian witness.

We are handicapped by some of the assumptions and attitudes of Christendom that are still very powerful in our minds and congregations. Our ecclesiologies of institutional maintenance and the tending of savedness are not adequate to the task that faces us now. We cannot evangelize under the assumption that most of what it means to be a practicing Christian is already handled by one's being born and raised in so-called Christian North America — so that all one needs to do is accept Jesus, join a church, and perhaps start tithing. Nor can we evangelize under the assumption that our culture prepares people for Christ, so that we merely need to recognize the "felt needs" that people bring to church with them. The "felt needs" of a society shaped by consumerism and the entertainment industry may, instead, generate a kind of church that continues the gospel reductionism already so deeply engrained in Western Christianity. What may then happen could be nothing more than a last, desperate attempt to recover the popularity by other means that Christianity seemed to enjoy during Christendom, a popularity that Christians continue to confuse with faithful witness and genuine mission. Genuine missional vocation today must take seriously that process of dilution that David Bosch aptly described when he commented that Western theology could be characterized as a process of explaining why the Sermon on the Mount does not apply to us.[16] Much of our evangelism is based upon unquestioned, undoubted versions of "cheap grace." And much of our understanding and practice of the church's calling and ministry is based upon a reductionist ecclesiology that cannot pretend to be "evangelical" because it is not "missional."

That process of theological reorientation has been emerging for a long time. Although the Reformation does not generate an explicitly missional theology for Christendom, the first resources for such a theology can be traced in Luther's vision of the priesthood of all believers and Calvin's radical understanding of God's grace effecting our justification, our forgiveness, and our sanctification in an inextricably intertwined process that generates public witness affecting every area of the community's life. It advances in Kierkegaard's attack upon Christendom[17] and P. T. Forsyth's comprehensive

16. "Indeed, this sermon expresses, like no other New Testament passage, the essence of the ethics of Jesus. Through the ages, however, Christians have usually found ways around the clear meaning of the Sermon on the Mount"; Bosch, *Transforming Mission*, p. 70.

17. Søren Kierkegaard, *Attack Upon "Christendom,"* trans. W. Lowrie (Princeton: Princeton University Press, 1968).

understanding of the formation of the congregation of believers for faithful witness as service.[18] It is certainly accelerated by the beginnings of the Ecumenical Movement at the Edinburgh Conference of 1910 and the subsequent study and exploration under the aegis of the Faith and Order movement, the Life and Work movement, and the International Missionary Council.[19] Karl Barth recognized by the early 1920s that "the idol is tottering,"[20] and that it was time to rethink all of Christian doctrine from the perspective of what serves the formation of the church for its faithful witness in an increasingly post-Christian and even hostile world — the result is a *Church Dogmatics* rather than a "systematic theology."

With regard to the challenge of developing a missional ecclesiology, there appear to have been two major factors that have shaped the process. On the one hand, there was the theological significance of the emergence of new and autonomous churches in the non-Western world, as the result of the modern missionary movement. It is widely acknowledged that the planting of new churches in previously unevangelized cultures was undertaken with a very inadequate ecclesiology. Most modern mission was undertaken by voluntary societies, not by the established churches of the West. There was virtually no theological attention given to mission by the Western academic guild, and so the mission societies had little ecclesiological equipment to guide the formation of new churches. Thus, Christendom's focus upon the salvation of individual souls shaped the proclamation of the modern missionary movement, and so the newly formed mission churches figured largely as a kind of ecclesiastical receptacle for converts. Since Western ecclesiology did not operate under the fundamental principle that the church is called, gathered, formed, and sent to be God's witnesses in the world, we did not initially form churches with that sense of missional vocation. The question of missional calling was really forced upon the emerging global church by the reality of being minority churches in completely non-Christian settings and illumined by their own interaction with Scripture as translations into vernacular languages made this possible.

18. See, e.g., P. T. Forsyth, *The Church and the Sacraments* (London: Independent Press, 1947, 1917).

19. A comprehensive survey of these ecumenical developments is found in W. Richey Hogg, *Ecumenical Foundations: A History of the International Missionary Council and Its Nineteenth Century Background* (New York: Harper, 1952, repr.: Eugene, OR: Wipf & Stock, 2002).

20. Letter from Karl Barth to Eduard Thurneysen of April 20, 1920, in Ernst Wolf et al., *Antwort: Karl Barth zum siebzigsten Geburtstag am 10. Mai 1956* (Zollikon-Zürich: Evangelischer Verlag AG, 1956), p. 856.

As representatives of Christendom, used to the privileges and protections of majority status, we had little to offer our new sister churches as they began to take up the challenge of their calling in their contexts. But as they received the Bible in their own languages and began to grasp how this story was now their story and that the missional mandate of the New Testament church defined them as well, they began to address the ecclesiological deficiencies exported from Christendom. The urgent concern for Christian unity pressed upon the complacent denominations of Christendom by the sister churches in the non-Western world grew out of their clear understanding that their divisions invalidated their witness. The issue was well summarized in the statement on "Mission and Evangelism" drafted by the Commission on World Mission and Evangelism of the World Council of Churches and adopted in 1982: "The present ecumenical movement came into being out of the conviction of the churches that the division of Christians is a scandal and an impediment to the witness of the church. There is a growing awareness among the churches today of the inextricable relationship between Christian unity and missionary calling, between ecumenism and evangelization. 'Evangelization is the test of our ecumenical vocation.'"[21]

The other factor forcing the issue of a missional ecclesiology has been the disintegration of Christendom in the West and with it a growing sense of the deficiency of the ecclesiologies we inherit. It is gradually becoming clear that the Christian church in the West can no longer assume that it has a cordial Christian context within which it can go about its duties. When confronted by the secularism and paganism of Western cultures today, both the traditional inherited church structures and the theological systems that inform them find themselves largely at a loss. But our theologies of the church do not prepare us for this missional challenge in our own previously Christianized territory. Before we can turn our theological attention to themes like ordered ministry, sacraments, and spiritual disciplines, we have to grapple with the basic questions: Who is the church of Jesus Christ and what is it for? As I have shown, the ecclesiological mindset we inherit tends to define the church in terms of the benefits it provides its members, as Avery Dulles explained in his classic *Models of the Church*.[22] Thus, mission had to be interpreted as all those activities that build and expand the church. Such

21. World Council of Churches, *Mission and Evangelism: An Ecumenical Affirmation* (Geneva: World Council of Churches, 1983), §1.

22. Avery Dulles, S.J., *Models of the Church* (Garden City, NY: Doubleday Image, 1978), pp. 45-47.

ways of thinking, which we group together as ecclesiocentric theologies of the church, are necessarily having to give way to another theological center of gravity. Since the 1930s, the consensus has gradually emerged that the church is not about itself, as though it were a self-justifying end, but the church must be defined and must act as part of the larger mission of God.

The theology of the *missio Dei* defines the church within the framework of the doctrine of the triune God. David Bosch has described this theological consensus succinctly, explaining that mission is "understood as being derived from the very nature of God. It was thus put in the context of the doctrine of the Trinity, not of ecclesiology or soteriology. The classical doctrine on the *missio Dei* as God the Father sending the Son, and God the Father and the Son sending the Spirit was expanded to include yet another 'movement': Father, Son, and Holy Spirit sending the church into the world."[23] The fundamental assumption here has to do with the revealed nature and purpose of God: ". . . mission is not primarily an activity of the church, but an attribute of God. God is a missionary God."

It is not possible in this chapter to explore all the twists and turns of the *missio Dei* debate since it became a focusing theme of missiological discussion in the 1950s.[24] It is intriguing, however, that this theological consensus emerges as Christendom is unraveling in the West. Scripture discloses that God's mission is the outworking of God's love for his entire creation, which God translates into purposeful action to bring about the healing of his broken creatures, restoration to himself and to his good design, and incorporation into his kingdom as its witnesses and servant. The theology of the *missio Dei* is making clear that our ecclesiology, if it is truly to be a doctrine for the church that is continuing the apostolic witness, must be rooted in God's nature, purpose, and action. It must be developed out of the mission of God as the One who calls and empowers his people to be the sign, foretaste, and instrument of God's new order under the lordship of Christ. This ecclesiology understands the church as Christ's witness, living in continuing community with him in its midst, prepared by his word through Scripture to be sent by him into the world which he loves and for which he died. Such a doctrine must serve the formation of the "community of the word" for

23. Bosch, *Transforming Mission*, p. 399.

24. For a thorough review of the *missio Dei* discussion in the latter half of the twentieth century, see the edition of the *International Review of Mission* 92, no. 367 (October 2003), titled "*Missio Dei* Revisited: Willingen 1952-2002," for a series of informative articles examining this tradition from diverse perspectives. See also chapter 2 above.

comprehensive missional witness. In short, *to be authentically "evangelical," our ecclesiology must necessarily be "missional."*

If our concern is faithful witness to the gospel, then our doctrine of the church must be built upon and expound the mission for which the church is called, formed, and sent, according to the biblical witness. As I said, the point is God's love for the world and the concrete demonstration of that love in the incarnation, ministry, death, resurrection, and ascension of Jesus Christ. The divine strategy for the healing of the world is the calling, setting apart, formation, and sending of a particular people whose witness has, as Newbigin puts it, "universal intent." God's gospel is to be made known to all people as an invitation to healing and to enlistment in the service of God as part of his witnessing people. Christian vocation is not merely to individual savedness, but to the service of God's mission to bring healing to the nations. Therefore, Christian witness is corporate in order that it can also be individual and personal. God calls a people into discipleship, formation by Jesus, in order to send it out as an apostolic community, so that each of its members can be an apostolic witness with that flame of the Spirit ignited on every head. The community of the word is neither a safe enclave nor a colony walled off from the world, although it is, to be sure, always an alternative community within its context. It is a people *in via,* en route, on a pilgrimage definitively shaped by the incarnation, ministry, message, death, resurrection, and ascension of Jesus, moving with him along his narrow path toward the certain consummation of God's work of salvation. The church that Jesus intended is a community that lives its message publicly, transparently, vulnerably — that is why it is called *ecclesia,* an assembly set apart to do public business in view of the watching world.[25] Its public witness has its dynamic focus on its gathered worship and proclamation of the Sent One. In Word and sacrament, Jesus encounters us in this central event of inward and focused devotion with the explosive outwardly thrusting commission, "So I send you." The ancient greeting that ended the liturgy, "Ite missa est," must be understood not merely as "go, you are dismissed," but rather, "go, you are sent."

To be authentically evangelical, I repeat, our ecclesiology must be missional. Such an ecclesiology will function then theologically as an integrative discipline, drawing all of the theological discourses into constructive interaction for the sake of building up the body of Christ and equipping it for its

---

25. John Howard Yoder, *Body Politics: Five Practices of the Christian Community Before the Watching World* (Nashville: Discipleship Resources, 1992, 1997).

service (Eph. 4:11f.). Rooted in the Trinitarian nature and action of God, this ecclesiology derives its purpose from God's mission. It defines the way it goes about its work by means of God's self-disclosure in the history of Israel and supremely in the earthly ministry of Jesus. As an ecclesiology of Pentecost, this doctrine confesses the church's dependence upon the empowering work of the Spirit as it enables witness to Christ in all that the church is, does, and says. It will be the work of the Spirit to guide the missional church in its disciplined engagement with God's Word as the instrument God uses for the continuing formation of the community of the word for its vocation. As a result of that biblical formation, the community will grow in its understanding of how its corporate public witness must be practiced, and at the same time, how each member will lead his or her life as an apostolic missionary in the daily neighborliness of witness to Jesus Christ.

Such an ecclesiology pays particularly close attention to the "as" and the "so" in John's missional summary: "As my Father has sent me, so I send you" (John 20:21). God's incarnational action in history provides the church the content of its witness and defines how it is to be carried out. "Mission in Jesus' way" has become a much-explored theme in missional theology these last decades, and such thinking should shape our missional ecclesiology.[26] Theological ethics should school the missional church to practice witness with integrity. It should guide the community to discern how, in fact, we are to "live our lives worthy of the calling with which we have been called."[27] The dominical and apostolic formation of the missional church focuses upon the concrete obedience of the called community and of all its members; it works intentionally on the transparency and integrity of its common life and its scattered life in an often-hostile world.

There is particular urgency today for a missional ecclesiology to reclaim the profoundly eschatological character of the church's calling. The theological reductionism of both gospel and church has been accompanied, over the centuries, by a great loss of that future tense of faith that should powerfully shape our present life and action. In place of fruitless speculation about

26. Commission on World Mission and Evangelism, *The San Antonio Report: Your Will Be Done: Mission in Christ's Way* (Geneva: WCC Publications, 1990); Lesslie Newbigin, *Mission in Christ's Way* (New York: Friendship Press, 1988); "Turn to the Living God: A Call to Evangelism in Christ's Way," in Office of Theology and Worship, *Selected Theological Statements: Presbyterian Church (U.S.A.) General Assemblies (1956-1998)* (Louisville: Presbyterian Church [U.S.A.], 1998), pp. 617-34.

27. Eph. 4:1; see also this fundamental theme in Paul's community formation in Phil. 1:27 and the theme of "imitation" generally in that epistle; 1 Thess. 2:11-12; 2 Thess. 1:11; Col. 1:9.

events that have not yet happened, we must focus upon the certainty of our hope that enables us now to witness to Christ fearlessly and point away from ourselves modestly. A missional ecclesiology will always be candid about its penultimate nature; the continuing conversion of the church will necessitate obedient and serendipitous revisiting of all our theological formulae and propositions. This does not mean that the gospel is not sufficient to the task; it means that the church lives with the open confession that its grasp of and response to the gospel is always partial, that there is yet more healing to be done, more conversion to submit to, more wonder to worship.

Paul wrote to the Corinthians, after a particularly evocative exposition of the gospel's vocation (in 2 Cor. 4:1-14), "All this is for your sake" (2 Cor. 4:15) — and Christendom would like to stop there, would like to leave us as Christians enjoying the benefits of our salvation and working away at the threats to our blessedness that arise both out of the world and our own rebellions. But the text has no period there. It says, "All this is for your sake so that grace, as it extends to more and more people, may increase thanksgiving to the glory of God." The purpose of God's mission is ultimately the acknowledgment and enjoyment of the glory of God; it happens as grace extends to more and more people; the evidence of that spread is growing thanksgiving to God which displays before the world the loving character and purposes of our God. It is the task and privilege of a missional ecclesiology to serve God's glory by guiding the church to an ever-growing understanding of who it is and what it is for. Thus, every classical theme of ecclesiology, the doctrine and practice of the sacraments, of proclamation, of ordered ministry, of membership, of stewardship, of spiritual disciplines, will be drawn into and redefined by the foundational vocation of the church to be Christ's witness, to lead its life worthy of its calling, to be Christ's letter to the world, to be, as Peter summarized it, "a chosen race, a royal priesthood, a holy nation, God's own people, in order that you may proclaim the mighty acts of him who called you out of darkness into his marvelous light" (1 Pet. 2:9).

CHAPTER 5

The Nicene Marks in a Post-Christendom Church

Dislocation and Opportunity

The issue that is either openly addressed or subtly at work in all our discussions about a denomination like the Presbyterian Church (U.S.A.) is the fact that Christendom is over. Wherever one is located on the theological or ecclesial spectrum, this is the common ground that links us together. The grant proposal that led to the funding of the "Re-Forming Ministry" project put it very succinctly:

> Mainline Protestantism is no longer the religious expression of American society, the culture's *de facto* established church. The social and religious climate has altered dramatically, pushing denominations such as the PCUSA out of the center of American Christianity, and pushing Christianity itself to the margins of a culture that is increasingly secular, pluralistic, and indifferent to the institutional church. (p. 20)

The "Christianity" referred to in the last sentence is the Christianity of European Christendom, that partnership of church, state, and society

---

This proposal to reread the Nicene marks in the reverse direction first emerged in the last chapter of the book I edited, *Missional Church: A Vision for the Sending of the Church in North America* (Grand Rapids: Eerdmans, 1998). I developed it further in the context of a funded research project of the Presbyterian Church (U.S.A.), which addressed the theology of the practice of ordered ministry in the Reformed tradition. It was published together with two other papers generated by that project: C. Wiley, K. Park, and D. Guder, *The Nicene Marks in a Post-Christendom Church* (Louisville: Office of Theology and Worship, 2005); that version makes up this chapter. In the final chapter of this book, I revisit the theme in order to take account of its role in the ongoing missional conversation of which I have been a part.

initiated in the fourth century under the Emperor Constantine. This project resulted in the shaping and definition of Western cultures as "Christian," symbolized by the parish church at the center of every village, town, and city. The Christian churches of Christendom have been legally "established" and the Christian religion socially and culturally privileged, to such an extent that the terms "European," and later, "North American," have been equated with "Christian" in common usage.

The proposal's language is a good, clean summary of a broadly held consensus — at least among schooled observers of our context. It is debatable whether or to what degree the general membership in Presbyterian congregations (or in any other mainline congregations) really grasps this paradigm shift. Christendom may well be over legally (disestablishment became the law of the land with the ratification of the Bill of Rights!), but the mentality and attitudes of Christendom still flourish in our churches, our popular imagination, and much of our public culture. The popularity of the song "God Bless America" witnesses to that cultural reality.

My concern is how we, within the Presbyterian Church, appreciate or work with this contextual change in which we find ourselves today. More pointedly, I would like to know how or whether we, in fact, see this paradigm shift as a theological opportunity. Can we understand that the end of Christendom opens up to us a way to begin to reassess the Western theological tradition from the liberating perspective of the actual and unquestioned end of Christendom? Can we grapple with the very significant challenges and problems as well as great benefits inherited from this long, fascinating, and complex history?

Why the Church?

It appears that the end of Christendom raises particularly unsettling questions with regard to the theology of the church. That should not surprise us. Both the institutional and intellectual shapes of the Christian movement have obviously been profoundly affected by the position of privilege and protection guaranteed across the centuries of Christendom. As we learn to look at what that project has done to us theologically, we also have to ask what can perhaps now be changed, or needs to be changed, as a result of that learning. This is no easy task, since ecclesiological issues are very complex and comprehensive. The wording of the grant proposal suggests that the end of the church's eminence and the decline of its influence, which we are all experiencing, have led to confusion about the church's identity. If legal establishment and cultural privilege should no longer define the church, then what should? What should be the criteria for our definition of both the purpose and the shape of the church? Should the church, because of its long history of cultural compromise and even captivity, distance itself from contemporary culture? Or should it find other ways to relate to its context when it no longer has automatic access to cultural power? In light of the diminishing numbers of people on our rolls, should our theology and worship be shaped to attract outsiders, or should they focus primarily on the needs and wants of those who are still faithful members? Are these two strategies necessarily incompatible, and beyond that, are they even appropriate expressions of a biblical theology of the church? What forms of mission or faith articulation are appropriate in a changing world? What are the characteristics of leadership needed in the changing church, and how are these characteristics identified and encouraged?

Ultimately, this massive paradigm shift confronts us with the most basic of questions: Why is there a church at all? That was the very same question that was formulated by Coulter, Mulder, and Weeks at the end of their six-volume study, *The Presbyterian Presence*, when they reviewed the theological agenda for the reforming of the Presbyterian Church. The fourth question on their list was "Why, after all, is there a church — an ordered community of Christians?"[1]

Interpreting the Legacy of Christendom:
Ecclesiology without Mission

As a teacher of future pastors and leaders of our church, I am very committed to reading our Christendom legacy in a balanced and fair way. There is a great deal of reckless "Christendom-bashing" going on, and we do need to be theologically attentive and responsible in the way that we read our legacy. It will not do to imply, somehow, that the Holy Spirit left the earth around the fourth century, when Constantine came to power, only to reappear in the modern group or movement with which we may now be affiliated. If God is faithful to his purpose and calling, then God has been present and at work

---

1. Milton J. Coulter, John M. Mulder, Louis B. Weeks, eds., *The Re-Forming Tradition: Presbyterians and Mainstream Protestantism*, vol. 6 of *The Presbyterian Presence: The Twentieth-Century Experience* (Louisville: Westminster John Knox, 1992), p. 283.

through this very ambiguous history that we call Christendom, just as God was present and at work through one thousand years of kings in Israel, most of whom the ancient Chronicler found wanting.

As we have already emphasized, we have to learn a certain dialectical skill in order to read and interpret this legacy that shapes us. Having said that, however, I contend that the end of Christendom exposes the fact that it is in the area of ecclesiology that we confront the greatest problems. To be sure, many have argued, as I have done, that Christendom's Christianity is defined by pervasive reductionism, especially with regard to our understanding of God's promised and completed salvation. There are, in fact, reductionist problems in all of the classical, theological themes. Having granted that, it seems to me that the most profound issues arise out of the problematic impact of salvation reductionism and its sweeping implications for the theology of the church. To concentrate a complex analysis in a brief summary, the reduction of the gospel of cosmic salvation to the focus upon the savedness of the individual is directly linked to an understanding of the church that centers on the administration of that salvation to the individual believer. From the onset of the Constantinian project, this gradually expanding reductionism of the theology of the church has been institutionalized, supported by the various forms of the church's cultural adaptation and compromise. Now we can see this more clearly than we have for a very long time. The telling point for this reductionism is the place and importance of mission in any Western theology of the church (ecclesiology).

It is important to stress that mission has never been absent from the church's work within the world. Kenneth Scott Latourette devotes the second of his seven volumes on the "History of the Expansion of Christianity" to what he calls "A Thousand Years of Uncertainty, 500-1500 AD."[2] There is much significant mission activity to trace across these centuries, but one looks in vain for a theological focus upon mission in the emerging ecclesiologies of Western Christendom. This is a fundamental theological problem for the Western church. It puts this tradition in direct tension with the biblical understanding of the character and purpose of the church within God's mission. Based on the New Testament, it is abundantly clear that the fundamental assertion we must make about the church of Jesus Christ is that it is, in the words of Vatican II, "missionary by its very nature."

---

2. Kenneth Scott Latourette, *A History of the Expansion of Christianity,* 7 vols. (New York and London: Harper & Brothers, 1937-1945).

The Missionary Nature of the New Testament Church

The character of the New Testament church was a community called and formed to be Christ's witnesses. Most of those wonderful images of the church that Paul Minear develops in his study of these images[3] can be described as fundamentally missional. What does it mean to be Christ's letter to the world (2 Cor. 3:2-3)? That's a missional definition of the purpose of the Corinthian congregation. Luke's theology of the early church is summarized in the Ascension Day promise to the gathered disciples, "You shall be my witnesses in Jerusalem and in all Judea and Samaria and to the end of the earth" (Acts 1:8). John's theology of mission as sending reaches its climax in the Easter command of the risen Christ: "As my Father has sent me, even so I send you" (John 20:21). If Luke confirms that the Christian vocation is witness, then Paul consistently focuses upon the formation of the missionary congregations to which he writes as a challenge "to lead their lives worthy of their calling" (e.g., Phil. 1:27; Eph. 4:1). The loss of a theology of mission defining Constantinianism's ecclesiologies is a loss of the very heart of the New Testament's understanding of the church.

To use classical creedal language, the church was from its very inception apostolic. It was sent to continue the ministry of the Apostles, the "sent ones," who had been the first missionaries founding churches. Each congregation was formed with the express purpose of continuing the witness that had brought it into being. As heirs of Christendom, we have been reading this biblical witness regarding this church without any kind of missional lenses. As I tell my students, it has not made sense for millions of Christians in the Western world to read in 1 Peter that we are "aliens and exiles" (1 Pet. 2:11). As the privileged religious institution of Christendom, we could not have had the vaguest idea what Peter meant when he described the Christian community as alien in its setting. We are now beginning to learn it again because the end of Christendom is making that possible. Our sister churches in the non-Western world read this text with great clarity, because in almost every context they are marginal, a minority, and they know that they are aliens and exiles.

3. Paul Minear, *Images of the Church in the New Testament* (Louisville: Westminster John Knox, 2004 [1960]).

Addressing the Absence of Mission

This lack of mission characterizes both the way we have written ecclesiology and the way we have done our confessions, these two forms of doctrinal enterprise in the church. To reiterate this fundamental point: one cannot find the theme "mission" in any classic, systematic theology written before the twentieth century. One needs only to scan Charles Hodge's volumes on systematic theology. This highly respected professor of theology at Princeton Theological Seminary, who regularly preached on mission, wrote brochures on the topic, was enthusiastically committed to the growing Presbyterian mission, sent his sons together with hundreds of missionaries who went out from Miller Chapel to become a part of the missionary enterprise of the nineteenth and early twentieth centuries, wrote a systematic theology in which the word "mission" never once appears. His three-volume *opus major* never deals with the church's purpose as God's missionary people.[4]

When we look through our *Book of Confessions,* the most missional statement we find before the year 1903 is the Nicene Creed, with its emphasis upon the apostolicity of the church. The themes that are formative for our Reformation confessions include the universality of the church; the church as the community of the elect and thus the community enjoying the benefits of the gospel; the community of salvation; the distinction between the visible and the invisible church; the criteria for the true church; the marks of the church as Word and Sacrament; and the ministry appropriate to the true church. There are a few mentions — very few as we scan those documents — about the church having something to do with the service of God. There is a great deal of polemic against the Roman Catholic Church and its misunderstandings of the church woven throughout.

I often ask groups of Presbyterian pastors or my own students, "When is the first time that the theme 'mission' actually occurs in the *Book of Confessions*?" I have yet to have anybody give me the answer to that question. That is because most people are not aware of the process in the old northern stream of American Presbyterianism that added paragraph XXXV to the Westminster Confession in 1903, titled "Of the Gospel of the Love

---

4. Under "soteriology," Hodge discusses "the means of grace" in four subsections: the Word of God, Baptism, the Lord's Supper, and Prayer. Charles Hodge, *Systematic Theology,* 3 vols. (New York: Charles Scribner's Sons, 1903), vol. 3, pp. 466-709. Under "church," the index refers to several places where some aspect of the church is discussed. There is no mention of mission, and there is no section of the work that is expressly devoted to the doctrine of the church.

of God and Missions." Significantly, this paragraph is placed at the end of the Confession, not in the section that deals with the theology of the church. This illustrates how our thinking continues almost automatically to separate mission from the theology of the church. That parallels the history of modern mission as a largely nonecclesial movement, carried out by lay-dominated mission societies rather than established churches — for at least its first century. Thus, we inherit a very Christendom-shaped interpretation of mission, rooted in the assumptions of established Christianity. It is really Thesis 6 of the *Barmen Declaration* that first signals the entry of "mission" in its fully ecclesial sense into our *Book of Confessions*. It then becomes a major theme in the *Confession of 1967*. But in the *Brief Statement of Faith* it appears as "witness" among several functions of the church, with little definitive impact on the way our most recent statement does its ecclesiology.

To address this doctrinal and confessional gap, the discussion that has emerged within the Gospel and Our Culture Network proposes that we read the Nicene marks in the reverse order, in order to restore missional purpose to our theology of the church. This suggestion actually emerged in a conversation in 1996 in my study at the Louisville Seminary when George Hunsberger and I were discussing the book *Missional Church,* which I was editing for publication. He said, "I wonder what would happen if we just thought Nicea in the opposite direction. Why don't you think about that?" As a result of his suggestion, I did propose this reading in the book, and I have been pursuing its implications ever since. It has been a significant challenge to my understanding of "missional theology" and "missional ecclesiology" to read the Nicene marks in this order: "I believe [in] the apostolic, and therefore the catholic, holy and one Church."

"I believe the apostolic church"

It is a simple yet revolutionary proposal. The crux is the understanding of "apostolicity." By "apostolicity," we do not merely mean "the church descended from the apostles," as important as that is. We mean "apostolicity" in the active sense of the New Testament verb, meaning "to be sent out," and the noun "apostle" as the "sent-out one." The community formed by the Holy Spirit through the initial apostolic witness is called to be sent. It is apostolically initiated in order to continue the apostolic ministry. Its mission is rooted in its calling, its conversion, its submission to Christ as Savior and Lord, and thus is definitive of its very being. The canonic process that forms the New Testament is then understood as the acknowledgment of the apostolic and thus missional authority of these documents — all of them emerging out of the continuing formation process of communities that exist to continue apostolic witness. These scriptures work in the church as God's chosen instrument for the continuing formation of communities to be faithful to their vocation.

If we start our Nicene ecclesiology with apostolicity, then we end up defining catholicity and holiness and oneness in rather different ways — in ways closer to the sequence of formation that we find in the biblical documents. Our interpretation commences, biblically, with Pentecost, the event that is the necessary completion of Easter. The Easter story isn't fully knowable until the Holy Spirit equips the apostolic witnesses to make it known. And at that act of equipping, the apostolicity of the church is further defined as "catholic."

"Apostolic and therefore catholic . . ."

The "catholicity" of the church refers to its global and cross-cultural missionary commission. The message is to be made known to the ends of the earth, as Jesus commands, and it will be translatable into the life and experience of every ethnicity, as concretely demonstrated at the first Pentecost. Yet this highly diverse, multicultural, multilingual, multi-organizational extension of the witnessing people of God takes place *kat' holon,* that is, "catholically," centered on that which is the whole, the common ground of the gospel. That *holon,* that center and common ground, is the life, death, and resurrection of Jesus Christ. It is the event that demonstrates God's love for and healing of all the world in Christ. It is history that can be translated and continued in every ethnicity ("nation" is not a strong enough translation of *ethnos!*). Justo González has frequently emphasized this very dynamic understanding of catholicity as cultural diversity centered around the *holon,* as the once-and-for-all gospel event.

From the very beginning, the New Testament churches had to be "catholic" if they were to be truly "apostolic." They were by God's intent multicultural, but proclaiming always the same Christ in every context. They were multi-organizational, but in common submission to one Lord, rather than to any human hierarchy (there were no headquarters in the New Testament church!). Lamin Sanneh has constantly pointed out that the gospel is from the very outset fundamentally translatable.[5] Every culture is "destigmatized" by the gospel, so that every culture can become a vessel within which Christ can be confessed, the church can be formed, and witness can be made. But no culture is normative for the church catholic. That is classically addressed in the Jewish-Gentile struggle of the Jerusalem church in Acts. The Jewish Christian movement is converted to the understanding that, by divine design, there was to be catholic diversity as a hallmark of the apostolic church.

It is difficult to find organizational language for the apostolic and catholic church of the first century. The church's engagement in political and social power, a process played out over centuries, has made it exceptionally difficult for us to imagine a way of existing organizationally that is faithful to the biblical intention. The "church that Jesus intended" clearly differed from the structures of power, both in the Greek and the Jewish world, which characterized that context.[6] Thus, our polity vocabulary is handicapped by the Christendom legacy: terms like "voluntary association," "established church," "national church," "territorial church," and "denomination" all fail to convey the concrete reality of the apostolic and catholic church, which is our common source. How do we aptly describe the character, the sense of "organizedness," of the early Christian communities as reflected in Scripture? Perhaps the current language of "network" might most readily correspond to what was in fact the organizational shape of the early church! Certainly one of the hardest tasks we face, as we labor through the implications of the end of Christendom, is the question of our institutional shape that continues the distinctive kind of community that Jesus intended and actually established.

Catholicity is shaped by apostolicity, with the result that there is in the New Testament and pre-Constantinian church a centered, focused diversity, expressed in diverse approaches to catechesis, to church organization, and to liturgy and worship. All of the forms of the church's life were, in some way, related to its basic missional vocation. This centered diversity was reflected in the "Rule of Faith" in the first centuries of the church's history, which functioned dynamically as an expression of what is held in common, the center around which the church in its diverse expressions clusters. This understanding and practice of catholicity contrasts with contemporary pluralism, which can be described as parallel tracks that never meet and have no center.

---

5. Lamin Sanneh, *Translating the Message: The Missionary Impact on Culture* (Maryknoll, NY: Orbis, 1989).

6. See Gerhard Lohfink, *Jesus and Community: The Social Dimension of Christian Faith*, trans. John P. Galvin (Philadelphia: Fortress Press, 1984). The original German title is *Wie hat Jesus Gemeinde gewollt?* = How did Jesus intend the community?

"Apostolic and therefore catholic, holy . . ."

Catholic apostolicity expresses itself appropriately in the holiness of the church. "Holiness" defines the way in which God's Spirit equips the church to practice its vocation so that witness can be credibly made in the world. God's Spirit "sanctifies," makes holy, in order to create a community that can serve as "Christ's letter to the world." This understanding of holiness is not so much related to salvation, as evidence of savedness, as it is to vocation, as formation for obedience. It is the context within which we are to understand the imperatives of the New Testament, the "commandments" of Jesus which, according to John, we are to follow. Holiness has therefore to do with fitness for service, with usableness for God's mission.

If we read the New Testament missionally, then among the many questions we ask the text are "how questions": how shall we witness; how shall we be light, leaven, and salt; how shall "the life of Jesus . . . be manifested in our bodies" (2 Cor. 4:10)? This questioning unpacks these texts in terms of their purpose, which was to continue the formation of these communities for their apostolic vocations. As already noted above, this is clearly illustrated in the overarching theme of the Pauline epistles, which is the admonition to "lead your life worthy of the calling to which you have been called" (Eph. 4:1; see 1 Thess. 2:11-12; 2 Thess. 1:11; Col. 1:9-10; Phil. 1:27; Gal. 5:13). The calling is to apostolic witness. To carry it out, the community is instructed to lead its entire life in ways appropriate to that calling.

Thus, every dimension of the community's life is of importance, because all of it relates to the vocation of an apostolic, catholic community. If it is missional by its very nature, everything it does, how it lives, how it administers its money, how people relate to each other, how it resolves its disputes — all are potential demonstrations or witnesses to the rule of God in Christ in its midst. The task of the post-Christendom church in the West is to learn to read the New Testament imperatives, these imperatives of holiness, from the perspective of apostolicity and catholicity.

"Apostolic and therefore catholic, holy, and one"

Thus we arrive at "oneness." What would happen to our ecumenical concept of oneness if it emerged out of the apostolicity that is catholic and sanctified? What would the world see if the diverse forms of church presented a coherent and congruent testimony to the one gospel? If "unity" were understood missionally, then the focus would be upon the way that Christians, before a watching world, love one another, "being of the same mind, having the same love, being in full accord and of one mind" (Phil. 2:3). It is likely that the mark of "oneness" first emerges in the language of the Nicene Creed because Constantine's political interest was to restore the organizational unity of the church. In the sequence at the beginning of Ephesians 4, the oneness emerges out of our grappling with the task of living worthy of our calling, in which we are to be "eager to maintain the unity of the spirit in the bond of peace" (Eph. 4:3). The diverse forms of witness and of the organized church are to be perceived and experienced in the world as testifying to the same Jesus Christ. Their public witness is to carry out the same practices and disciplines of Christian discipleship in a great variety of ways: prayer, worship, praise, proclamation, reconciliation, acts of justice and mercy, endurance under persecution. When people in diverse cultures observe Christian communities in their midst living in these distinctive ways, they encounter the witness that points them to Jesus Christ. The unity of the church is expressed in that unified witness, all communities disclosing God's love for all creation, enfleshed in and through the story of Jesus. All apostolic communities continue the ministry of John the Baptist, pointing to Jesus, as illustrated by Grünewald's famous painting, the Isenheim Altarpiece.

Reading the Nicene marks in this way raises questions not only about the nonmissional nature of Western ecclesiology. It opens up a discussion about the strategies of the ecumenical movement, at least in the post-Christendom context, during the twentieth century. The process appears to have focused on unity with little attention to the foundational character of the church's apostolicity, its "sentness." Thus, the efforts have largely been directed toward questions of organizational unity, which have revealed heavy baggage accumulated through centuries of Christendom compromises with worldly power. While visible unity is an essential aspect of the church's obedience to its calling, the way that we understand and practice that unity will be different if we approach it from the perspective of essential apostolicity, expressed in catholicity and holiness, for witness to the world. Are we not really in need of an entirely new definition of Christian unity, which is based on the missional vocation of the church and liberated from the Christendom preoccupation with power and influence? Do we know what such unity, framed in terms of the witness seen and experienced by the world around us, would actually look like?

Word and Sacrament?

This discussion also raises questions about our interpretation today of the Reformation marks of the church, Word and Sacrament. It is important to remember that these formulations first emerged out of the attempt of the disputing factions to find common ground at Augsburg in 1530. The definition of the "true church" in terms of the proper proclamation of the Word and administration of the sacraments was a minimal formulation, proposed by the Lutherans as a place at which the Catholics, Zwinglians, and the Lutherans could meet. It did not succeed, but the Augsburg Confession became the authoritative confession for the Lutherans, and the Word and Sacrament formulation became the common currency of the Reformation. It does not convey the fuller ecclesiology of the Nicene marks; one must argue rather carefully to evoke apostolicity, catholicity, holiness, and unity from Word and Sacrament — although there are clearly connections. What is more problematic is the way that this more modern version of the marks of the true church has defined the church in largely clerical terms. Ordained ministers are the ones who proclaim the word and administer the sacraments. The effect has been to solidify the nonmissional cast of Western ecclesiologies, at least in the magisterial Reformation traditions (the Radical Reformation goes a very different route).

The Presbyterian decision, at the time of reunion (1983), to replace the older language of "teaching elder" and "ruling elder" with "Minister of Word and Sacrament" and "elder" contributed to the continuation of a theology of the church that focused upon the clergy and diminished the missional calling that joins all members of Christ's Body into a witnessing community serving its Lord. The subsequent restoration of the traditional language in the denomination's constitutional documents can be welcomed as the affirmation of one outcome of the Reformation that truly has missional significance. Such issues can be fruitfully probed by means of the reverse-order reading of Nicea. In the realities of our post-Christendom situation, such rethinking of our basic ecclesiology is the urgent order of the day!

CHAPTER 6

The Missional Authority of Scripture

My purpose in chapters 6 and 7 is to explore the emerging focus upon missional hermeneutics as a theme of growing significance in missional theology. Although it may be a bit of a repetition for those who are well read in the subject, I should at the beginning summarize what we mean by this term "missional hermeneutics." In November of 2007, we gathered in San Diego for the annual meetings of the American Academy of Religion and the Society for Biblical Literature. One of the "Additional Meetings" of the SBL was the sixth gathering of a network that has met annually to work on the theme of missional hermeneutics. The growing numbers of people who attend this "Additional Meeting" reveal that this theme, though still under development, is finding resonance across the theological and confessional spectrum.

When I use the term "missional hermeneutics," I am referring to the interpretation of the Scriptures in terms of the fundamentally missional vocation of the church of Jesus Christ. This approach to biblical interpretation is rooted in a consensus about the character of the apostolic strategy — what the apostles were actually intending as they carried out the Pentecostal mission (Acts 2 leading into the rest of Acts). As we have emphasized already, their strategy was the formation of witnessing communities whose purpose was to continue the witness that had brought them into being. It was, therefore, not the intention of the apostles in some narrow and personalistic sense

---

These lectures on missional hermeneutics were delivered at the Associated Mennonite Biblical Seminary in Elkhart, Indiana, as the first Wilbert Shenk lectures, November 30 to December 1, 2007. They were subsequently published in *Mission Focus Annual Review* 15 (2008): 106-21 and 125-42. The first lecture attempts to redefine the doctrine of scriptural authority as shaped by the assumption of missional hermeneutics. The second lecture addresses the authoritative role of Scripture in the formation of the witnessing community.

to save souls, although, of course, that work of salvation was always the result of their witness. Their intention was to form communities. They began the work of evangelization, understood as the discovery, as a result of their proclamation and witness, of those whom God's Spirit had prepared to become the first witnesses in a particular place. The necessary consequence of evangelization with its response was the gathering of these converts into a community for the continuation of that witness. Thus their evangelization inexorably moved into catechesis, into the instruction of the newly formed community so that it could be about its obedient and faithful witness in its particular setting. The self-understanding of every apostolic community was thus at its core and in a comprehensive sense missional.

An example of this apostolic strategy was the community in Antioch as it took the initiative to send out apostolic missionary teams while at the same time continuing its corporate witness in Antioch. When we speak of such apostolic strategy, the most obvious example is, of course, Paul, whom we experience in the New Testament in a variety of situations, virtually all of them related to the forming and the continuing formation of witnessing communities. We see that Pauline process continuing then in the catechetical disciplines of the sub-apostolic church from the *Didache* onwards. We observe especially how the apostolic strategy of continuing formation of missional communities became the motivation of their writings. The apostolic scriptures serve the continuing formation of these communities for their witness, in particular places. In the ongoing conversation about "missional hermeneutics," this is the basic assumption undergirding our interpretation of all New Testament literature: each community is defined by its missional vocation, which is its sense of itself as called into being for the continuation of apostolic witness. The actual task of these Scriptures, then, was to deal with the problems and the conflicts, the challenges and the doubts as they emerged in particular contexts, so that these communities could be faithful to their calling.

The Epistles carry out this formation through direct engagement with the challenges arising out of the contexts of the addressed communities. We see this engagement addressed through theological explanation, through argument, instruction, admonition, and pervasively through parenesis, exhortation, imperatives — "do this, do that." In a parallel fashion the Gospels are about the same fundamental task. They are carrying out this formation of witnessing communities as they engage congregations that are already shaped by Easter. The Gospel narratives guide them in the process of discipleship consisting of their joining Jesus' disciples and accompanying him

91

through his earthly ministry on the path to the cross. Every community for which a Gospel is intended is already Christian. It is already living in the light of Easter, as I said. But the Gospel narrative never begins with just the events of Passiontide. The story begins with (or soon comes to) the earthly ministry of Jesus, with the invitation for us to join the disciples as they respond to Jesus' summons to "follow me." In this preparation of disciples to become apostles, missional formation is happening in the Gospels.

The basic hermeneutical question that we are constantly asking the biblical text might be formulated in this way: How did this particular text continue the formation of witnessing communities then, and how does it do that today? This makes very clear how important context is for missional faithfulness. The importance of context in scriptural accounts illumines the translation process that each canonic text demonstrates. As we learn how they dealt with the Greek/Jewish controversy, or with the question of pagan practices, we are taught how, in an ongoing way, Christian communities have to learn together to discern what is truly excellent (Phil. 1:9). We might say that this hermeneutical enterprise combines interpretative translation with missional connectedness. Interpretive translation means that the gospel is constantly being interpreted into and for a particular context. In that process, however, it is the same gospel, the continuation of the same story, the same good news that connects every community to each other. In this nexus of interpretative translation and missional connectedness, we see in particular situations how the universal, multicultural, multi-organizational, multilingual church continues to carry out its apostolic strategy to be Christ's witnesses. We could say that "interpretive translation with missional connectedness" is a reiteration of the character and practice of "catholicity" as we discussed in the last chapter. Certainly, interpretive translation with missional connectedness is the constant task of the missional church. For it is always our obligation to make very clear that we are proclaiming the same gospel and carrying out the same Spirit-mandated mission. As disciples/apostles of Christ, we are continuing the same story that began in Palestine early in the first century. And we do that as interpreters by asking missional questions of the text. To repeat the basic hermeneutical question: We are constantly asking, how did this text continue the formation of witnessing communities then, and how does it do so today?

There is, then, an implied polemic in such missional hermeneutics. We are, as we explore Scriptures in this fashion, critiquing readings of Scripture that diminish the focus upon God's revelatory action and the empowered response and witness to it. We critique those approaches that would read

Scripture as a collection of abstract religious truths, or as an answer book to a great diversity of questions, or as we see in some forms of regrettably popular literature, as a book full of coded mysteries. From the perspective of missional hermeneutics we must polemicize against any dilution of the centrality of the Scriptures in the life and witness of the church. Missional hermeneutics invests the Reformation's *sola scriptura* with great urgency. Scriptural formation is the priority that must define the gathered life of the church. With this understanding of what we mean by "missional hermeneutics" we return then to the purpose of these two chapters (6 and 7), which is to explore the emerging focus upon missional hermeneutics as a theme of growing importance in missional theology.

What is the significance of this focus upon missional hermeneutics for our theological understanding of the authority of Scripture? Many expositions of Christian doctrine, especially in the Reformed tradition out of which I come, begin their discussion of theology with a chapter on the authority of Scripture. These discussions have, if you look at them over the centuries, virtually no reference in them to the missionally formative function of Scripture. In the theological expositions of the doctrines of the faith, mission is the noticeably absent theme — we have made this point from diverse perspectives in the previous chapters. To be sure, there are aspects of that missional formation that can be drawn out of reformational approaches to Scripture. To be very fair, one must say there is probably more groundwork for a missional interpretation of Scripture in Anabaptist writings about the theology of scriptural authority than in the other streams of the Reformation. In these comments, however, I will focus upon the missional thrust of the Reformed tradition.

Taking missional hermeneutics as a working hypothesis will have very great implications for our understanding of the ways in which Scripture is authoritative. How shall we then, theologically, approach this challenge? What are the hurdles to be negotiated? I've already alluded to some of them. Against the larger doctrinal background out of which we come, which in many ways shapes us still, we face a very real problem when we put the words "mission" and "doctrine," "mission" and "theology," in the same sentence. This is a major problem for the discipline we call "history of doctrine." In our argument up to now we have made it clear that this is a real concern: the absence of mission from the developed theological traditions of Western Christendom. But it is necessary to examine that polemic theme in terms of its implications for the doctrine of scriptural authority. We have referred already to the fact that Martin Kähler said over a century ago, in his very cogent and still very relevant studies of the development of early Christian theology, that "mission is the mother of theology."[1] Further, when one examines the early catechetical traditions it is clear that the theology the church taught was profoundly shaped by the missional realities in which that theology was being developed. The church was catechizing converts for their vocation to continue this witness. Catechesis was preparation for baptism, not as a rite of individual salvation alone, but as a rite of incorporation into the witnessing community that testified to its faith centrally by its regular gathering around the Lord's table. The apologetic task of early theology was basically missional. These apostolic Christians had to learn to engage the context of their emerging communities in such ways that they could carry out the interpretative translation of the gospel. That many-sided set of issues is too complicated to explore in detail, but let me make a few summarizing remarks in order to locate the missional question of the authority of Scripture.

The result of what we call the Christianization of Europe renders the fundamentally missional nature of the church a marginal theme. One does not find mission as an operative focus in the theologies that emerged from the Constantinian period onward. There is no trace of missional vocation in any of the traditional approaches to ecclesiology. To be fair to that history, however, one must note that there was mission going on. It is what Lamin Sanneh often calls "mission by diffusion," by which he means the expansion of an already-existing Christianized culture by spreading its influence and boundaries outwards.[2] One would scarcely want to legitimize Charlemagne's method for evangelizing the Saxons — "be baptized or be beheaded" — as a soul-winning tactic we would emulate today. At the same time, one could not gainsay the missional importance of the evangelization of Ireland under Patrick, or the labors of the Iro-Scottish missionaries in northern Europe in the Middle Ages. In a genuinely dialectical sense, there is throughout the course of Western Christianity the activity of mission in diverse ways.

It is not until the Reformation that we begin to see at least some anticipation of the doctrinal formulation of the church's missional vocation, and, as I said before, this is particularly the case in Anabaptist expressions. Generally, the sense of mission that we do see in the Reformation and thereafter has to do with what Christians might do when they move outside the

---

1. Martin Kähler, *Schriften zur Christologie und Mission* (Munich: Chr. Kaiser Verlag, [1908] 1971), p. 190; cf. David Bosch, *Transforming Mission: Paradigm Shifts in Theology of Mission* (Maryknoll, NY: Orbis, 2011), p. 16.

2. Lamin Sanneh, *Translating the Message: The Missionary Impact on Culture* (Maryknoll, NY: Orbis, 1989), pp. 28-34.

boundaries of Christendom. That Christendom mentality creates the idea that mission is what European Christians do when they enter into a non-Constantinian world. In a very oversimplifying way, mission is understood to happen when one enters into a world in which one encounters pagans, as though there were no pagans in Christianized Europe. Crossing boundaries to non-Christian or pre-Christian cultures is an essential aspect of mission so defined. In the modern missionary movement, that has very often been done in partnership with colonialism.

It is interesting that the vocabulary of mission reemerges in our Western European languages as a result of the onset of the modern missionary movement. Thus, we use the word "mission" for anything that is on the other side of the boundaries of Christendom. We also revive the word "evangelization," or in English, "evangelism." This term describes what we do inside the boundaries of Christendom with all the backsliders, of which we seem to have adequate numbers, because we assume that they are really culturally Christians as a result of their socialization and conditioning in the religious traditions of the West. Through evangelization, they become by persuasion what they really already are by cultural formation.

As a result of this process, the doctrinal *loci,* the various themes of theology, develop without any central emphasis upon God's missional purpose and action, or upon the church's missional definition, or upon the individual Christian's missional vocation. It has been my particular concern to focus upon the reduction that then ensues in our understanding of the gospel itself, and with that the reduction of salvation to an individual and personal benefit, with no emphasis upon the vocation of the believer to learn Christ as his disciple in order to carry out his mission as his witness.[3] This generates a multidoctrinal reductionism. There is reductionism in our understanding of soteriology — the gospel is primarily about the benefits that accrue to the individual believer as a result of responding to Christ's call. This focus upon individualistic salvation is preceded by and paralleled with an almost total disappearance of the theme of the kingdom of God from the evangelistic preaching of the church by the onset of the medieval period. There is, then, also a reductionism in eschatology, a loss of confidence in God's promised future, which invests our present life and ministry with hope and which gives our witness energy. Eschatology becomes pointless speculation about

---

3. See, in particular, Darrell Guder, *Be My Witnesses: The Church's Mission, Message and Messengers* (Grand Rapids: Eerdmans, 1985), and *The Continuing Conversion of the Church* (Grand Rapids: Eerdmans, 2000).

the unknowable sequence of future events, or a reduction to an apocalyptic sense of the future that renders the present largely meaningless, a trial to be endured — we think of the medieval image of the Christian life as a pilgrimage through a vale of tears.

There is a reductionism in Christology, a separation between the Saviorhood and the lordship of Christ. Much contemporary evangelism reveals this reductionistic separation at work. In some instances, the lordship of Christ is reduced to ecclesial hierarchy or to the assumption that a Christian culture makes adequately clear that Christ is Lord. And, out of all that, there is a profound reductionism of ecclesiology. The community called to witness to God's inbreaking reign in Christ becomes the church that receives, contains, and serves saved souls. The church becomes what the Germans call a *Heilanstalt* (salvation institution). In Catholic theology the church is defined as the perfect society that needs no mission because it already represents God's rule on earth. In Christendom, these processes constitute in reality a reductionism of the church to a partner of the state and thus a cultural agency captive to its environment.

The impact of these reductionisms upon Western theologizing is then the very serious loss of a missional dynamic that places the theological disciplines within and in support of our shared apostolic vocation. We are not confronted by a vocation shaped by the eschatological reality of God's saving action beginning with Abraham and reaching its great climax in Jesus Christ. The theological doctrines become propositional rather than formational. And with regard to Scripture, the question of its authority is primarily addressed in terms of permanent characteristics of Scripture, focusing upon propositions regarding its inspiredness, or even the method of its inspiredness. Authority may be something the Bible has, but it is not at all clear that it has anything to do with what the Bible does. This constitutes then a profound reductionism of pneumatology, of our understanding of the person and work of the Holy Spirit. These propositional and abstract approaches to the authority of Scripture obscure the way in which the Bible, through the Holy Spirit, works formatively in the witnessing community. This is what a missional hermeneutic is endeavoring to reclaim under the assumption that the original purpose of these written testimonies was to continue the formation of witnessing communities for their missional vocation.

Thus, the endeavor to develop a missional hermeneutic is, as I suggested, a massive critique of the Christendom legacy that shapes us. That is not a problem for a community in the Anabaptist tradition. With profound respect and gratitude for the prophetic Anabaptist witness that guides us in so many ways in this necessary critique and in which they have been the pioneers, I am addressing the question as a Reformed theologian and drawing on Reformed resources. This Reformed emphasis expresses itself in a commitment to read our legacy dialectally and to recognize God's faithfulness in the ambiguity of our very human and sinful history. We learn this as we recognize God's faithfulness to Israel in one thousand years of monarchs who generally got failing grades, while God's word was never absent because of the faithfulness of prophets. If the king would not do what God required, the prophet would proclaim the truth and its consequences. That dialectic applies to our Western history as well. The Holy Spirit did not depart from human history when Constantine came to the throne. The word of God continued to be heard, to be translated and to challenge the established expressions of the Christian tradition. One example would be the myriad forms of the monastic renewal movements. Another would be the aforementioned missionary movements in medieval Europe.

There has always been within the *ecclesia* some expression of the *ecclesia reformata semper reformanda secundum verbum Dei* — the "church reformed always being reformed according to the word of God." Speaking as a Reformed theologian, I would suggest that there is in our tradition a theological point of departure for the missional interpretation of Scripture that is of ecumenical value. This resource is articulated in many ways, but particularly in a book very recently published by Eberhard Busch in Germany, *Reformiert: Profil einer Konfession* (Reformed: Profile of a Confession).[4] There he describes as the basic principle of Reformed Theology a statement made in the earliest formulations of Reformation doctrine, especially in Switzerland. These doctrinal statements were formulated at a time when such actions were not a matter of academic study but concrete matters of life-and-death decision-making. They documented the process by which Swiss communities were debating whether or not they should adopt the rapidly spreading evangelical understanding of the Christian faith and practice. Such decisions had enormous consequences since they realigned these communities against the dominant Roman Catholic tradition and the institution of the Roman Catholic Church — with its political partners.

One of the very early formulations, shortly after Luther's first wave of publications in the 1520s, was made by the leaders of the emerging evangelical movement in the southeastern part of Switzerland in the canton called

---

4. Eberhard Busch, *Reformiert: Profil einer Konfession* (Zürich: Theologischer Verlag Zürich, 2007).

Graubünden, or the Grisons in French, in a little village called Ilanz in 1526. These early Swiss Protestants began their statement, their definition of the conviction they were now adopting as they became evangelical, with these words: "The Christian church is born out of the word of God. It should remain in it and not listen to the voice of any stranger."[5] This became a major defining thesis of Reformed ecclesiology: *Ecclesia progenita est ex verbo Dei, nec audit vocem alieni.* It reoccurs as the first thesis of the Bern disputation of 1538, but at that point two additions are made: the "should" in the second clause becomes indicative — "The church remains in the word of God," not "should remain in it." And the church's relationship to Christ is defined precisely by adding a clause regarding the headship of Christ. "The holy Christian church, whose only head is Christ, is born out of the word of God, and remains in it, not listening to the voice of any stranger."[6] The biblical background of the statement is, of course, the account of the good shepherd and those who hear his voice, in John, chapter ten. This was a primary scriptural motif in this Reformation movement.

We also see that Jesus is identified as the word of God together with the biblical witness which reveals him. Thus the "word of God" becomes a term that always means both Jesus and the Scriptures that reveal Jesus. Busch explains it this way,

> Thus the picture of the good shepherd and his sheep is connected to the head and his body. This makes clear that the Holy Scripture is the word of God because in it the voice of the living Christ, which defines everything, is heard, thus, the word of God and Christ are brought into a mutual relationship in such a way that two assertions must be made. The church whose head is Christ lives solely from the word of God, and does so in that it remains in him and is governed by him. And, the church born out of the word of God, has Christ alone as its head, is his property, his body in that it belongs to him, it listens to him and obeys him, and only him.[7]

Thus the church listens to and obeys him who is the word of God by means of the written word of God. This emphasis picks up on the ancient insight of the early church captured by its use of the term *kyriakon* to describe itself.

---

5. Busch, *Reformiert: Profil einer Konfession,* pp. 49-51.
6. Busch, *Reformiert: Profil einer Konfession,* pp. 55-57.
7. Busch, *Reformiert: Profil einer Konfession,* pp. 57-58.

It is "that which belongs to the Lord," and it is the word from which we get the word "church," and the Germans get "Kirche," and the Scots get "kirk."

Busch will later on argue that this principle is taken up by the Barmen Declaration in a clear continuation of this fundamental principle going back to the earliest stages of Reformed theological formation in Switzerland. It is memorably captured in the first thesis of Barmen: "Jesus Christ, as he is testified for us in Holy Scripture, is the one Word of God which we have to hear and which we have to trust and obey in life and in death."[8] This basic principle, as I suggested earlier, carries forward the *sola scriptura* already firmly established by Martin Luther. In the Reformed tradition, however, it shapes the life of the church concretely as the argument is made that only those doctrines and practices should be accepted in the evangelical church that are directly taught and mandated by Scripture.

The Radical Reformation will rightly insist that the Swiss Reformers did not take their approach radically enough or realign themselves seriously enough with the New Testament understanding of the church. And, as we all know, this leads to major debates, divisions, and conflicts not only with Roman Catholicism, with its insistence on the authority of tradition, but also with Lutheranism with its milder interpretation of the changes needed to accomplish reformation. For the purposes of the church's missional vocation, however, the full impact of this basic principle will not be fully grasped until the essentially missional nature of the church begins to be recognized and acknowledged again. That is a very recent development. The magisterial reformation of the sixteenth century sets the presuppositions for missional hermeneutics and in many ways actually begins to practice it. This can be seen, for instance, in the Genevan and Scottish concern for the discipline of the congregation. But only recently has the radical nature of this missional hearing of Scripture begun to assert itself in a way that actually corrects our doctrine.

The paradigm shift in twentieth-century missiology has been away from the ecclesiocentric understanding of mission shaped by Christendom to the theocentric and ultimately Trinitarian understanding of mission as the actual implementation by God's grace and empowering of God's saving purposes for all creation now made possible by the life, death, resurrection, and ascension of Jesus. The movement has been away from the maintenance of established Christianity as the church's purpose toward missional calling

8. Office of the General Assembly of the Presbyterian Church (U.S.A.), *The Book of Confessions* (Louisville, 1999), par. 8.11.

or vocation in which the church's gathered life is defined and oriented to its scattered life, its apostolate as light, salt, and yeast in the world. This paradigm shift has been away from tacit or explicit claims that particular traditions represent normative Christianity, toward the acknowledgment of the necessarily multicultural and multi-organizational and multilingual form of the church catholic, demonstrated today by the sheer diversity of global Christianity. The paradigm shift has been away from institutional and organizational understandings of unity towards the more martyriological practice of unity, demonstrating what God's love in Christ makes possible in communities of forgiven sinners, communities in which our humanly made walls of separation are being taken down.

In this major paradigm shift it is important and helpful to recognize, again, the key role of Karl Barth as a missional theologian. Certainly Barth is the major proponent of that Reformed tradition of the Word-based and Word-centered church, the principle of which was articulated at Ilanz and Bern. This basic commitment finds emphatic expression in the way that Barth's interpretation of the doctrine of reconciliation shapes his ecclesiology. In the massive fourth volume of the *Church Dogmatics,* the doctrines of reconciliation and ecclesiology are interwoven in terms of the reconciling gospel. He argues, at great length and much of it in small type, that the gospel must be understood as justification, sanctification, *and* vocation. And he parallels that argument regarding the character of the gospel by defining the church in terms of its gathering (justification), its upbuilding (sanctification), and its sending (vocation). Vocation and sending are inseparably linked, and all of them must be emphasized or one has a reductionist gospel. Christian identity is necessarily totally redefined. Critiquing the understanding of Christian identity as the enjoyment of the benefits of the gospel, Barth stresses that the purpose of Christian existence is that we be witnesses. Our vocation is to the life of witness as the crucial outworking of the gospel in one's personal life and in the life of the community. This effectively counters that reduction of the gospel which permeates inherited established Christianity in the West.[9]

This sets the stage now for reclamation of the missionally formative authority of Scripture. In repeated statements throughout the *Church Dogmatics* Barth underlines the fundamentally missional nature and purpose

9. It should be remembered that the phrase *beneficia Christi,* which is part of our Reformation vocabulary, was given to the theological vocabulary by Philipp Melanchthon. The exposition of vocation is carried out in par. 71 of the *Church Dogmatics* IV/3.2.

of the church. Although this emphasis is yet to be fully recognized by many Barth scholars, it is unmistakably the binding theme through the entire *Church Dogmatics* project. As he unfolds that argument, it becomes clear that for Barth the role and function of Scripture are the missional formation of the church, even though he does not use that phrase.[10] Biblical scholars are beginning to pay more attention to the way in which Barth, as a New Testament scholar, actually interprets Scripture, and it is proving rewarding to recognize how he sees the Scriptures forming communities for their sending. This can be observed in his 1920s commentary on Philippians, in which the role of the epistle in the formation of the Philippian community is especially emphasized.[11]

Let me conclude with some further thoughts about biblical authority and missional formation. At the heart of the challenge we face doctrinally is the question of what we mean by authority. The common understanding of authority is that it is a characteristic, a static definition, a criterion. Often negative in its implications, it is associated with arbitrary power. We need only think of the way we use the word "authoritarian." But there is another possibility for our understanding of authority. We need to negotiate a distinction between the wielding of power and the exercise of authority. To do that, we return to the original meaning of the term in Latin, *augere* and *auctor*, and *auctoritas*. This word family has to do with those actions or functions that bring about increase, encourage flourishing, instigate growth. Our word "augment" is derived from these roots. Thus, authority is that function, that instance, that agency which brings about increase, movement, flourishing, and growth. The author is one who increases human capacity and knowledge by the product of one's work. If scriptural authority is understood in that dynamic way, then it has to do with the way in which God's Spirit works through these written testimonies so that certain things happen. Scripture's authority resides in the ongoing event in which Christ is encountered in scriptural testimony as God's Word; that Word can be heard and listened to, and by virtue of the Holy Spirit's empowering, responded to and obeyed. Faith and discipleship emerge as the Scriptures work with their distinctive authority.

God's Spirit calls people to Christ to become Christians, followers of Christ in order to become Christ's witnesses as part of the called and sent

---

10. It should be noted, however, that a digital search of the text of the *Church Dogmatics* reveals that the vocabulary of mission, both in German and English, is pervasive.

11. Karl Barth, *Epistle to the Philippians*, trans. J. W. Leitch, 40th Anniversary Edition (Louisville: Westminster John Knox, 2002).

community, the *ecclesia,* the *kyriakon.* These communities are to continue the story, which they have now encountered and entered into as their own story. They participate with Christ in his mission. And thus the Scriptures continue their work of formation for which they were originally written. They teach the understanding of the gospel so that there can be renewal by the transformation of the mind (Rom. 12:2). The presupposition of this process is the honest recognition that we are all shaped by the conformities that we bring with us when we encounter Christ. Following Paul's admonition in Romans 12:2, those conformities can be brought to a point where they no longer hold us captive, so that we "conform no longer to this world but are transformed by the renewing of our mind." We are given, through the work of the Holy Spirit, the possibility of receiving entirely new presuppositions for our thinking, presuppositions that emerge out of the gospel. This is the process of *phronesis,* the "mindedness" that is so central to Paul's formation of the Philippian community through his epistle to them. One interpreter explains this "mindedness" as the "thinking, acting, and feeling which was also displayed in Christ Jesus."[12]

These Scriptures work with such a formative authority in order to teach the practice of the gospel, which God's Spirit actually makes possible; it is a process one can call "enabled obedience." The discipling that happens in the four Gospels results in the apostolate. That is its purpose — the disciples are not called and formed by Christ merely to meet their own religious needs! The imperatives of the gospel are not there to mock us because they are totally un-obeyable; they are there because God's Spirit intends to make them happen. These Scriptures form people to be witnesses. Karl Barth loved the great painting by Grünewald, *The Crucifixion,* which is displayed in the museum in Colmar, France. John the Baptist is depicted stretching out his bony finger toward Christ on the cross. That gesture is linked to his statement, "He must increase while I must decrease." This is what the Scriptures equip us to do: to point to Christ, to give evidence of the gospel, evidence that serves as the basis for the decisions that others will make. In this exercise we never move from the witness seat to the judge's bench. The Scriptures teach the language of faith as the narrative story of what God has done and what that story now means, so that it can be translated interpretively into every culture into which Christian witnesses are sent by God's Spirit.

Thus, what I am arguing is that God's missional calling of the apostolic communities included the scriptural witness as the means by which God's

---

12. See Stephen Fowl, *Philippians* (Grand Rapids: Eerdmans, 2005), p. 88.

Holy Spirit continued these communities' missional formation. The Scriptures' authority resided in their capacity to be the Spirit's instrument for the continuing calling, conversion, equipping, and sending of the saints into the world as Christ's witnesses. That authority revealed in their formative power ultimately led to the Scriptures' universal acknowledgment as canonic, as the criteria, the canon, for continuing missional witness, proclamation, and practice.

A few years ago I was meeting with a group of students who were in their senior year in Princeton and who were preparing to graduate and move on into ministry. This group was gathered in a process of mentoring with a colleague and myself. We met once a month and, together, we examined the Presbyterian ordination vows, which these young people would take as they responded to their various calls to ministry. We were talking at this meeting about ordination vow two in our book of order. "Do you accept the Scriptures of the Old and New Testaments to be, by the Holy Spirit, the unique and authoritative witness to Jesus Christ in the church universal and God's word to you?" We asked the students to talk about this concept of the authoritative witness to Jesus Christ. There was a long pause. They did not want to say something offensive, but they finally began to admit that the wording bothered them. It sounded as though the Scriptures were authoritarian, some kind of dictatorial tool. They talked about problematic ideas such as submissiveness and obedience. They suggested that such language made Scriptures sound like a cudgel, a schoolmaster's rod, a code of behavior that separates grimly the sheep from the goats. That is not an uncommon reaction. A missional hermeneutic proposes that the authority of Scripture lies in its wonderful and releasing power to bring about the increase of faith in practice. Its task is to empower the practices of obedience that God uses as part of his strategy to heal the broken creation. The authority of the Bible is not a claim set over us as a threat, but the real power of God's Spirit in our midst. That Spirit makes possible our renewal by the transformation of our minds, which equips us to recognize what is good and acceptable, the perfect will of God. And what the Spirit enables us to recognize, to "prove" (Rom. 12:2), is what the Spirit enables us to do, in full view of our brokenness and sinfulness and in all our ambiguity. Scripture is by the Holy Spirit truly the unique and authoritative witness to Jesus Christ which calls together the church and equips each community to be a part of the universal movement of God's people towards the completion of God's healing of creation.

CHAPTER 7

The Scriptural Formation of the Missional Community

Ever since the book *Missional Church* appeared, the constant response in virtually every discussion has been, "The theology resonates, but how does it translate?" How does it enter into the life and practice of real congregations? We often hear very encouraging reports about how that is, in fact, happening. But we also frequently hear about and encounter a great deal of resistance and lethargy; there are frequently questions that betray skepticism about the realism and translatability of this missional theological vision. It is these concerns that I would like to address as we consider the relationship between the congregational calling and the scriptural role in its formation.

The Congregation between Individualism and Corporate Calling

We will begin these considerations about the missional vocation of the congregation by thinking about congregation itself. Perhaps one of the most widely held convictions among missiologists of virtually all traditions is that God's chosen instrument for mission is the particular community, the congregation. That emphasis upon the corporate and the communal, which the congregation represents, clashes with powerful components of the culture that shapes us. It is especially challenged by modern individualism. We turn

---

In this second Shenk Lecture, delivered in 2007 at the Associated Mennonite Biblical Seminary in Elkhart, Indiana, I build upon the understanding of the scriptural formation of the missional community as the hermeneutical key to biblical authority. The guiding question with which this essay grapples is the concrete challenges of translation into the life and practice of the church.

first, then, to the tension between individualism and the corporate Christian calling, recognizing that it is a truism to define our society as profoundly individualistic. This is a characteristic of our society that is acclaimed and praised as well as strongly criticized. On the one hand, there are manifold reasons to be thankful for the liberation of the person from social roles, predispositions, and structures that have over the centuries been very restrictive. When I was teaching in Germany years ago, my students would talk with me about how important it was for them to leave their little home villages up in the Swabian Alb and come into the city to live. It was only then that they could become the persons they wanted to be. Their village cultures were defining and restrictive, and the expectations they were to fulfill were overwhelming. They had to leave for the sake of their freedom to be and to become.

We moderns celebrate that freedom and the possibility of such personal liberation. But at the same time, we bemoan the loss of the bonds and the shared identity of committed communities upon which we can rely. There is a certain intentional nurturing of the self-centeredness of the modern Western person that is an obvious theme in our societies, particularly in our advertising. Yet we also recognize that to nurture that self-centeredness is to weaken the common life. The intellectual legacy of the Enlightenment is often blamed for the rampant individualism of Western modernity. May I suggest that the Enlightenment critique, presently a favored intellectual game, is a very ambivalent enterprise? Who would earnestly argue that we should, somehow, do the historically impossible and return to a pre-Enlightened world? I, for one, do not want to continue believing that a disease is a result of evil spirits when in fact, it is a problem of bacteria in the pond. Once we take care of bacteria in the pond, we do not have to deal with that disease any longer. Such an enlightened way to live is vastly preferable to its alternatives.

Clarifying the Enlightenment Legacy

Further, when we address the Enlightenment and the powerful ways it continues to shape us, we have to be good historians. There are good historical reasons for the Enlightenment's suspicions about organized religion. After all, it is an intellectual period that follows over a century of brutal religious wars that were undeniably horrible and left deep and lasting scars. Yet, they were the outworking of the Reformed, Catholic, Protestant, and

Lutheran dissension after the Reformation. Obviously the problem of the Constantinian partnership of church and state cannot be underestimated when we try to understand this traumatic period. Be that as it may, the Enlightenment quite consciously interprets itself as the coming of light into a dark situation. It was one of the few periods of human history that actually defined itself while it was still happening. Towards the end of the Enlightenment, Immanuel Kant wrote his famous essay *Was ist Aufklärung?*, "What is Enlightenment?" There, he described that intellectual period as a passage in which humans were lifting themselves up and out of their self-imposed immaturity. There can be no question that we have benefited greatly from many aspects of that Enlightened movement to intellectual maturity. There have been profoundly salutary effects of the Enlightened emphasis upon human rationality, upon human educability, upon the capacity for virtue. We are all indebted to the development not only of theories but of practices and structures that honor inalienable human rights. We are all helped by systems of society today that restrain communities from imposing too much upon and restricting too many of their members. We recognize, particularly today in a global society so fraught with dissension, how profoundly we are shaped by our common commitment to tolerance and forbearance. We have an increased appreciation of human diversity nurtured by the Enlightenment. So it is, as I said, an ambivalent exercise to critique the Enlightenment. We have no business doing what I have been accused of as a student of Lesslie Newbigin; we have no business being "Enlightenment bashers."

But there is at the same time no question that the intellectual inheritance and the cultural implications of the Enlightenment pose profound problems for a corporate understanding of our Christian calling. The problems are well known. They include the outworking of: the anthropocentricity of the Enlightenment — the understanding that the human person is the measure of all things; the optimism about the human condition; the unrestrained belief in progress and in the human capacity to control the cause-and-effect nexus; the unquestioning reliance upon human reasonableness. All of these have powerfully shaped the individualism of Western modernity, and they have taken their toll with regard to patterns and traditions of communal life that are of very great value. Here, as in so many related instances, we need to learn how to interpret our Enlightened legacy dialectally. We have to learn how both to receive and to critique this legacy, if we are going to be intellectually honest about how it conditions us.

Deeper Roots of Western Individualism

Moreover, I would suggest that the roots of Western individualism are deeper; they go far back beyond and before the Enlightenment — although the Enlightenment certainly propels this basic thread in Western culture into its dominant place today. The reductionism of the Christian understanding of salvation, which we have already discussed, prepares the way for modern individualism. The focus upon "my" salvation, upon where "I" shall spend eternity, and how "my" religious needs are met — that individualism is reflected in the church's role of providing all that is needed for the individual's religious needs. This is that *Heilanstalt* understanding of the church of which we have spoken. This reductionistic individualism propagated over the course of Christendom is then intensified especially in the American social context and the particular and complex chemistry of our own enlightenment. It is a powerful brew made up of Puritanism, Revivalism, Pietism, and emerging Capitalism, along with the scientific revolution and optimistic anthropocentricity. This process shapes the diverse American Christian movement with its free-market denominationalism in very profound ways. Institutional religion in the United States has been disestablished for two hundred years. Disestablished churches in America have generated entrepreneurial churches. The state as the guarantor of the church, which it still is in a few structures in Europe, has been replaced by Social Volunteerism with powerful effect. The partnership of church and state is often, today, replaced by the partnership of church and marketplace (and one wonders who is winning). The evidence of this is the contemporary influence of consumerism upon churches. Is not the seeker-friendly, member need-driven church a totally American consumerist innovation? Having said that, this entrepreneurial church system must also be appreciated as a remarkable thing! Those of us who have lived in other countries, if only on the other side of the North Atlantic, are well aware of the profound difference in the culture of church inside Christendom on both sides of the Atlantic.

There is a tremendous sense of engagement and of ownership in our churches in America. People in our country speak of "my" church in a way Germans never speak of their parish church. There is an enormous willingness on the part of our population to invest and support their churches. And there are very strong expectations directed towards our various congregations. There is a pervasive focus upon the benefits that our churches are supposed to provide their members. This is, in fact, supported by a strong ecclesiological tradition. Still widely read and valued is Avery Dulles's useful

Dulles
5 church models

analysis of Western ecclesiology in his book, *Models of the Church,* which is one of the best tools to sort out the ecclesial process in our Western traditions.[1] In his initial edition of that book, he described five basic models of the church analyzed in terms of various descriptive categories. Two of those categories have to do with the benefits and the beneficiaries of a particular model of the church. What are the benefits provided by the church defined by a particular model and who are the beneficiaries of those benefits in this model? The first three models, which are generally aligned with the Roman Catholic tradition, are institution, mystical communion, and sacrament. It is intriguing that in all three of those models the beneficiaries of the church are its members and the benefits are the salvation assured to its members. We see that the member-driven, need-meeting understanding of the church also, like individualism, has very deep roots.

The deterioration of the English language in the last centuries, which has resulted in a loss of expressive power, has also resulted in additional problems with regard to the corporate understanding of the church. Modern English basically fosters individualistic thinking by virtue of the loss of the distinctive vocabulary to express the plural "you." When we gave up the King James Version of our Bible, we forfeited the distinction between "thee" and "ye." When we hear or use the pronoun "you," we customarily think of the individual, not the assembled body. Thus, when we listen to Scripture read, we are not predisposed to hear accurately the predominance of the plural "you" in biblical discourse. Nowadays there are modern English translations of the Bible with footnotes to indicate whether the "you" in the text is singular or plural, because it is so important for proper understanding. The corporate character of biblical faith is more readily expressed and experienced in other languages such as German or French, where people hear very differently when they are addressed as "ihr" or "vous" over against when they are spoken to as "du" or "tu." When we listen to Scripture in English today and hear the pronoun "you," we almost always think in terms of the individual and often the isolated individual.

Reclaiming the Corporate and Communal

If, to summarize, there is that aforementioned consensus among missiologists that the particular congregation is the primary instrument of God's mission,

---

1. Avery Dulles, *Models of the Church* (Garden City, NY: Image Books, 1987).

we face a very great challenge in a society characterized by individualism and controlled by consumerism. Christian analysts of the contemporary situation agree that we have lost in profound ways the corporate sense of God's people as formed by God's calling. We have great difficulty accessing the drama and the urgency of the biblical story in which the call of Abraham is the calling of a people, is the initiation of a people's story, is a narrative in which the legacy is personified generation after generation in the shared faith and practices of the people of God. We have difficulty grasping how significant it is that Jesus calls twelve, as the intentional continuation of the story of the people of God. All through the New Testament, the church is understood fundamentally as community, as koinonia, as gathered people, as *ecclesia,* as assembly. In that great missional text in 1 Peter, we hear a masterful summary of the powerful images of the people of God across both testaments: "You are a chosen race, a royal priesthood, a holy nation, God's own people" (1 Pet. 2:9). The inescapable conclusion of the missional reading of the Bible is that God is carrying out his saving and healing purposes for the world through gathered communities, through congregations. First Peter begins in its salutation by addressing specific communities in Pontus, Galatia, Cappadocia, Asia, and Bithynia. And it is as such concrete communities that they are to hear the "you" that follows that great summary of corporate images: "You (plural!) are a chosen race, a royal priesthood, a holy nation, God's own people, in order that you (plural!) may declare the wonderful deeds of him who called you (plural!) out of darkness into his marvelous light. Once you (plural!) were no people but now you (plural!) are God's people; once you (plural!) had not received mercy but now you (plural!) have received mercy."

The net effect of the complex individualism we have been discussing constitutes one of the great challenges for the biblical formation of the missional community. It puts lenses in front of our eyes that make it very hard to read Scripture on its own terms — which means, to read and hear Scripture as a community being formed by God's Spirit through that Word. It is an urgent matter that Christian communities learn how to hear and respond to the missional formation carried out by Scripture in the plural sense, as communities who are called and sent together. It is essential for the called community to understand that its common conduct before a "watching world" (John Howard Yoder!) is its first and most powerful form of witness to the gospel. In my own ecclesiastical tradition, it is a major responsibility of the teaching eldership, which is our best term for the ordained minister, to guide the corporate biblical formation of congregations and to school Christians to hear the plural "you."

Continuing Conversion from Individualism to Missional Community

Our experience of the discussion of the book *Missional Church*[2] since it appeared in 1998 has evidenced deeply rooted resistance to the vision of missional calling and the witnessing community intended by that calling. This resistance surfaces especially when the hallowed convictions of our individualism begin to be questioned. Missional formation always entails a process of continuing conversion. The salvation of the Christian person is not so much a state as it is a process, a pilgrimage whose outcome and destination are certain. Many Christians, as a result of the reductionist history that shapes us, understand their Christianity to mean primarily that they are "in," they are saved, they are the beneficiaries of the benefits, and they are primarily then interested that the church should help them maintain that status.

The problems created by our Christendom legacy are more complicated than mere issues of reorganization and relabeling. It is not something that gets done in a Saturday workshop — although such church-renewal seminars and workshops are a lucrative cottage industry in the United States. This merits a bit more exploration. When I emphasize, in a community of Anabaptist friends, that Christendom places obstacles before our experiencing our corporate calling, I am certainly bringing coals to Newcastle. Perhaps your hearing a Reformed theologian grapple with these issues might at least reassure you that what you have been advocating for a very long time is now being sought and valued by many others within the larger family. Constantinian Christianization leads to a geographical and cultural redefinition of the church, and in the process, the calling to missional witness disappears. In its place, birth, location, geography, and the processes of socialization become the way that the church reproduces itself; mission continues automatically, from generation to generation, in a so-called Christianized culture. This social and cultural and territorial process parallels the disappearance of mission from the church's theological self-understanding, which we have discussed frequently thus far.

When Charlemagne, in the eighth century, divided the Holy Roman Empire into parishes, he set up a system in which everybody lived within the hearing range of church bells. That is the basic system of European Christendom. I well remember, in a remote valley in southeastern Switzerland, going

---

2. Darrell L. Guder, ed., *Missional Church: A Theological Vision for the Sending of the Church in North America* (Grand Rapids: Eerdmans, 1998).

into a magnificent Romanesque church that had been built in 800 and in which Mass had been celebrated every day since then. That's stability! And in that little village there is a sense of identity that is profound. The church in this long and complex process has accepted responsibility for the provision of what the Germans, in a wonderful phrase, call *flächendeckende Dienste*. This describes the expectation that the institutional church will provide all the religious ministrations needed by all the population in a particular region. To be a Christian in such a society is to be entitled to these rites and rights. Just as all should live within hearing range of the bells, one should be able to count on the church's provision of appropriate services for every major passage of life.

The European states from Charlemagne on would work with and even fund the churches and ecclesial structures to make sure that this was done. To repeat my earlier point, a church whose purpose is to meet the needs of its members is deeply rooted in Western Christianity. Thus, the church's mission is a matter of generational incorporation into the already-existing Christian society. One is born into the church; one experiences Christianity as a culturally absorbed identity for which there never was an option. And therefore, it is not the response to a calling; it is not the turning from one way of life to another; baptism is no longer the celebration of God's faithfulness in the continuing building of his church. It is rather the individualistic rite and right of entry that provides the mark of salvation while losing its original sense of calling and catechetical formation and set-apartness for God's service. This stands in very great contrast to the admirable disciplines of catechetical instruction in the church of the first centuries.

↑ Jerry's book

General Vocation and Special Vocation

In the emerging Roman Catholic Middle Ages, the sense of vocational baptism for all is replaced by the vocation and profession of priests and members of religious communities. One is baptized into salvation, and some are ordained or consecrated into vocational ministry. The clergy-lay distinction jeopardizes the church's sense of its universal missional vocation. We end up with an ecclesiastical society made up of levels or ranks of spirituality, commitment, and identity. But everyone has a sense of belonging, because of one's identity with the geographical parish in a Christianized culture. With that emphasis upon geography and locality, the actual lived reality of congregations is more defined by social and cultural, by economic and racial factors, than by the radical calling of the church to be the gathered witness to the inbreaking reign of God and Jesus Christ.

Our inherited gospel reductionism focuses upon my salvation, and dilutes any commitment to the radical otherness of kingdom communities that actively demonstrate what the alternative rule of Jesus Christ actually looks like. The individualism that conditions us fosters understandings of the gospel and even practices of evangelism that focus upon what Jesus and his gospel do for me, while leaving aside or never even encountering the call to take up one's cross and follow Jesus as part of a new kind of community where human walls of separation are, in fact, being dismantled by the gospel reality of the kingdom of God.

Now, with the passing of Christendom, that sense of geographical Christian identity has been modified and is, for many, a relic of the past. Yet I wonder if it is not far more persistent than we are perhaps aware of. Although we have good reasons to claim that Christendom is over, is that entirely true? While once visiting in Elkhart, Indiana, I heard the weather person report that the winter storm that was coming in that night would go through so quickly that "you will be able to go to church in the morning." That would never be said on a television station in California or in the state of Washington. In many parts of our country it is inappropriate to assume in a public medium that the watching audience would be going to church in the morning. But, apparently, in northern Indiana, that is still possible. Is that not, in an obviously superficial sense, evidence that Christendom, like some phantom, is still haunting our society?

Parish systems continue in several mainline traditions. We have at least advanced to the point that we, in some instances, have what we call comity arrangements where the denominations negotiate the placement of their congregations so that they do not compete too obviously with each other. That contrasts with the other American model so baffling for our European visitors: the crossroads in an American town with different churches on all four corners. Denominational church-planting strategies often reveal the persistence of Christendom mindsets. The standard wisdom in my denomination has been, until recently, that a Presbyterian church can be founded when a presbytery has sufficient funds in the bank for the land and building needs of a future congregation. I've searched the Scriptures in vain for the validation of this understanding of missional church (and fortunately, that kind of thinking is now rapidly changing). The congregation that meets the needs of its members and provides all their religious ministrations betrays the ongoing influence of the Christendom legacy. It is present in attitudes, in structures, in unquestioned assumptions — and in great frustrations as the rapid changes in our society prove, again and again, that Christendom is certainly disintegrating if it is not yet entirely over.

The great challenge to be faced in our post-Christendom world is to liberate congregations from the mindsets of Christendom that obscure why congregations exist as the core strategy of God's mission. The continuing conversion of churches is beginning to happen when members of a congregation start to understand who they are, and what they are for, differently. They are changing when they begin to define themselves in terms that theologians might describe as corporate missional calling. I encourage my students when they go into their field education congregations to ask the members of the congregation, why are you a member of this congregation? Why did you join this particular Presbyterian church? The typical responses are always rather deflating for a missiologist. People join churches because Grandma had been a Presbyterian, because of the wonderful program for children and youth, because the church had adequate parking, because this church didn't talk about Jesus too much, because it was a friendly congregation and made it possible to meet people quickly. It is difficult to find any sense of missional calling in such a spectrum of motives for being part of a local congregation. One does, then, also encounter congregations where people's responses indicate that missional conversion is happening.

Missional Conversion: A Process, Not a Model

Missional conversion is a theme and a process, however, that needs to be approached carefully. One of the books in the Gospel in Our Culture series, the book titled *Treasure in Clay Jars* edited under Lois Barrett's very able leadership,[3] started out with a plan to find models of missional congregations. We collected a great deal of literature, we wrote some very fine papers, and we developed some criteria for missional congregations. As we were doing this, we became aware that we were betraying how our thinking was shaped by the Enlightenment. The idea of "models of missional congregations" reveals an Enlightened belief in method, in strategy, in the human capacity to solve the problem. What we needed to do was to define the problem, chart

3. Lois Barrett et al., eds., *Treasure in Clay Jars: Patterns in Missional Faithfulness* (Grand Rapids: Eerdmans, 2004).

out its dimensions, set aside the proper resources, and enlist the experts to resolve it. Chastened by this insight and in response to Scripture (especially 2 Corinthians), we moved from the idea of identifiable replicable models to an investigation of "patterns of missional change" in congregations. The emergence of such a pattern is signaled when a member of the congregation says to me, "I think I'm in this congregation because God brought me here." "We're gathered, so that we can learn together to live out our calling more faithfully, particularly the calling that we carry with us when we are not together." "We're gathered in this particular place because God has something for us to do in this particular place." "We're trying to learn here together how to see the world and our neighbors through the eyes of Jesus."

My students and I find, as we continue this conversation in churches around the country, that there are Christians and congregations becoming aware of the American-ness of their understanding of the gospel and are beginning to grasp the difficult challenges of our cultural captivity. There are many ways this is happening, one of which is through the growing role of the so-called "mission trip." I am not a fan of the mission tourism that has become a common part of congregational programs these days. There is good reason to be concerned about what happens in our sister communities in the Caribbean or Latin America as a result of our mission trips. But it is certainly clear that those experiences with Christian communities in the non-Western world are profoundly converting for culturally captive North Americans. Seeing ourselves and our culture through the lenses of other cultures sensitizes us to our cultural captivity and begins to change our understanding of the character of sin. As painful as it is, this learning process helps us to recognize the ambivalence of our structures and assumptions. Conversion is happening when members can deal with the fact that even in the church, systemic sin is at work, and it generates an array of ecclesiastical capacities to justify a reductionist gospel. That conversion is happening when our members begin to discriminate between different ways of interpreting what it means to say, "I am a Christian," and can articulate how Christian profession might well mean becoming countercultural. It is happening when participants in Bible studies recognize that there are profound differences between "the community Jesus intended"[4] and our ecclesial reality. David Bosch suggests that Western theology can be described

---

4. Gerhard Lohfink, *Jesus and Community: The Social Dimension of Christian Faith,* trans. J. Galvin (Philadelphia: Fortress, 1984). The German title of the original book, when translated, is "How Did Jesus Intend the Community?"

as a sequence of learned attempts to explain why the Sermon on the Mount does not apply to us![5]

In some expressions of the so-called emergent movement there are signs of an awakening of the missional gospel's call to conversion from reductionist and individualistic piety to kingdom witness. But, in that emergent movement, there are also many evidences of the strong sway that Christendom captivity still has, albeit now evidenced in culturally post-Christendom forms. One must constantly ask, What is the gospel that is proclaimed? What is the outcome of response to that gospel? How are the benefits of faith in Christ inseparably linked with the vocation to witness to his inbreaking rule? And, how does this community equip its members to see and engage the difficult mission field in which we find ourselves in post-Christendom America?

This challenging process of corporate missional conversion needs to be focused on the biblical emphasis upon witness linked with the corporate character of Christian vocation. As we have emphasized, the biblical story centers on the calling and setting apart of a distinctive people as God's agents for God's mission. With the passing of Christendom and the revision of the assumption that the society and everyone in it is already Christian, the corporate character of Christian vocation is reasserting itself today as crucial for Christian faithfulness. That corporate understanding of our vocation is most powerfully shaped by the Luke-Acts emphasis upon witness. For Luke-Acts, Christian vocation and identity are defined by Jesus Christ on the Mount of the Ascension: "You shall be my witnesses" (Acts 1:8). This is a profoundly holistic definition of who and what we are as Christian persons and as the Christian community. It is always dealt with as a plural concept. The entire community is made up of persons who are defined as witnesses. Yet witness itself is not merely an activity of these persons, so much as it defines comprehensively who they are. The text does not say, "You shall give testimonies." It defines who and what a Christian is: a witness. The essential integration of the personal and the corporate is symbolized in Acts 2 in that these first Christians are gathered as one community in one room, sharing the experience of the wind while something like a flame of fire is seen over every head, and they all subsequently become translators of the gospel into all the tongues spoken by the multicultural gathering of Jews in Jerusalem.

---

5. David Bosch, *Transforming Mission: Paradigm Shifts in Theology of Mission* (Maryknoll, NY: Orbis, 2011), p. 70: "Through the ages, however, Christians have usually found ways around the clear meaning of the Sermon on the Mount."

Out of that common event emerges the proclamation of the gospel as a corporate undertaking — but with a spokesperson. We should note that Peter speaks, "standing in the midst of them," the voice of the Eleven and their gathered community.

The term "witness" defines both persons in their distinctiveness and in their common impact upon their context. They are sent singly and together into the world as witnesses. The word family includes *marturos,* the person as witness, *marturia,* what the watching world experiences because these witnesses are present and active, and a cluster of verbs based on *marturein,* the various ways in which witness actually happens as action and communication. Every dimension of their life is to be an expression, an outworking of their calling. I have defined this theology of witness as a matter of being, doing, and saying.[6] It was for this multifaceted vocation to witness that the apostolic strategy was the formation of communities. These assemblies were called *ecclesia* in order, among other things, to emphasize that their vocation was to public witness. The primary task of a missional hermeneutic then is to provide a particular congregation the formation it needs to be able to live out both its gathered life and its scattered life faithfully.

In the Pauline literature, vocation to witness is most trenchantly explained and developed in the emphasis upon living one's life worthy of one's calling. If our concern is how Scripture works in the congregation so that this calling to missional witness actually happens, we find guidance in the repeated injunction that we are to live worthy of the calling with which we have been called, as Ephesians 4 puts it. It is a common theme in the Pauline epistles, found in varying articulations in Philippians, First and Second Thessalonians, Ephesians, and Colossians. There are echoes, with other terminology, in Romans and especially in the first five chapters of Second Corinthians, dealing with the integrity of the apostolic vocation as it defines the life and practice of the entire community. Clearly, theologically, the calling comes first: God's initiating action is testified to in the apostolic witness. God's action results in the calling of people to become followers of Jesus Christ and to become part of his continuing mission carried out by his people, the *ecclesia/kyriakon.* The calling empowered by God's Spirit generates appropriate responses, ways of living that correspond to and give evidence of the healing that is the purpose of that calling. If the calling is to witness to God's love for the entire world, then to live worthy of that calling

---

6. Darrell Guder, *Be My Witnesses: The Church's Message, Mission, and Missionaries* (Grand Rapids: Eerdmans, 1985).

is to live together lovingly. If the calling is to be agents of God's peace, then to live worthy of that calling is to live together peacefully as peacemakers. If the calling is to point to the healing that is God's intention for all creation, then to live worthy of that calling is to live together in ways that foster healing, restoration, and reconciliation. The purpose of the calling defines the character of the respondents' life and action.

Of course, this calling results in personal faith, that is, in the personal transformation that redefines who I am now in terms of God's salvific revelation in Christ. But this faith is neither a thing nor a status nor a possession. It is a new way of walking. It is a living hope. It is the capacity to join a pilgrimage going in a new direction. This gift of faith initiates our continuous conversion, that transformation by the renewing of our minds spoken of in Romans 12:2. And that continuing conversion happens through the parallel continuing repentance that comes about as we discover more and more how culturally captive and conformistic we actually are. This faith, which God's Spirit enables, is more than an assent; it is more than merely saying "yes" to creedal propositions; it is more than a confessional tradition or a particular theological position. This faith that God gives us becomes expressive and active. It becomes a transforming knowledge that results in action. To use a statement constantly emphasized by Karl Barth, it is a gift that becomes a task *(Gabe — Aufgabe)*. Or, to use Peter's language in his first epistle, it becomes a hearing to which we respond with action — which is what Petrine "obedience" is all about. Such obedience is a dependent and enabled action, a real action, because God has spoken and we can hear. The imperative of obedience is an enabled response to what God has done, is doing, and will complete. "Having purified your souls by your obedience to the truth for a sincere love of the brethren, love one another earnestly from the heart" (1 Pet. 1:22). The community can practice that mutual, earnest, heartfelt love, because God's truth has engendered their obedience and made "the sincere love of the brethren" a new possibility.

One way some of us talk about this living worthy of the calling is in terms of the incarnation. There is an understandable nervousness in the theological world about language that encroaches upon the uniqueness, the once-and-for-allness of the life, ministry, death, resurrection, and ascension of Jesus. When I use the adjective "incarnational," I am not talking about a prolongation of the unique event of the incarnation. There is nothing more that needs to happen to accomplish God's saving purposes for the world. The work is, truly, completed on the cross and at the empty tomb. But there is in this incarnational language recognition that Jesus has taught us how to carry forward his mission by the way he conducted his ministry. That is part of the importance of the Gospel narratives: they demonstrate that the message and its demonstration cannot be separated. That is why it is important for us to understand the process of rabbinic discipling as the model for the formation of an apostolic community. This we learn from watching Jesus as the disciples learned from watching Jesus. We see how "living worthy of our calling" actually happens as we follow Jesus from encounter to encounter in the four Gospels. Those first called disciples basically learned everything that Jesus said and watched everything that he did in order to be empowered by him to continue his ministry and to be sent out by him to proclaim his message. There is this necessary congruence that we learn in the Gospels between the content of the gospel and the way it is communicated, which expounds, I suggest, what Paul intends with the admonition that we are to live our lives worthy of the calling with which we have been called.

We return again to our basic question: How does the scriptural formation of communities that live their lives worthy of their calling actually happen? To borrow language from Lesslie Newbigin, how do congregations truly become "the hermeneutic of the Gospel"?[7] Such scriptural formation is clearly a task that takes time and hard work. Peter's first imperative is to "gird up the loins of your minds" (1 Pet. 1:13, King James Version) — which speaks of the rigorous discipline that will be required for the formation that will now be addressed in detail. Such rigorous discipline requires, I suggest, the reclamation of Sabbath for the sake of our missional formation. The goal is the kind of scriptural literacy that enables us to be translators of this story, to live bilingually, as Newbigin says, speaking both the language of faith and translating that language into our lives and actions in our various mission fields.[8] Such scriptural formation happens in communities that are consciously united around their missional vocation. They know, or they are learning to know, who they are and what they are for. Their identity is beginning to be defined for them by the biblical accounts of witness, of being Christ's letter to the world, of being disciples now who are being sent out as apostles, as being those that bear Christ's cross. To put it another way, their identity is defined by God's calling and not by their own religious needs, or the continuation of their religious tradition or their ethnicity or whatever the other agenda might be. God's active and constant intervention is sum-

7. Lesslie Newbigin, *The Gospel in a Pluralist Society* (Grand Rapids: Eerdmans, 1989), pp. 222-33.

8. Newbigin, *The Gospel in a Pluralist Society*, p. 65.

moning this community to its mission. And such scriptural formation takes the public life of the community seriously.

In the Philippians 1:26 version of the injunction to live worthily, there is a very interesting variation in the verb. The usual translation puts it: "Let your manner of life be worthy of the gospel of Jesus Christ." The verb is political, *politeuein*, from *polis*, and it is very difficult to render clearly. It is emphasizing the public character of the community's life. One might translate it, "Conduct your public life worthy of the gospel of Jesus Christ," which is the sense of the term *ecclesia* as well. The concern is for a witness that is understandable. It may not be welcome in that public world, but it is understandable. It makes the point. It is a legible letter to the world, so that the community, the watching world, will know what it needs to know about the gospel because this community of witnesses is there, being, doing, and saying good news. It is a witness that is credible as it points to God's healing love at work in our own lives. It shows how that love enables the community to follow Paul's formative injunctions: "Do nothing from selfishness or conceit, but in humility count others better than yourselves. Let each of you look not only to his own interests but to the interests of others" (Phil. 2:3-4). It is not a matter of our merely liking each other. It's about practicing decisional and active love before a watching world.

Such scriptural formation will then relate our gathered worship of God to our apostolic scattering in the world. The test of missional formation in the gathered community is the lay apostolate. The concern is for how our members live and why they live that way when we are not gathered. The concern is how we gather for one-seventh of our time in order to be equipped for the apostolate of the sixth-sevenths of our time. Such scriptural formation for that lay apostolate focuses our attention constantly on our neighbor, picking up on a major theme in the Gospels. Our neighbor is the one to whom God is sending us because we can't avoid that person — the man in the parable of the Good Samaritan lying, unavoidably, across the road. Such scriptural formation shapes our thinking in radically new ways, generating that *phronesis,* the missional mindedness advocated by Paul, which entails the conversion of our thinking and our attitudes as well as of our practices.

Finally, that scriptural formation happens through the gifts of Christian sisters and brothers who serve as mentors — a scriptural theme rarely alluded to. Who can guide missional apprenticeship in the community? Who is worthy of imitation, that *mimesis* that is another central theme in the Pauline formation of the missional church? Karl Barth lists twelve activities of the sent community of the Holy Spirit, in his discussion of the "service of the community."[9] He has no theology of ordered ministry, although obviously there are ordered and credentialed ministers to carry out the preaching, teaching, and theological disciplines about which he speaks. But he has a whole section on modeling, on mentoring, on the gifts of mentors and apprenticeship, for the formation of a faithful community.[10] He speaks of these gifted people as "definite personal examples of Christian life and action." These people are Christ's gift to the church to enable the community as a whole to live in such a way that their "love abounds more and more, with knowledge and all discernment, so that [they] may approve what is excellent and may be pure and blameless for the day of Christ, filled with the fruits of righteousness which come through Jesus Christ, to the glory and praise of God" (Phil. 1:9-11).

---

9. Karl Barth, *Church Dogmatics* IV/3.2 (Edinburgh: T. & T. Clark, 1962), pp. 865-901.

10. Barth, *Church Dogmatics* IV/3.2, pp. 887-89.

CHAPTER 8

The "Worthy Walk" of the Missional Community after Christendom

Introduction

In this chapter and the chapter that follows, I shall attempt to address a theme that relates missionally to what we do in seminaries as we prepare missional leaders for the church after Christendom. I do this as a missiologist who, in the first two seminaries in which I served as a full-time faculty member, was part of the Practical Theology Department. Now, as a member of the Theology Department and especially as Dean of Academic Affairs (2005-2010), I am as a missional theologian particularly concerned with the way in which the theological formation we do relates to the missional vocation of the church and to the realities and challenges of the mission fields into which our graduates are going.

This chapter comprises the first of two Payton Lectures I delivered at Fuller Theological Seminary, May 2-3, 2007. The content of the two lectures was published as a single essay under the title "Walking Worthily: Missional Leadership after Christendom" in *The Princeton Seminary Bulletin*, new series, 28, no. 3 (2007): 251-301. The content of the second lecture appears as chapter 9 in this volume. In these lectures, the exploration of missional theology, and especially of missional ecclesiology, turns to the missional practice of the gathered community. Based on the exposition of the entire community's walking worthy of the calling with which we are called, I investigate the issue of the leadership needed for the formation of the witnessing community. This might be regarded as a move from classic doctrinal themes to the perspective of "practical theology." It should, however, be clear by now that the distinction between doctrine and praxis is highly problematic. Missional theology can only function in the service of God's mission in that it is practiced, and its theoretic formulation must be shaped by that practice.

The Concept "Missional" and Its Intended Polemic

We have thus far examined the concept and scope of "missional theology" from several perspectives. Permit me to summarize that argumentation. When we gave our study the title "Missional Church" back in 1998, our little group of missiological researchers affiliated with the Gospel and Our Culture Network was attempting to state the implications of the classic consensus statement advanced by Vatican II in both *Lumen Gentium* and *Ad Gentes Divinitus:* "The church on earth is by its very nature missionary since, according to the plan of the Father, it has its origin in the mission of the Son and of the Holy Spirit."[1] By adding the suffix "al" to the word "mission," we hoped to foster an understanding of the church as fundamentally and comprehensively defined by its calling and sending, its purpose to serve God's healing purposes *for* all the world as God's witnessing people *to* all the world. We were obviously engaging in a polemic endeavor. We were critiquing theologies of the church that neglect the church's essentially missionary nature. We were critiquing reductions of mission to one of several clusters of activities that are proper to the church: worship, fellowship, service, and, in some cases, mission. We were following through on Wilbert Shenk's assessment that Western Christendom is Christianity without mission, although we moderated that statement by concentrating on the curious silence about mission in Western ecclesiologies — a theological lacuna that characterized virtually all systematic theologies in the West until Barth made mission the pervasive theme of his *Church Dogmatics.*

Avery Dulles illustrated this theological problem with the analytical method he adopted in his classic *Models of the Church.*[2] He explained each of the five models (in the revised version, he presented six models) in terms of various categories, at the center of which are two: What are the benefits afforded by a particular model, and who are the beneficiaries of it? The answer for the first three models, the Institutional Model, the Mystical Communion model, and the Sacramental model, is the same. The benefits that accrue from the existence of the church in each of these models are the gift and reality of salvation — eternal life — and the beneficiaries are the members of the church. The church is basically inwardly oriented, focused

---

1. "Decree on the Church's Missionary Activity," Vatican II, *Ad Gentes Divinitus, 7 December 1965*, in *Vatican Council II: The Conciliar and Post-Conciliar Documents*, ed. Austin Flannery, O.P. (Collegeville, MN: Liturgical Press, 1975), p. 813.

2. Avery Dulles, S.J., *Models of the Church* (Garden City, NY: Image Books, 1978), esp. pp. 39-79.

upon itself and its members, and their savedness. Its activities concentrate on the mediation and maintenance of their salvation, along with the preservation of the institution itself. I have attempted to show at some length that this understanding of the church reflects a reductionistic soteriology and ecclesiology. At the heart of these reductionisms is a weakening of the centrality of the kingdom of God as the central theme of the gospel. God's saving purposes for the world have been, in effect, reduced to God's salvation for the members of the church; the purpose of the gospel is the formation of the church as the community of the saved.

From Maintenance to Mission

This reductionism, which is broadly characteristic of the thought and practice of Western Christendom both within our so-called Christian societies as well as in the modern missionary movement, has been criticized, of course, for much of the twentieth century. Much of this critique has arisen out of the ferment of the emerging global church that resulted from the missionary movement, especially within the ecumenical theological discussion under the aegis of the International Missionary Council. Just as the demographic center of world Christianity has shifted from the North Atlantic to the global south, the understanding of the church has moved from seeing it as an end in itself to understanding it as God's called people sent as witnesses to God's gospel "in Jerusalem, Judea, Samaria, and to the ends of the earth." But the shift from a member-centered, vertical salvation–oriented, "who-is-saved" and "who-is-not-saved" understanding of the church is, for traditions shaped by seventeen centuries of Western Christendom, slow and painful. The pressure is enormous to "keep on keeping on" within the reductionisms of Western soteriology and ecclesiology. The institutional viability of our churches appears to be linked to their capacity to meet the religious needs of their members. The mindset of religious consumerism does not welcome the missional probing of the church's purpose and actions. While the emphasis upon the "missional church" has evoked much discussion and appears to have resonated with many who are struggling with the implications of the end of Christendom in the West, it also evokes a great deal of resistance in late-Christendom churches when its radical implications begin to be understood.

Granting that such resistance is certainly there, there is a consensus that Western Christendom has ended, or is still ending. Ever since the 1920s it has been clear to perceptive observers across the theological spectrum that the "idols are tottering."[3] What started out in 1900 as "The Christian Century" in the West certainly did not end that way in 2000. What we have discovered in the discussions of the missional church since 1998 is that the mindset of Christendom is much more resilient than its crumbling structures. The reclamation of the church's missional vocation is not an easy process, a thematic workshop that can turn your congregation around after one Saturday session (at $500 a head), or a twelve-step method, or any of the myriad add-water-and-stir approaches to church renewal that are on the market — and I choose that venue advisedly. It is for that reason that I described my own further exploration of the challenge of missional vocation as "the continuing conversion" of the church, to make clear that we are not talking here about technique or strategy or manageable change, but about the Spirit's mysterious and powerful work to bring about repentance and both the desire and the ability to walk in a new direction. For congregations and denominational structures focused on maintaining what has been, this is a truly daunting challenge.

The implications of the shift to missional ecclesiology are as daunting for theological education as they are for the practice of particular congregations. If we are educating for the inward-oriented sense of the church, then our graduates should be equipped to deal competently with the religious needs of the churches' members and to maintain the structures and traditions of the institutions that exist to address those needs. We continue to need ecclesiologies that focus upon the attainment and preservation of the individualistic assurance of personal savedness, upon rites and sacraments, polities and ordered ministries, the provision of services and programs to the religious consumer, and the preservation of religious customs and celebrations valued by our secularizing culture. If, with Lesslie Newbigin, we are challenged to recognize that our own context has become, within an astonishingly short period of time, a post-Christian mission field, posing enormous challenges to the received forms and attitudes of Western Christendom, then that inward-oriented, church-maintaining approach to theological education will not work. Education for maintenance is not the same thing as education for mission.

---

3. Karl Barth, *"Der Götze wackelt": Zeitkritische Aufsätze, Reden, und Briefe von 1930 bis 1960*, ed. K. Kupisch (Berlin: Käthe Vogt, 1964).

The Goal: The Formation of the Missional Community

If it is the mindset of Christendom that results in our seminaries educating for maintenance, then we need to explore together how the end of Christendom profoundly changes our educational goals, or to use the current academic jargon that dominates the world of accreditation, our academic outcomes. It was not hard to fashion the outcomes of theological formation for the maintenance of Christendom. What needed to be done was to keep on keeping on. There was little perceived break between the theological theory that we taught, the ministry that we practiced, and the cultural context in which it all happened. After all, we have been a church in Christian societies; we have been a part of cultures that have privileged our faith; we have lived in partnership with the state and have at times even been the dominant power shaping corporate human affairs. We have become used to clout, accustomed to a consensus of favor and endorsement — and, in the process, we have become culturally captive. The paradigm shift through which we are moving is confronting these givens of the Christendom legacy, the concessions to power, influence, wealth, and privilege that we have made, and the institutions they have generated. It is, as I constantly remind my students, a difficult task to learn how to deal with our legacy within the liminal passage in which we find ourselves. We constantly stress that it is a dialectically shaped challenge, to be addressed with both modesty and conviction as we seek to discern how God has been faithful and how we have been unfaithful in the same story — and yet God's Spirit has never left the church, and the gospel has not ceased to be heard and the vocation passed on.

But how will we determine the impact of this paradigm shift to the missiocentric church upon our theological education? The academic enterprise theology is, in terms of the history of Western education, classically defined with two other university disciplines, law and medicine. All of them produce "professionals," holders of advanced degrees at the level of at least a master's degree, whose life and action are defined by what they profess. As Christendom continues to decline, however, a significant difference emerges between the academic disciplines of law and medicine on the one hand, and theology on the other. This difference has to do with the actual purpose, the intended outcomes, of these academic enterprises. My hunch is that the educational strategists who develop the outcomes for the study of medicine think primarily in terms of the proficiencies and competences that must characterize a professional medical doctor. I doubt that they devote much attention to the idea that the real outcome of their work should be a healthful and wholesome society. Similarly, lawyers should graduate from our law schools competent in all the complexities of the formulation, interpretation, and application of public law. I doubt that they are focused upon the desirable outcome that we should live in a just, well-governed, equitable society.

But, from a missional perspective, the outcome of theological education is *not* the competent well-equipped professional clergyperson. Or, to put it in its historical dynamic, that cannot be our point of orientation in a post-Christendom world in which the focus upon the maintenance of the church must be absorbed into and redefined by the overarching missional purpose of the church. Rather than just the clergy, it is the entire missional community that is the central agency God's Spirit uses to bring about God's healing purposes for the creation. The test of missional theological education is the equipped and faithful witness of called and sent communities. The people of God in concrete assemblies and fellowships must be the focus of missional theological formation, and not merely the incumbents of ordered ministry structures. To borrow Lesslie Newbigin's now-classic phrase, it is the community which is the hermeneutic of the gospel.[4]

The Apostolic Strategy and the Missional Community

This understanding of the missional community derives from the original apostolic strategy that brought about the initiation of the Christian movement in history. We recall the argument made in our discussion above of "the Christological formation of missional practice." This strategy begins with the earthly ministry of Jesus, where according to Gerhard Lohfink we can learn about the "community that Jesus intended."[5] From the moment that Jesus appointed *twelve* disciples, it was clear that the ancient emphasis upon God's calling and setting apart a *people* for his service was finding its continuation in the strategy of Jesus. That ancient variant on Mark 1:14 which, in our modern translations, wanders back and forth between the text and the footnotes, documents this continuity from the calling of Israel through Abraham to the formation of the church: "And he appointed twelve, *whom also he named apostles,* to be with him, and to be sent out to preach and have

4. Lesslie Newbigin, *The Gospel in a Pluralist Society* (Grand Rapids: Eerdmans, 1989), pp. 222-33.

5. Gerhard Lohfink, *Wie hat Jesus Gemeinde gewollt?* (Freiburg/Basel/Vienna: Herder, 1982); ET: *Jesus and Community: The Social Dimension of Christian Faith,* trans. J. P. Galvin (Philadelphia: Fortress Press, 1984).

authority to cast out demons." For the disciples who went to school with the Rabbi Jesus, graduation would mean apostolate. And the apostolate, initiated by the Twelve who are the core of the people of God sent into the world, was equipped and commissioned to form witnessing communities. The apostolic mission was not merely the saving of souls and their collecting into communities of the saved. The apostolic strategy, whose message was the event of salvation accomplished in Jesus Christ and whose method was defined by the earthly ministry of Jesus, was the formation of witnessing communities whose purpose was to continue the witness that brought them into existence. They were to "disciple the ethnicities" (Matt. 28:19), which meant that they were to reproduce in every newly formed church in whichever culture they were engaging what they had experienced with Jesus; they were to "teach them to observe everything that [Jesus had] commanded [them]" (Matt. 28:20), after these communities had been set apart for God's mission by their baptism in the name of the Father and of the Son and of the Holy Spirit. They were to implement the definition Jesus gave to the church on the Mount of the Ascension: "You shall be my witnesses" — and they would be enabled to do this by the empowering work of the Holy Spirit: "You shall receive power when the Holy Spirit has come upon you" (Acts 1:8). They were to be "a letter from Christ delivered by [the apostolic missionaries], written not with ink but with the Spirit of the living God, not on tablets of stone but on tablets of human hearts" (2 Cor. 3:3).

The Apostolic Scriptures and the Continuing Formation of Missional Communities

The apostolic strategy, the formation of equipped and empowered witnessing communities, finds its continuation in these ancient documents written to such communities, which over time were collected and became the canonical New Testament. This was the central thrust of our discussion of "missional hermeneutics." It is frequently observed that there are virtually no evangelistic or missional imperatives in the New Testament. Even the celebrated Great Commission describes what Christians are to be doing all the time, wherever they may be, as they are going about in the world — the text is really a summary of the entire gospel message of this book, and the apostolic ministry it summarizes is a comprehensive definition of the entire life of the witnessing community. Matthew 28:16-20 does not intend to generate a narrow, individualistic, benefits-centered evangelism. Here is a vision of the missional church that is centered in the authority given to Jesus in heaven and on earth. Here is a definition of discipling that is happening wherever Christians go in the world and is intentionally multicultural. Matthew's Gospel, like the other three, invites the Christian community into a relationship of intense personal formation, a process of discipleship paralleling the three years of schooling of those first followers of the Rabbi Jesus. The outcome in every instance is to be a repetition of Jesus' ministry with these disciples: This formation is to flow into apostolic witness, into making the good news known to the world. To be called to Jesus will always result in being sent out by him. Like the first disciples, every Christian community is to learn from Jesus and with Jesus both his message and how it was to be communicated. They were taught to see the world through his eyes and to understand the whole course of human history from the central event that he was and is. Each of the four gospels is an immersion learning experience in missional vocation.

The epistles function in a similar way. They continue the formation for apostolic witness that the first missionaries were doing in the weeks and months they spent in each newly formed congregation. They react to the challenges and problems these fledgling missional churches were experiencing. They encourage and admonish these communities as they struggle to discern how they shall be Christ's witnesses in Jerusalem, Judea, Samaria, and to the ends of the earth. They are all occasional writings, but basically they are all linked by the same occasion: the missional vocation of the congregation. So, there are no evangelistic or missional imperatives because the assumption that informs the New Testament is that each of these communities, be it Thessalonica, or Colossae, or Ephesus, or Corinth, or Rome, or the Matthean or the Johannine or the Marcan community, or one of the seven churches to whom John the Seer sent his letters, understood itself as existing to continue the mission that had brought each one into existence. All of them, living in the light of Easter and mobilized by the confidence that Jesus Christ had truly been raised, were shaped by the dominical claim, "As my Father has sent me, so I send you" (John 20:21). As George Hunsberger has argued, the New Testament functions as the "warrant" for the missional vocation that defined every first Christian congregation.[6]

If we want to know, then, what a missional community looks like, our primary resource is the New Testament. To repeat the argument already

---

6. George Hunsberger, "Is There Biblical Warrant for Evangelism?," *Interpretation* 48 (April 1994): 131-44.

made above, we interrogate the text from the perspective of a missional hermeneutic. Assuming that the purpose of every New Testament scripture is, in some way or another, the continuing missional formation of particular communities with particular challenges in particular places, we constantly ask each text some version of the question, "How did this text equip the missional church then for its vocation, and how does it do that today?" Each New Testament book will render distinctive insights when explored in this way. The concrete situation of any congregation that, in today's rapidly changing world, wants to be faithful to its missional vocation will be illumined in radically converting ways by this rigorous scriptural formation.

Biblical Formation of the Missional Community: "Walk Worthily"

If there are no evangelistic imperatives addressed to the emerging Christian movement in the New Testament communities, there certainly are imperatives. Jesus defined his missionary movement with the "commandments" so often referred to in John's Gospel. Matthew's commission stresses that these apostolic communities emerging in every ethnicity should observe all that Jesus had taught them. All of the epistles arrive, at one point or another, at the pivotal "therefore" that leads from the exposition of the gospel to its implications for the witnessing community. There is, in particular, a pervasive and thematic imperative in these documents in which Paul continued the formation of his missional communities. It is formulated in a variety of ways beginning in the earliest epistle, 1 Thessalonians, where Paul reminds the people of the formation they had received during his initial and prematurely interrupted visit in their city: "You are witnesses, and God also, how holy and righteous and blameless was our behavior to you believers; for you know how, like a father with his children, we exhorted each one of you and encouraged you and charged you to lead a life worthy of God, who calls you into his own kingdom and glory" (1 Thess. 2:10-12). In 2 Thessalonians, this pervasive theme shapes his prayer for this community: "To this end we always pray for you, that our God may make you worthy of his call, and may fulfill every good resolve and work of faith by his power so that the name of our Lord Jesus may be glorified in you, and you in him, according to the grace of our God and the Lord Jesus Christ" (2 Thess. 1:11). He prays in a similar way in his epistle to the Colossian community: "And so, from the day we heard of it, we have not ceased to pray for you, asking that you may be filled with the knowledge of his will in all spiritual wisdom and understanding, to lead a life worthy of the Lord, fully pleasing to him, bearing fruit in every good work and increasing in the knowledge of God" (Col. 1:9-10). The text that many regard as the thematic center of the Philippian epistle takes up the same motif: "Only let your manner of life be worthy of the gospel of Christ" (Phil. 1:27). Finally, this theme forms the bridge in Ephesians from what John Mackay called the rhapsodic statement of the gospel to its implications for the life of the witnessing community: "I therefore, a prisoner for the Lord, beg you to lead a life worthy of the calling to which you have been called, with all lowliness and meekness, with patience, forbearing one another in love, eager to maintain the unity of the Spirit in the bond of peace" (Eph. 4:1-3). "Walking worthily" appears to be a key description of the life and conduct of these communities as they continue the apostolic witness that is their very reason for being. They are to walk worthy of God, of his call, of the Lord, of the gospel of Christ, of the calling to which they have been called. The missional congregation may be defined as the community that walks worthy of the calling to which it has been called.

Vocation as the Defining Center of Biblical Ecclesiology

If, then, we are going to develop a biblical ecclesiology for the missional church, the theme "vocation" will be its defining center. Understood against the backdrop of the biblical drama of God's calling, God's election, God's setting apart of a people and within it of particular persons for the carrying out of God's blessing of all the nations, we understand the missional church to be created and defined by its calling, its vocation. Just as the original community of twelve, representing the continuation and extension of the whole people of God, resulted from Jesus' calling them, the church is the response to God's initiation, God's calling, God's invitation, and God's empowering. It is God who calls, and God's Spirit who enables our hearing and responding, and the triune God who determines that this unlikely community will be the agent, the foretaste, the firstfruits of the inbreaking kingdom.

Karl Barth incorporates this understanding of the fundamental ecclesiological importance of vocation into the great design of his theology of reconciliation. In that project, which is the topic of the several books making up volume IV of the *Church Dogmatics*, he expounds the gospel of reconciliation in terms of justification, sanctification, and vocation. These actions of God are all essential components of the gospel that we have been enabled to believe and to which we now witness. But our grasp of the gospel is too small if we

130

stop with justification and sanctification. To do so is ultimately to fall into that individualism and reductionism that characterizes Western Christendom's central theological and missional problem. The good news of God's gracious accomplishment of salvation for all, which we appropriate as God's justifying us and sanctifying us exclusive of any merit on our part, must necessarily define who we are and what we are for as those who have received these benefits. The justified and the sanctified are, by virtue of their enabled response to God's gospel, the called. If, according to Luther, the Christian should start every day by touching his or her head and saying, "I am baptized," then he or she should necessarily continue with Jesus' Easter announcement, "As my Father has sent me, so I send you." We enter into the world into which we are sent defined by Jesus' statement, "You shall be my witnesses."

In placing vocation in this theological linkage with justification and sanctification, Barth laid out the doctrinal framework for the missional church. With this emphasis upon vocation, he challenges what he calls the "classic definition of what it means to be a Christian." That classic definition dwells primarily on the benefits of the gospel, what the Christian receives by virtue of the life, death, and resurrection of Jesus. These are the benefits summarized by our classical theologies of justification and sanctification: reconciliation with God through Christ, restoration of wholeness, forgiveness of our sins, removal of our guilt and abrogation of our deserved punishment, the gift of eternal life and the promise of eternity with Christ and his people in heaven, and the victory over sin, Satan, and his minions. All of these benefits testify to the fact that God's radically new reign in the kingdom of Christ is breaking in now in those who are the firstfruits, the earnest, the *arrabon* of the gospel. Those who respond in faith and obedience to that calling receive the sealing work of the Holy Spirit, assuring them of their salvation and granting them the confidence that God will complete what God has begun. These benefits are wondrous and merit our constant praise, worship, and thanksgiving. They are the motivation and the grand theme of our assembled worship. They are the lyrics of the church's song and the good news to be shared with every neighbor. All of this is summarized and expounded theologically by the doctrines of justification and sanctification in their distinctive and yet essentially interlocking character.

But Christians are defined by more than their reception of these benefits, as sure as they may be that these benefits are undoubtedly theirs. God's

---

7. See discussion in Darrell Guder, *The Continuing Conversion of the Church* (Grand Rapids: Eerdmans, 2000), 121-31.

calling is not solely for the benefit of the called who are incorporated into the called-out people, the *ecclesia*. God's calling of a particular people is for God's saving purposes for the world, for Jerusalem, Judea, Samaria, and the ends of the earth. For God so loved the *world*. God was in Christ reconciling the *world*. And for the sake of that *world*, created and fallen, God's calling creates, forms, equips, commissions, and sends the church to carry out the witness for which it exists. Its vocation, then, is centered and defined by God's salvific mission for the world, and its action is in service of that vocation. One cannot use Christian calling legitimately in any other sense than as calling to the life and service of witness.

The Vocation to "Walk Worthily": Not Works Righteousness

The missional community carries out its calling by walking worthily. The question then is what walking worthily is all about. It's a phrase that appears to receive precious little attention in the lexical resources, even though it is obviously a prevailing theme in the Pauline corpus. It is certainly possible to talk about what it is not. It is clear that worthy walking does not imply some merit or spiritual accomplishment on the part of the called Christian. Works righteousness is not reentering ecclesiology by the missional back door. Markus Barth says it plainly in his commentary on Ephesians: "Those called possess no worthiness of their own."[8] The reclamation of the church's missional vocation is not a reversal of the great soteriological battle fought and won in the Reformation. There is to be no compromise of the doctrine of justification by faith alone: *sola gratia, sola fide, sola scriptura* all stand and must not be diluted. But the fact remains that the missional vocation of the church is the pervasive, shaping theme of the New Testament scriptures, reflecting, I believe, the central thrust of the apostolic mission and the purpose of Jesus' own formation of the disciples. We are to understand the imperative to walk worthy of the calling to which we have been called not as an act of spiritual accomplishment but as evidence of empowered obedience. The imperatives, and the conduct they form, have to do with the church's missional calling to be, to do, and to say witness. Markus Barth again: "Imperatives can be a means of preaching the gospel."[9] They are, he suggests,

---

8. Markus Barth, *Ephesians: Translation and Commentary on Chapters 4–6*, The Anchor Bible, 34A (Garden City, NY: Doubleday, 1974), p. 454.

9. Markus Barth, *Ephesians*, p. 455.

an outworking of the transforming goodness of the gospel: ". . . the way in which Paul introduces his exhortations shows that he *honors* his readers by expecting of them a specific conduct. His very imperatives imply a privilege the saints can enjoy, not a burden they ought to bear."[10]

The Vocation to "Walk Worthily": Not the Perfected Community

"Walking worthily" is, moreover, not to be construed as a claim that the Christian community is perfect. The sanctification that is, with Calvin, the inseparable outworking of justification is ongoing. Worthy walking takes place in that protected and empowered space between what God has already done and what God will most certainly do. It is the nature of our pilgrimage, the kind of life we live as followers of the Way. It takes place in the confidence expressed by Paul to the Philippians, "I am sure that he who began a good work in you will bring it to completion at the day of Jesus Christ" (Phil. 1:6). It is the vocation of those who, as Peter describes us, "are born anew to a living hope through the resurrection of Jesus Christ from the dead," who are thus certain of that "inheritance that is imperishable, undefiled, and unfading, kept in heaven" for us, while we "are guarded by God's power through faith for a salvation ready to be revealed in the last time" (1 Pet. 1:3-5). Walking worthily does not ignore the frailty of those joined together on this pilgrimage. It is shaped by the earthly ministry of Jesus who dealt as much with the disciples' obtuseness and competitiveness as with their insight into their calling. Those walking worthily are enjoined to forgive each other seventy times seven. We are to know that we are but "earthen vessels" who are afflicted, perplexed, persecuted, struck down, but in all that not crushed, not driven to despair, not forsaken, not destroyed. Instead, in our forgivenness we are enabled so to "carry in our body the death of Jesus that the life of Jesus may also be manifested in our bodies" (2 Cor. 4:7-10). Walking worthily happens as a constant demonstration of dependence upon God's grace, a determination with Paul "to know nothing among you except Jesus Christ and him crucified." Thus, the apostolic model in our midst is one of "weakness, much fear, trembling," not relying on "plausible words of wisdom" but upon the "demonstration of the Spirit and of power," for our faith does not "rest in the wisdom of men but in the power of God" (1 Cor. 2:2-5).

10. Markus Barth, *Ephesians*, p. 455.

The Vocation to "Walk Worthily": Not Institutional Success

Just as worthy walking is not to be misconstrued as personal or corporate claims to spiritual or moral perfection, it is not a matter of institutional success. To be sure, it is the apostolic intention that the gospel be made known and that the movement of witnessing communities should grow. Paul follows his realistic depiction of our earthen vessel character with this strong and confident assertion: "For it is all for your sake, so that as grace extends to more and more people it may increase thanksgiving, to the glory of God" (2 Cor. 4:15). The purpose of that extension of grace is the increase of thanksgiving, of *eucharistia*, so that God may be glorified, may be made known, acknowledged, and served in the restoration of the relationship of Creator and creature, which is the actual shape of the new creation. This apostolic longing for the extension of grace to more and more people is tempered by our Lord's clear instructions that kingdom planting is our task, but not kingdom harvesting. We are to sow in all kinds of soil, not conduct feasibility studies to determine where it would make sense to sow. The harvest, when it comes, will be God's, and it will be out of all proportion to any of our labors. It is also the harvester's responsibility to separate the weeds from the good wheat, not ours. Just as witnesses betray their calling when they attempt to slide over onto the judge's bench, kingdom sowers disobey their Lord when they claim that they can either strategize or produce the kingdom harvest. Church growth is not so much the New Testament concern as it is grace growth, thanksgiving growth, and growing attestation of the glory of God. This growth is summed up in Paul's prayer for the Philippians: "And it is my prayer that your love may abound more and more" (Phil. 1:9).

"Walking Worthily": What "Walking" Is About

The compelling emphasis of Paul's injunction that we walk worthy of the calling to which we have been called is that the action is one of walking. This favorite Pauline verb speaks of purposeful movement accompanied by distinctive conduct. We struggle with its translation, looking for ways to capture its comprehensive character. In the RSV proposal, several passages render the peripatetic nature of our calling as "leading a life." The one Pauline passage that does not use the Greek verb translated as "walk," Philippians 1:27, presents even greater challenges. Here our English text speaks of "letting our manner of life be worthy of the gospel." The focus here is political, public, having to do with the way that our calling shapes our entire shared life and conduct before a watching world. Taken together, the focus upon walking conveys that the calling of the missional community is an ongoing process, a discovery mixed with struggles, a growth that is both gradual and yet at times granted sudden leaps of insight. Precisely as walking, it is formed by the biblical imperatives that focus upon *how* the community walks, *how* its public conduct is to be congruent with its public testimony, and *how* it incarnates the good news that God wants all people to experience because "God sent the Son into the world, not to condemn the world, but that the world might be saved through him" (John 3:17).

"Walking Worthily": What "Worthy" Is About

That "how" seems to be the thrust of the defining concept "worthy." It is puzzling that there appears to be so little attention to this little adverb *axios*. It is, as far as I can tell, not discussed in Kittel's *Theologisches Wörterbuch*. But some recent commentators, whose work reflects a growing awareness of the missional formation that is actually the scopus of these New Testament texts, are helping us to grasp the enormous importance of "walking worthily." Karl Barth, lecturing on Philippians in Göttingen in 1924, dwelt upon the public and corporate meaning of "walking worthily" in Philippians 1:27. The root of the verb here is *polis*, and Barth works with that "political" understanding of worthy walking when he translates, "Your state must be worthy of the gospel of Christ."[11] He explains, "In their state, their 'form,' their bearing, under the invisible discipline of that kingdom, they must be en route here and now, moving along in ways corresponding with the 'state' that is to be reflected in their conduct, 'worthy' of the gospel, the gracious message that in Christ was issued to them and received by them concerning that kingdom."[12] Stephen Fowl proposes a translation that also picks up on the public and political nature of worthy walking: "Order your common life in a manner worthy of the gospel of Christ," which he explains as Paul's "enjoining them to act in a manner consistent with or appropriate to the community's identity in God."[13] He goes on to say that "walking worthily entails that the members of

11. Karl Barth, *Epistle to the Philippians*, trans. J. W. Leitch (Louisville: Westminster John Knox, 2002), p. 44; see also Karl Barth, *Erklärung des Philipperbriefes* (München: Chr. Kaiser Verlag, 1928), pp. 378.

12. Barth, *Epistle to the Philippians*, p. 46, revised.

13. Stephen E. Fowl, *Philippians* (Grand Rapids: Eerdmans, 2005), pp. 59-60.

the body display certain types of habits, dispositions, and practices toward one another"[14] — to which I would like to add "that demonstrate before a watching world what the inbreaking kingdom of God is really all about."

The meaning of "worthily walking" is expounded in the whole range of imperatives directed towards missional communities to continue their formation for their calling. It is striking that the paranetic passages in the epistles, those translations of the gospel into conduct that follow upon the key "therefores" in the arguments, deal consistently with the corporate life of these communities. There is this constant concern about the public nature of the missional community, which is emphasized by the apostolic use of Greek terms like *polis* and *ecclesia* for the church. Their conduct toward one another is to be congruent with the message they proclaim. In the context of Philippians, for instance, the thematic injunction to "order your common life in a manner worthy of the gospel of Christ" is followed within a few verses by the instruction that the people should "have the same love, being in full accord and of one mind, doing nothing from selfishness or conceit, but in humility counting others better than yourselves, looking not to your own interests but to the interests of others" (Phil. 2:2-4 paraphrased). Worthiness has then to do with the ways in which the community practices its calling towards each other. It has to do with the "mind" they are to share in the imitation of Christ, what Fowl translates as "the pattern of thinking, acting, and feeling."[15]

Immediately following the Ephesian version of the injunction, the apostle focuses upon the way in which the community displays before a watching world the gospel at work in its relationships: worthy walking is characterized by lowliness and meekness, patience, forbearing one another in love, and eagerness to maintain the unity of the Spirit in the bond of peace. We could examine all of the paranetic passages in the epistles to document how this concern for the witnessing character of the community's life is an overarching and constant theme. This is how the gospel is to be made known, through Christian communities walking worthy of their calling. What they say about the gospel arises out of and is expounded by how they live as called and sent communities. In this emphasis, the epistles expound the same fundamental understanding of the witnessing power of the community's shared life that we find in John's Gospel: "By this all people will know that you are my disciples, if you have love for one another" (John 13:35).

14. Fowl, *Philippians*, p. 63.
15. Fowl, *Philippians*, p. 88.

"Walk Worthily" as Congruence

The congruence between their communication of the gospel with their visible conduct is a further crucial dimension of "walking worthily." This is often a matter of the integrity of their life and witness — speech and act cannot be separated. In 1 Thessalonians, Paul is concerned that they have learned from the apostolic example practiced in their midst, by which the "declaration of the gospel of God" took place without error, uncleanness, guile, attempts to please humans, not with words of flattery, nor as a cloak for greed, nor seeking glory from men (1 Thess. 2:2-6). Communication with integrity is connected to relationships that demonstrate the gospel's healing power at work. Their walking worthily took the shape of a gentle, nourishing, caring self-giving in relationships, illustrated by the image of a mother nursing her child or "a nurse taking care of her children": "Being affectionately desirous of you, we were ready to share with you not only the gospel of God but also our own selves, because you had become very dear to us" (1 Thess. 2:8). The love that the Christian community practices toward each other enables the demonstration and explication of that love as good news to their neighbors, those next to them and those to whom they are sent.

Models of "Worthy Walking"?

In a study that followed after the Missional Church project, a small group of us asked the question, What would a model of a missional congregation look like? We discovered in the process that we were being archetypically Western, late modern, and American pragmatist with our "model" question. We were looking for the solution to a problem, the stencil that could reproduce the successful missional church. We were operating from classical cause-and-effect thinking. We were forgetting everything we had learned from David Bosch and Lesslie Newbigin about modern mission shaped by Western Enlightened assumptions. We turned to Scripture and found in 2 Corinthians a different world of inquiry. We were challenged to think about ourselves as clay jars, as unlikely vessels whose unlikeliness was precisely part of the witness to the extraordinary power of God that was, by his grace, at work in us. Guided by these texts that David Bosch had powerfully expounded for Mennonite missionaries many years earlier as a "Spirituality of the Road,"[16]

---

16. David Bosch, *A Spirituality of the Road* (Scottdale, PA: Herald Press, 1979).

we turned away from the self-confident search for models and began to look for patterns that witnessed to God's Spirit converting congregations to their missional vocation. In a great diversity of congregations, we found that the formative role of Scripture was a central factor in the change processes that were going on. But we also found that this rigorous scriptural formation was always hard, demanding, challenging — and that it often evoked resistance.[17]

The Imperative as Missional Formation

Especially when we pay attention to the imperatives in the New Testament do we find ourselves getting nervous. When obedience becomes the theme, our Reformed antennae begin to vibrate as we pick up suspicious hints of works righteousness and legalism creeping back into our discourse. It is, in fact, from the problematic lessons of Christendom that we have rightly learned to be cautious about how we read the Bible, knowing full well that we are very prone to reduce the gift of faith to a program that we manage and control. That proclivity has only been intensified by the centuries of silence about mission in the church's theological reflection about itself and its purpose. The New Testament imperatives are not so much soteriology in a causative sense as they are ecclesiological, focusing upon the witness to salvation, which is our calling, not our efforts to cooperate in our salvation.

As the Holy Spirit's instrument for the formation of witnessing communities for their vocation, the New Testament is necessarily and gloriously full of imperatives. Jesus told his disciples in the Great Commission to "teach them to observe all that I commanded you" (Matt. 28:20), so that they could, indeed, "disciple the ethnicities." He assures his disciples in John's great missional formation discourse that "if you love me, you will keep my commandments" (John 14:15), because Jesus "chose them to go and bear fruit, fruit that will abide" (John 15:16, adapted). Paul admonishes the Philippians to imitate Christ, to imitate Timothy and Epaphroditus, and to imitate himself. Using the same verb that we translate as "lead a life worthy of the calling" in Ephesians 4, the apostle also says earlier in that epistle that "we are his workmanship, created in Christ Jesus for good works, which God prepared beforehand, that we should walk in them" (Eph. 2:10). Conduct, obedience, visible alternativeness — these are all clearly essential dimensions of the

---

17. See Lois Barrett et al., eds., *Treasure in Clay Jars: Patterns in Missional Faithfulness* (Grand Rapids: Eerdmans, 2004).

New Testament missional church. The sense of an imperative is that it must be obeyable — unless the purpose of the text is to render us hopeless and despairing. What God's Spirit requires of God's people, God's Spirit equips them to do. It is an equipping that centers upon God's gracious acceptance of us "while we were yet sinners." It is not perfectionist but is still confident: "God who has begun a good work in you will bring it to completion at the day of Jesus Christ" (Phil. 3:6). It lives out of forgiveness and humility and profound gratitude for the unmerited and healing power of God's love made real and personal in the person and work of Jesus Christ.

"Walking Worthily" as a Parable of the Gospel

When Karl Barth arrives at the point in volume IV/3.2 of the *Church Dogmatics* where he weaves all the emerging strands of his missional ecclesiology together — in paragraph 72, titled "The Sending of the Community of the Holy Spirit" — he addresses in quite concrete terms just how this community understands itself and functions as God's people sent into the world. This leads to some highly perceptive insights and formulations in the subsection titled "The Community for the World," which can guide the missional congregation theologically to recognize and reject the false equations and reductionisms to which we are so vulnerable as heirs of Western Christendom, while still claiming our calling as witnesses. The missional community does not equal the gospel. It does not constitute the kingdom of God. Its vocation and holiness do not abrogate its human fallenness. It does not believe *in* itself as an object of its creed but rather believes itself to be in reality what God the Holy Spirit both calls and enables it to be. The third article of its creed states *credo ecclesiam,* and not *credo in ecclesiam* — the limitations of English will always make this hard for our congregations to understand.

Barth emphasizes, first of all, that the Christian community recognizes that its emergence and its continuation can be attributed solely to the particular power of God, upon whose constant newness it is completely dependent for its future.[18] The venerable traditions and valuable insights of the movement of the church over time do not replace its constant dependence upon "birth from above" as the community is called and gathered by God's action.

---

18. Karl Barth, *Kirchliche Dogmatik* IV/3, part 2 (Zollikon-Zürich: Evangelischer Verlag, 1959), pp. 899-900; ET: *Church Dogmatics* IV/3.2, trans. G. W. Bromiley (Edinburgh: T. & T. Clark, 1962), pp. 786-87. The paraphrases in the text are my free renderings of the German.

Further, it recognizes, empowered by the Holy Spirit, that what it can really do, effect, and bring about in its creaturely spontaneity is focused entirely in its profession of its commitment to Jesus Christ.[19] That is what the missional community is for. Thus, it recognizes that its profession of its commitment to Jesus Christ as its particular and distinctive action, to which it is empowered by the Holy Spirit, can only be, in all its human and natural spontaneity, its thankful response to the fact that Jesus Christ has professed his commitment to it, continues to do so, and will continue to do.[20]

This clear delineation of the theological sense that the missional community can and must have of itself and its purpose leads then to a creative interpretive proposal that relates the biblical word to the process of divine vocation and Spirit-empowered response. The missional community is enabled to — and, in fact, it should — understand itself as a *parable* in the full New Testament sense of that concept.[21] It shows the watching world what the kingdom of God is like. It conveys in understandable pictures and explanations the "wonderful deeds of him who has called us out of darkness into his marvelous light" (1 Pet. 2:9). The divine reality of the gospel as event comes first, and in response to it, in interaction with it, as witness to it, the church represents parabolically and provisionally what this good news is all about. It is preceded and followed by that reality, portraying it imperfectly, inadequately, both illuminating it and at times casting it in the shadows. Its witness can describe the inbreaking kingdom of God in Christ, but never in a way that fully captures this wonderful event. But like the parables in the Gospels, it can disclose essential aspects of the kingdom of God that is coming and is now very near. It can render this overwhelming good news in such ways that the Holy Spirit can awaken faith and extend that calling that results in the growth of the missional community. This community, as we have said already, cannot duplicate the salvation event that has happened once and for all in Christ. It neither equals the gospel nor the kingdom. But the community is derived from that event, is shaped and called by it, lives to make it known, and thus participates in it, in spite of all its imperfections. As parable of the kingdom, the community's witness is God's instrument to draw others into the same encounter with the loving God who calls and empowers the response of obedience. The reality that the community as parable reports to the world begins with the resurrection of Jesus and looks forward

---

19. Barth, *Kirchliche Dogmatik* IV/3, part 2, p. 901; ET: p. 787.
20. Barth, *Kirchliche Dogmatik* IV/3, part 2, pp. 903-4; ET: p. 790.
21. Barth, *Kirchliche Dogmatik* IV/3, part 2, p. 906; ET: p. 792.

to the ultimate and consummate revelation of the kingdom, which Barth describes as the "establishment of the sole, all-encompassing, all-pervasive and all-defining rule of God, of the Word, of the Spirit of God, in the entire creation. Jesus Christ himself is this kingdom in its total perfection."[22] And the confessing, witnessing, missional community is his parable, reflecting his truth to the world into which it is sent in its actions, its communication, its visible dependence, and its equally visible fallenness. Understanding itself as gospel parable, the missional community can practice its vocation with the appropriate and necessary combination of modesty and conviction that God uses to build his church.

"Walking worthily" may then be understood as parabolic witness, the demonstration of the truth of the gospel in what the community says and does, including the evidences of its human frailty and its dependence upon the grace of forgiveness. Understood with the earthen-vessel realism that is characteristic of the biblical word, the community can respond to the imperatives that shape missional witness with confidence in God and modesty about its own capacities. The power of parables lies in the work of the Holy Spirit who interprets them to the heart and mind and makes them into instruments of gospel exposition and invitation. The parables in Jesus' proclamation were vehicles of prophetic proclamation and explication. Barth says, "A parable, in the sense and power of the one who creates and uses it, refers beyond itself to that which He wants to point out and represent by using it."[23] That is at the heart of what it means to walk worthy of the calling to which we have been called. The missional community is invited and formed by Jesus to be his parable, to be an illustration for the watching and listening world of what the Good News that has already happened and that is yet to happen really means. As such a parable, the missional community points not to itself, but to the Lord who continues to tell the story and to illustrate it with and through his called-out people. The parable and the witness, two powerful and formative New Testament concepts to interpret the church's purpose and action, always function like St. John the Baptist in Grünewald's great painting of the crucifixion in the Isenheim Altarpiece, which Barth loved so much. Like John, the missional community points as parable and witness to Christ, testifies to Christ, makes Christ known, anticipates Christ, and rejoices in both his truth and his presence in their midst. In doing that, it is walking worthy of its calling.

22. Barth, *Kirchliche Dogmatik* IV/3, part 2, p. 906; ET: p. 792.
23. Barth, *Kirchliche Dogmatik* IV/3, part 2, p. 909, ET: p. 794.

CHAPTER 9

Missional Leadership for the Formation of the Community's "Worthy Walk"

Missional Leadership Based upon Missional Community

Having examined at some length the priority of the missional community as the strategy God's Spirit uses to carry out God's mission, we turn now to the leadership of such communities. There is theological significance in this sequence. The general vocation of the missional church must be dealt with before we turn to the special vocation of those who carry out the ministry of leadership within it. This parallels the ecumenical consensus about baptism: The corporate celebration of baptism is the community's acknowledgment of God's faithfulness in building his church, one by one. It is as such the act of calling and the setting apart of each Christian for his or her vocation as a witness within the missional community. We are becoming used to speaking of baptism as the general ordination of all Christians to their shared calling before we think about the special ordination of some. The latter is dependent for its meaning upon the former. This understanding of baptism is thus the framework for the theology and practice of the so-called ordered ministries. Special ordination is a subset of general ordination, and the vocation of the entire people of God precedes, surrounds, and shapes the vocation of its specialized servants.

This is, of course, all based on the conviction that the "church is missionary by its very nature," and its corollary, that the particular or local missional community is the primary agent of that vocation. Another way of framing the

---

This chapter comprises the second of two Payton Lectures I delivered at Fuller Theological Seminary, May 2-3, 2007. The content of the two lectures was published as a single essay under the title "Walking Worthily: Missional Leadership after Christendom" in *The Princeton Seminary Bulletin*, new series, 28, no. 3 (2007): 251-301. For more information, see p. 121.

missional theology we are discussing is to understand mission as the concrete implication of the good news that God's love for the creation results in God's action to restore, heal, reconcile, and make new this rebellious creation. The event of Jesus Christ is the culmination of that action, and now, the salvation accomplished on the cross and ratified at Easter is to be made known to all people. For that to happen, God continues the strategy of calling a particular people to be his witnesses, to make it known that God so loves the world that he has sent Jesus. The gospel of salvation generates the called and sent people, the *ecclesia;* mission, as Martin Kähler famously argued, is the mother of theology.[1] God's mission necessitates a missiological ecclesiology.

This understanding of the missional church implies a radical revision of traditional ecclesiologies, which have, as I have argued, largely neglected the central biblical theme of mission. The doctrinal challenge is to develop every theme and subtheme relating to the theology and practices of the church from the central and foundational understanding of the church's missional vocation. Whether we are discussing the church's worship and liturgy, its structures and organizational forms, its practices and disciplines, or its ordered ministry (to use the technical term), the thematic door by which we enter is the missional vocation of the church. Thus, we could move at this point to a discussion of the assembled life of the community and especially its worship, and we could explore how these essential practices of the church both demonstrate missional vocation and equip all members for their living out of their calling. It would be especially important to address the central and defining role in missional equipping that is carried out in very distinctive and unique ways by the sacraments of baptism and the Lord's Table. We could examine the practices of faith formation, the resources of spirituality, and discover their crucial importance for the actual practice of walking worthily. And we could talk about the corporate life of the community, its visible koinonia in terms of the collective witness it presents to the world of its neighborhood. We could examine the community's acts of prophetic challenge in interaction with the world into which it is sent, its conscious alternativeness in its larger context, as worthy parables of Christ's kingdom breaking in. In all these dimensions of the life and practices of the local congregation, the calling to walk worthily can be exemplified, and worthy walking can be learned and practiced. Our focus here is on missional leadership because missional leadership is of such profound importance for

1. Martin Kähler, *Schriften zu Christologie und Mission,* Theologische Bücherei, 42 (München: Christian Kaiser Verlag, 1971), p. 190.

the worthy walking of missional communities. But, we must ask, why and how is missional leadership of such importance for the worthy walking of witnessing communities? To get into that question, we will first consider, very briefly, the roots of "ordered ministry" in Christendom, in order then to assess the situation in which we find ourselves after Christendom.

The Roots of "Ordered Ministry" in Christendom

Without any claims to comprehensiveness, I will paint in broad strokes the process of the ordering of ministry within the Western Christendom project. My purpose is to place in high relief the situation within which we find ourselves today as Christendom is ending. We begin with the theme of "office in the New Testament scriptures" — bearing in mind that the term "office" is itself a construct of ecclesial tradition imported into this discussion. Our theme is set against the background of the apostolic mission strategy as we have described and interpreted it from diverse perspectives. That strategy was (and is) to form communities of witnesses whose calling is to continue the apostolic witness that brought them into existence, and who do so by, together, walking worthy of the calling to which they have been called. The New Testament investigation of this apostolic mission strategy makes clear that these witnessing communities had leaders. Knowing that this is somewhat risky, I will, for the sake of our discussion, propose some summarizing statements about the way that the Scriptures address this leadership, these "ordered ministries" within the formation and continuing activity of faithful missional communities. Although there is not a lot of detailed documentation, it can be argued that structures of leadership were an essential part of the early Christian movement. The apostolic missionaries who planted communities to continue the Christian mission in particular places identified those whom they discerned to be the Spirit's gifts to these communities for various ministries of leadership. They are described in diverse ways with terms such as apostles, overseers, elders, deacons, or ministers. The pastoral epistles address the qualifications and practices of these "officers" explicitly, but there are several references scattered throughout the epistles and Acts that would allow one to conclude that while structured leadership was a given, perhaps a necessity, the structures themselves were diverse. The emphasis in all four Gospels upon the calling and formation of the disciples clearly underlines their particular importance for the subsequent apostolic mission. In general, however, the structures of leadership do not really form the central emphasis of the New Testament scriptures. They appear, rather, to have been part of the contextualizing of the various communities in their particular locations. The necessary functions of leadership are in some way carried out so that the witnessing communities can function in their particular settings, but the shapes and forms of that leadership vary. It is, indeed, striking that the one mention of overseers and deacons in the unquestioned Pauline epistles is in the salutation to Philippians, after which they are never mentioned again, and the entire epistle clearly focuses upon the entire community and not solely upon its leadership.

In their desire to reengage the mandate of the apostolic church, Reformed ecclesiologies tend to gravitate to Ephesians 4:1-16 for their scriptural understanding of the ordered ministry. Markus Barth calls this section "The Constitution of the Church."[2] Verses 11-12 are the crux. Here is how Barth translates them: "He [Christ] is the one who appointed these to be apostles and those to be prophets, some to be evangelists and others to be teaching shepherds to equip the saints for the work of service for building up the Messiah's body. . . ." The purpose of these appointments is especially important: to equip the saints for the work of service for building up the Messiah's body. That is, if you will, the missional mandate of every particular community: to do the work of service or ministry that builds up the body of Christ before a watching world. It is a definition of the practice of walking worthily. And that work needs to be equipped. How will that happen? It happens through the distinctive persons whose functions are laid out at the beginning of the text. Christ gives gifts to the church in the form of certain persons. These persons are all, as Markus Barth points out, ministers of the Word — they share the common task of speech in the service of God's message. In diverse ways, they serve the proclamation of the Word, be it apostolically, prophetically, evangelistically, or pastorally and pedagogically. It takes, as it seems, a range of gifted people to provide the Word formation that truly equips the saints for their shared calling, which is the work of ministry that builds up Christ's body. What these ministers of the Word do, in their various ways, enables the missional community in a particular place to walk worthy of its calling — which is the overarching theme with which the Ephesian "Constitution of the Church" begins. The power of these ordered ministries is the power of the Word at work in the community. Formation by the Word makes it possible to respond to the apostolic imperatives as a privilege and an honor, a Spirit-enabled obedience.

---

2. Markus Barth, *Ephesians: Translation and Commentary on Chapter 4–6,* The Anchor Bible, 34A (Garden City, NY: Doubleday, 1974), pp. 425-96.

Whether they are called apostles, or prophets, or evangelists, or teaching pastors, or overseers, or bishops, or elders, or deacons, their work is subservient to the missional calling of the communities they lead. Markus Barth again: "... the task of the special ministers mentioned in Ephesians 4:11 is to be servants in that ministry which is entrusted to the whole church. Their place is not above but below the great number of saints who are not adorned by resounding titles. Every one of the special ministers is a *servus servorum Dei.*"[3] They are not mediators between their communities and Christ, although they certainly proclaim Christ. They are not primarily liturgists, although their communal worship is reflected in the citation of corporate prayers, creedal affirmations, and hymns that are scattered throughout the texts. They are not custodians of arcane mysteries to be preserved for the initiates, although they certainly recognize the difference between milk-drinking and meat-eating Christians and deal with it sensitively. They are continuing the rabbinical ministry of Jesus, teaching the disciples in each community what it means to know this Jesus now as risen Lord and to be his witnesses where they are sent. The only power they have as they carry out their task is the power of the Holy Spirit who uses their frail human efforts to evoke faith and enable obedience and draw together one missional community after another. The only tangible resource they will ultimately have is the Scriptures that begin to appear and be collected: Gospels and epistles mainly addressed to or formulated for particular missional communities. The credentials for such missional servants are not standardized. It is not who they are but what God is making them into that counts. Their authority is not innate but conferred, not so much their essence as their function, an outworking of the Word, which they proclaim, and expound, and demonstrate.

That basic pattern of missional leadership undergoes enormous changes in the course of Christendom. As the church moves from the margins to the center of society, as it is given the mixed blessings of wealth, and property, and power, the diversely ordered ministries of the missional church in the apostolic and sub-apostolic period change. Much of this change is appropriate contextualization — as we said, there is no specific polity or structure for church leadership laid out for us in the New Testament. With the essentially multicultural character of the church, which is both intentional and struggled-for reality from Pentecost on, come diverse ways of organizing the body of Christ for its missional vocation in particular places.

3. Markus Barth, *Ephesians*, p. 481.

But much of the change is also, as we look back upon the centuries of the Christendom project, problematic. What was originally missional leadership becomes something different when the sense of the missional vocation of the church begins to fade. The ecclesiastical terminology that emerges in Christendom is evidence that the church no longer understands itself as "missionary by its very nature." The word "presbyter," or elder, which becomes the most widely used concept for missional leadership in the particular community, evolves ultimately into the modern term "priest." The legacy of Christendom is, however, that this does not mean "elder" in the New Testament sense. The concept has the etymological shell of the biblical presbyter, but its kernel is the *hiereus,* the *sacerdotes,* the priest of sacred rites and prerogatives, whose ministrations do not so much equip the saints as supply the saints what they need for their own salvation. This office, within the now-essential historic succession of bishops who alone can make men into priests, evolves gradually into a human-divine institution whose special functions are dogmatically necessary for the salvation of the people. The separation between clergy and laity becomes a divinely maintained order, and ordination becomes a sacrament. The church is identified with its hierarchy, from pope, to bishop, to priest, to deacon. The ecclesial hierarchy administers salvation in a church now defined by its geography, its cultural hegemony, and its partnership with the state. In a Europe in which everyone lives within hearing range of church bells, mission disappears from the theology of the church. But the theologies of office become ever larger and more complex.

The Reformation challenges those centuries of institutional evolution with its strong assertion of the "priesthood of all believers" and its emphasis upon the essential teaching ministry to equip the saints. Although there is no language of mission here, there is something profoundly missional in the Reformers' commitment to the biblical literacy and doctrinal understanding of the entire faith community. Luther and Calvin translate the Bible into the vernacular and write catechisms and *Institutes* to teach the faith to the laity. That catechetical formation always moves from doctrine to practice, so that the concern to walk worthy of our calling is present, even though our calling is not redefined as missional. As Alan Roxburgh notes, the dominant model of church leadership shifts at the Reformation from priest to pedagogue.[4] The New Testament emphasis upon teaching ministries to equip the saints

4. Alan Roxburgh, "Missional Leadership: Equipping God's People for Mission," in *Missional Church: A Vision for the Sending of the Church in North America,* ed. Darrell L. Guder (Grand Rapids: Eerdmans, 1998), pp. 183-220, especially pp. 190-93.

is reclaimed, but it functions differently in a Christendom that is largely un-challenged in the magisterial Reformation. Calvin devotes much attention to the relevance of Ephesians 4:1-16 for the formation and structuring of the church. But after centuries of Christendom, he has some problems with Christ's gifts of some to be apostles, prophets, and evangelists. So, he argues, ". . . these three functions were not established in the church as permanent ones, but only for that time during which churches were to be erected where none existed before." He acknowledges that there might be special situa-tions in which these offices become necessary again, but they will remain in his view "extraordinary." But, he goes on, "Next come pastors and teachers, whom the church can never go without."[5] Of lasting significance is, of course, the massive reorientation of the understanding of office away from an onto-logical priesthood that is theologically necessary for the spiritual welfare of the believers, to a more functional understanding of office that focuses upon the service of the church, the upbuilding of the believers, and the integrity of the community. The Reformed churches saw in the great diversity of terms and structures of office in the New Testament a rationale for diverse and complementary ministries in the service of God and his people. They also welcomed patterns of ordered ministry that eschewed the accumulation of both temporal and spiritual power in one person, especially the bishop. The result has been the Reformed polities of complementary offices: the teaching elder, the ruling elder, the pastor, and the deacon.

In the almost five hundred years of Protestantism, there has been an enormous proliferation of concepts and structures of office, in which the old patterns of Christendom and revisions of the Reformation are inter-twined and adapted. For all the talk about the priesthood of all believers, there are many traces of Christendom's legacy in the ways that the ordered ministry actually functions. The clergy-laity distinction persists in spite of all Protestant affirmations that we are all a part of the laos, the laity of God. Congregants still tend to think that their ministers are there to provide the services that meet their religious needs, based on the assumption that their ordinations, however celebrated, conferred a special spiritual status on them. One might say that the pedagogue model of the Reformation did not replace the priest, but merged with it. That merger continues on in the modern metaphor of the minister as professional, as suggested by Alan Roxburgh,[6]

---

5. *Calvin: Institutes of the Christian Religion*, ed. John T. McNeill, trans. F. L. Battles, The Library of Christian Classics, XXI (Philadelphia: Westminster, 1960), IV.3.4, p. 1057.

6. Roxburgh, "Missional Leadership," pp. 196-98.

with priestly attitudes and expectations operative, whether the emphasis is on the professional technician, or therapist, or manager.

Ordered Ministry after Christendom

As Christendom ends and the Western world becomes an ever more difficult mission field, the churches are challenged to reclaim their missional calling. That is the vocation of the missional community as we have been describing it. This process means that their inherited forms of leadership are also subject to review and change. And change is happening, although not without a lot of resistance. Those priestly attitudes and expectations are, as I just noted, very resilient. The drive to maintain Christendom, or even to return to it, is widespread, across the spectrum from right to left. There are examples, of course, of very successful Christendom maintenance if the measure of success is numbers, budgets, well-attended programs, and satisfied members. Much of our formal theological education still has the Christendom priest/pedagogue/professional in view, in spite of all our protestations that we are in touch with the changing context. However the focus upon organizational maintenance may take concrete shape, it effectively obstructs any movement toward continuing conversion to missional calling. It appears that maintenance leaders rarely equip saints for missional vocation.

If, however, Christendom over time generated ministry structures oriented to hierarchical power, to rank and title, to privilege and position, to the trappings and perquisites of office, what happens to all of that when the Christendom project begins to disintegrate? What happens to these inherited orders of ministry where the Spirit does surprise a community with conversion to missional vocation? Communities *are* beginning to move from reaction to the end of Christendom to explore what missional obedience might now look like. Questions about the cultural captivity of Western Christendom *are* raised and discussed, as threatening and unsettling as they are. Ministers with their members *are* beginning to read the Scriptures with different questions in mind, questions about vocation, and alternativeness, and liberation from idolatry. There is a growing awareness that there are basic patterns of missional faithfulness that can be nurtured and tested.[7] Out of this ferment there is emerging a willingness to examine new and yet

---

7. Lois Barrett et al., *Treasure in Clay Jars: Patterns in Missional Faithfulness* (Grand Rapids: Eerdmans, 2004).

very old understandings of the purpose and practice of the ordered ministry. Communities *are* recognizing that there are people who, as ministers of the Word, do, in fact, "equip the saints for the work of service for building up the Messiah's body," but that what they do is intimately related to the ministry of the entire community, and not something just done on its behalf. How many congregations are trying to change these deeply rooted patterns of office and authority, as they describe in their worship bulletins all the members as the ministers, and put up signs over the exit doors reminding their members that they are now entering the mission field, and they are sent? As the disintegration of Christendom continues and these explorations of missional vocation after Christendom gain traction, they will have far-reaching implications for our ministerial polities and our theological education.

Borrowing the concept of patterns from the project coordinated by Lois Barrett that produced the study *Treasure in Clay Jars: Patterns in Missional Faithfulness,* I will suggest three patterns of missional leadership that, as I see it, are crucial to the continuing conversion of the church to its vocation of witness and crucial to the community's walking worthy of its calling.

The Equipping Priority of the Word

Missional leadership is centered upon and shaped by the Word of God written. The initially verbal testimony of those apostles, prophets, evangelists, and teaching shepherds that equipped the first saints for the work of service was formally captured in the various documents that ultimately became the New Testament canon. We reiterate the claim that the apostolic Scriptures became the Holy Spirit's instrument for the continuing formation of missional communities for their calling. That formation happens as their leaders serve as the interpreters, the catalysts, the resources for the exposition of that Word in all its formative power. For the Reformed concept of divided and complementary offices, this means that ruling and teaching elders, pastors, and deacons are all to function as Word-equippers. All ordered ministries are needed for the equipping of the saints for the work of ministry. Every Christian is a witness who belongs to and represents Christ.

There are, however, subtle ways that we resist this broad and inclusive understanding of the ways that the Word equips the saints. Again, our vocabulary itself reveals a lot. Terms like "preaching" and "proclamation" tend to narrow our understanding of the enormous variety of ways in which, in the New Testament, the communication of the scriptural Word actually works in the community. Gerhard Friedrich pointed out that Martin Luther used one German verb, "predigen = preach," for the translation of more than thirty Greek verbs having to do with verbal communication.[8] If only the few who are clerically qualified can validly articulate the Word of God, then missional formation is not likely to happen. Certainly if we Reformeds are to take missional vocation seriously, then we should emphasize that not only are the elders, deacons, and pastors all Word-equippers in their various ways, but all Christians are called to share in the communication of the gospel and should be equipped to do so.

I am persuaded and have often said that we in the Reformed tradition need to reclaim the teaching eldership. The Presbyterian Church (U.S.A.) jeopardized that distinctive understanding of congregational leadership when it replaced "teaching elder" with "minister of Word and Sacrament" in its formal polity from 1983 until 2011. Its new Form of Government has restored the title and practice of "teaching elder" to its proper place. But I am not concerned about the reclamation of the teaching eldership for reasons of authority or office. The purpose of this particular ordered minister is not to entrust the Word to the credentialed few so that everyone else might be dependent upon them. That is yet another way to preserve the priestly office of Christendom. It is the priority of the Word for missional formation that requires that we all have the opportunity to engage the Scriptures in all the fullness and power of their meaning. For that, we need "learned clergy." By that, I mean that we need students and expositors of the Word who are themselves convinced that the Scriptures are the Holy Spirit's instrument for the ongoing missional formation of the community. And they are equipped with the tools to expound the Scriptures missionally. They contribute to the equipping of the saints by helping the community explore how the Spirit formed missional communities then and continues to do so now.

The missional community will be formed through the work of Word-equippers who, in a great breadth of ways, can guide congregations into the risky confrontation with the Bible. We have to risk unchaining the Bible, risk real biblical literacy in our communities rather than dependence upon the learned few, and risk the freewheeling conversation about what the Spirit is really saying to the churches through these Scriptures. It is risky constantly to ask the text missional questions. It is risky to allow Scripture to become the

8. G. Friedrich, "κηρύσσω," in *Theologisches Wörterbuch zum Neuen Testament*, ed. Gerhard Kittel (Stuttgart: W. Kohlhammer, 1938), vol. 3, pp. 701-2.

lenses through which we see ourselves and our neighborhood. It is risky to move forward in the conviction that we are to walk worthy of our calling, and that the biblical documents not only show us what that looks like but tutor us in the practices that are truly worthy. The risk is that we might discover how that really happens, what that really means. The risk is that we might find ourselves being converted. We might be confronted by the discovery that our cherished and secure notions about who we are as church and what we are for need to be revised. We might find ourselves being transformed by the renewing of our minds as the encounter with the Scriptures reveals our conformities and God's Spirit enables us to put them aside.

Such expectations of the encounter with the biblical Word are countercultural, to be sure. There are widely favored approaches to scriptural interpretation that do not start with God's mission or the missional vocation of God's people. They are not interested in the contention that this is what the biblical testimony is really all about. There are those who move rather from the context, from the human experience, from assessments of human religious need, to the text, asking questions that more often than not filter out the missional mandate and replace it with various responses calculated to meet those needs. And there are those who assume from the outset that the Bible is about my vertical relationship with God, my savedness, my eternity, and whose filters effectively evade all the claims about our mandate to be witnesses to the inbreaking reign of God in the Lord Jesus Christ. Even after Christendom, there is great resistance to recognizing that the biblical story is, from beginning to end, about God's mission and the calling of his people to be the witnesses and the parable of that mission.

Missional teachers of Scripture can guide the community to engage the Word of God as the lenses through which we learn to see ourselves and our world. Through the biblical lenses, we learn not to see lepers and Samaritans, publicans and prostitutes, Pharisees and centurions, procurators and executioners, the clean and the unclean, the Jew and the Gentile. We see people made in the image of God, people in darkness for whom light has come, people who need to be made whole and for whom God's loving purpose is that healing. We learn to "see the crowds" the way Jesus did, as recorded in Matthew 9:36: "When he saw the crowds, he had compassion for them, because they were harassed and helpless, like sheep without a shepherd."

The missional leader who is qualified as a biblical equipper and committed to its priority and urgency will help the community to discover the new creation intended by the gospel as it is expounded by the New Testament imperatives. The biblical imperatives describe a real option for frail and sinful Christians, God's Spirit will enable us to hear, and hearing, to obey. And God's Spirit will continue to convict us of our sinful stumbling, assure us of our forgiveness, and enable us to take the next steps of obedience. This is how we learn to walk worthy of our calling. The command to love will cease being an abstraction or a sentimentality as the community learns the concrete actions that express God's love for us. God's love toward us is translated immediately into the practice of love that the followers of Jesus are enabled to have for each other — that is the special emphasis of the missional formation that Jesus carries out in the great final discourse in John's Gospel. Those concrete actions are, however, not limited to the company of the elect and the called. The way that God loves the world is demonstrated by Jesus' encounter with people of all sorts and conditions, and we, with the disciples, learn how to continue that witness by watching and imitating Jesus. We are taught by him, through the word, that our neighbors are the people we cannot avoid, the people we have to deal with, the unsightly and unseemly who are stretched across our path and whom we have to go to great lengths to walk around. We learn that we are sent to our neighbors, that our mission field begins with those next to us.

In the missional community, we need to experience the equipping power of the word in the diverse ways laid out in Ephesians 4. We need to be confronted by the biblical witness as it shapes us *apostolically* — that is, as the word roots us in our Lord's mission and joins us to his sent-out people as those who continue the apostolic vocation. We need to encounter the *prophetic* formation of the word — the word becoming flesh in our concrete situations, throwing the bright light of God's justice on the situations of injustice that surround us. The prophetic ministry of the word equips the saints for the work of kingdom ministry that gives evidence of the goodness and newness of the reign of God in Christ now breaking in. The *evangelistic* ministry of the word equips the saints by showing us how to tell the story to those who have not heard it, how (as John Mackay put it back in 1928) to "win a right to be heard,"[9] how to "share with you not only the gospel of God but also our own selves, because you have become very dear to us" — as Paul describes gospel ministry in 1 Thessalonians 2:8. The *pastoral and pedagogical* ministries of the word equip the saints for the work of service

9. John Mackay, "The Evangelistic Duty of Christianity," in International Missionary Council, *The Christian Life and Message in Relation to Non-Christian Systems of Thought and Life,* The Jerusalem Meeting of the International Missionary Council (New York and London: International Missionary Council, 1928), vol. 1, pp. 393-95.

by practicing the healing and restorative power of the gospel, by engaging in the cure of souls as a ministry of witness-making, and by confronting our weakness and frailty and brokenness as arenas of God's action that generate witness to the goodness and grace of God's salvation. There is critical agreement that these last two terms in the catalog of five forms of word ministry are not distinctive but hyphenated: pastoral teaching, or teaching pastors. All pastoral ministry, all work of caring and nurturing and restoration, shall in some way teach the word so that the saints are equipped. All teaching shall be characterized by the care and oversight of attentive and responsible shepherds — so that the saints are equipped. These are concrete ways of formation that turn us and our world around. They require and bring about "transformation by the renewing of our minds." They entail that "mindedness" Paul speaks of in Philippians that would lead us to risk imitating the mind of Christ in the ways that we relate to each other. This biblical formation is what the missional community needs in order to walk worthy of its calling, and it is the defining priority of every form of ordered ministry. It is the central task of missional leadership.

The Collegial Character of Missional Leadership

The theological work done by the Consultation on Church Union left some important resources for a missional theology of ministry, even if the organizational outcomes of that project are not overly edifying.[10] Their definition of the collegiality of ordered ministry, if read through missional lenses, is helpful. "All ministry in the uniting church will be *collegial.* Baptism and ordination alike associate the individual with others who share the same call. The ministry is a single task common to many. Thus no minister is independent or autonomous. Collegial relationships obtain among persons in different ministries as well as among those of the same ministries. Such relationships include lay persons as well as bishops, presbyters and deacons. The interpersonal character of collegiality is a basis for partnership in governance and gives life and substance to the institutional structures of the Church." Collegiality is defined by the many other terms in this statement that expound it: sharing, interdependent, inclusive, interpersonal, partnership. Although the term is hackneyed, it applies here: collegial ministry is

10. *In Quest of a Church of Christ Uniting: An Emerging Theological Consensus; Chapter VII: Ministry* (Princeton: Consultation on Church Union, 1980), esp. pp. 39-46.

relational, takes place in networks of relationships, and demonstrates the nature of God's love through the way that these relationships actually work.

Seen through missional lenses, the collegiality of leadership is a basic form of witness that guides the entire community in its formation to be Christ's witnesses. How the leaders of the community interact, how they love and serve one another, how they "do nothing from selfish ambition or conceit, but in humility regard others as better than themselves" (Phil. 2:3, adapted), equips the entire community for its work of service. Community formation happens through the mentoring and modeling that is the constant responsibility of the leadership community, the collegium of persons with distinctive gifts that are needed for the equipping of the saints. If the community is to respond faithfully to its biblical formation, if it is to walk worthy of its calling, then the biblical formation that is the priority of the missional leadership needs to be supported and fleshed out in the collegial relationships of equippers of the saints.

The collegial character of missional leadership is a pervasive theme throughout the New Testament. When Jesus came to that time in the disciples' formation for missional leadership when they needed some field education experience, he sent them out two by two. When Peter stood up to proclaim the gospel at Pentecost, the text notes that he was "standing in the midst of them" — in the community on behalf of whom he proclaimed. When Paul set out on his mission from Antioch, he went with a team, as he always did on all his apostolic ventures. Most of the New Testament epistles are authored by an apostolic team: Paul and Sosthenes, Paul and Timothy, Paul and all the members of God's family who are with him, Paul, Silvanus, and Timothy. Missional leadership in the New Testament is expressly and intentionally collegial. Since it is a message of healing love, of reconciliation, new beginnings, and thus of transformed relationships, its witness is always and essentially relational. The gospel is good news that can and must be acted out wherever it is received and passed on. The proposition of agape love is made known by the demonstration of agape love that begins in the apostolic teams and becomes the essential DNA of the newly formed missional community. The enabling of koinonia is essential to the witness, and it starts with the collegiality of missional leaders, whose own practices shape the collegiality of the communities they serve. The imperatives of the New Testament relate mainly to the way that the community's relationships function, and thus to the corporate witness that the watching world can observe. As the missional leadership of the community walks worthy of its calling, it equips the entire community of saints to do so. The practiced collegiality of the missional leaders of the community will render questionable and ultimately passé the mindsets of the old clergy-lay distinction.

To implement such collegiality for the missional formation of communities will mean that much that we inherit from Christendom will be subject to critique and change. The privileges and spiritual specialness of ordained office need stringent review. The clergy-laity distinction is not simply a useful difference in function. It still connotes a church with two castes. As I already emphasized, in spite of almost five centuries of Protestant emphasis upon the "priesthood of all believers," Christendom attitudes about office are still powerfully present in our congregations. Try as we will, especially in the Reformed legacy, to correct the impression that there is something sacerdotal, some necessary mediatorial givenness in the ordained minister, our members still want to put us on priestly pedestals. Although Presbyterians ordain teaching elders, ruling elders, and deacons with basically the same ordination rite, our members by and large look upon their ministers, their pastors, as a distinctive and spiritually privileged breed. Those attitudes, those remnants of Christendom, obstruct the practices of collegiality. They fortify the impression that the words and actions of ordained clergy are more Christian, more holy, and more effective than what "ordinary" Christians do. They diminish the central importance of the public witness of the entire community by focusing on the actions and personality of particular office-holders.

How shall we liberate both congregations and their ministers from these constrictive mindsets? It's obviously a profound theological problem. But we could start with language. We spoke of the translation problem with regard to the enormous variety of ways the gospel is communicated in the Greek narrative of the New Testament, and the reductionist mindset that results when our members always hear "preach" and "proclaim" and don't see themselves doing either. We could examine our speech to see how many ways we violate or diminish the fundamental collegiality of missional vocation. We could refuse to use the term "solo pastor." We could question what possible sense there still is in the use of the term "Reverend." We might look at questions like vestments. Do our congregations understand that Geneva gowns signal that there is a credentialed teacher standing in front of the congregation — and nothing more? We Reformeds might ask ourselves how the collegiality of missional leadership could be made more explicit in the ways that we practice the diverse and complementary offices. We could make the discipline of the selection of ruling elders and deacons as careful and painstaking as the selection of teaching elders. We could require that these ordained officers be rigorously educated and credentialed for their responsibilities as part of the missional leadership of the church. We could ask ourselves searching questions about the restriction of sacramental presidency to ordained ministers. If the Lord's Table is the central encounter with the risen Lord in our midst, meeting us, nourishing us, and sending us, then should we not model there the collegiality of missional leadership?

But the collegiality of missional leadership is jeopardized not only by the momentum of Christendom keeping priestly images alive in our minds and communities. There is a further chemistry at work that creates even more problems for the collegiality of ordered ministers. Missional communities in our culture are handicapped by some of the distinctively American factors that shape us. The congregation as private association, as voluntaristic society, as member-funded and member-owned for the benefit of its members, has a hard time recognizing the missional collegiality essential to walking worthy of our calling. Every Presbyterian session has heard someone say in the last twelve months, "What this church needs to do is run itself like a good business." I suspect that this comment is also heard in vestries, boards of deacons, and church councils. There are undoubtedly important dimensions of stewardship addressed here, but there are also cultural influences that get in the way of missional collegiality. What is happening to the collegial ministries that equip the saints for the work of service when we adopt the language and values of the corporate world and describe ministers as Chief Executive Officers, Heads of Staff, Executive Pastors, Directors of this and Directors of that? Why is it that ministers' studies have become offices? Those may be more superficial evidences of the problem. There is, at a much deeper level, reason to speak today of the crisis of ordered ministries, especially in traditional denominations. Anyone who labors within the structures of the organized church has discovered evidences of this crisis. One-third of our Presbyterian pastors do not go on from a first call to a second call. Since becoming a seminary faculty member, I have dealt with a disturbing number of my graduates who went on to appointments as associate pastors only to experience in often devastating ways the failure of collegiality, especially with senior pastors. Burn-out is one of the most frequently discussed crises affecting those in ordered ministry.

The ethos of the corporate world joins with the values of the marketplace to complicate even further the practice of collegiality. I have contended that, in the United States, the partnership of church and state has been replaced with the partnership of church and marketplace, and the marketplace appears to be winning. What is going on when members are treated like customers and begin to understand themselves that way? What is the theology of mission that propagates mission statements intended to function primarily as advertising slogans? What kinds of ecclesiology have we developed if our sense of ourselves is that we should be user-friendly, full-service, consumer-sensitive churches? What shall we make of the practical redefinition of the ordered ministries as a mixture of narrow-gauge behavioral therapist, organizational development expert, and program impresario? I remember a church in Louisville that proudly announced its express worship service, in and out in thirty minutes.

The centrality of the missional community that we emphasized in the last chapter finds its parallel here: missional leadership must itself be and function as missional community. That is what the pattern of collegiality is all about, as it shapes the community's witness before a watching world.

Missional Leadership and the Personal Apostolate

We have discussed the role of missional leadership in terms of the priority of the Word for the equipping of the saints, and the essential collegiality of leadership that models and mentors worthy walking. Up until now, we have stressed primarily the communal character of the missional community's vocation: how its life together witnesses to the gospel before a watching world. It is unquestionable that this is a major emphasis of the Scriptures. There are, however, two fundamental, interactive dimensions of the missional community. There is the dimension of its gathering, and there is the dimension of its scattering, its sending. With the gradual establishment of Christianity in Western Christendom, the focus was more and more on the gathering of the church. The more we assumed that our entire culture had been Christianized (curious term!), the less important was the dimension of our scattering — because wherever we went, we were still within the Christian culture at whose center stood the church. Thus, we were most Christian when we gathered, but we were still Christian when we were scattered. And there was no real reason to think about being sent. We lost any sense of that ancient final injunction of the liturgy: *ite, missa est* — Go, thou art sent. Why would we think about ourselves as sent? Our culture was already Christian. The apostolic mission had been accomplished. The kingdom of God was actually here in the structures and offices of the church. Thus, what we did when we assembled in our ecclesiastical buildings came to be seen as the real reason we existed. Our liturgies, our sacraments, our music, our priestly action all gained a spiritual worth that was an end in itself. They lost any sense of equipping for the work of service. The primary service of God was the gathered and ordered worship of the community. To walk worthily meant to engage in the gathered life of the church faithfully, to participate in the sacraments, to share in the assembled worship and praise of God. Isn't it still true that, for most people, "becoming a Christian" is equated with "starting to go to church"?

The problem is not the emphasis upon the gathered church. The problem is the loss of the essential linkage between the gathered church and the scattered church. That we have no sense of sentness is, in effect, the expression of the loss of missional vocation in both our theology of the church and our practice of the faith. Now, with the end of Christendom, that essential sentness reasserts itself every time we walk out of the church into the secularized, post-Christian world, which is now our mission field. If the gathered life of the church is about our discipleship, then the sending is about our apostolate. Like the biblical disciples, we go to school with Jesus as we gather in his name, in order to be sent out by him to proclaim the message. Missional leadership, centered upon the Word and practiced with evangelical collegiality, must serve the gathered church by preparing each member for his or her apostolate. However one calls it, the ministry of the laity, ministry in the workplace, Christian living Monday through Saturday, the presenting issue for the missional community is this: How do we equip each other to walk worthy of our calling in the personal apostolates into which God sends us every time we make the transition from gathered to scattered community?

If a missional community is going to grasp this constant missional movement from discipleship to apostolate, and back again, then it will be essential that its missional leaders help it to encounter Scripture as it equips them for this apostolate. This will require some retooling on the part of the missional leaders. We became very adept, over centuries, at reading the biblical Word in such a way that the obvious could be ignored. In Mark's account of the calling of the Twelve, the missional understanding of vocation may be seen as exemplary of the pervasive missional orientation of the New Testament Scriptures. We have already referred earlier to the reference in Mark 3:13-15 to the calling of the disciples to become apostles. We need also to pay attention to the dimensions of missional calling clearly delineated in this text: "And he appointed twelve, whom he also named apostles, to be with him, and to be sent out to proclaim the message, and to have authority to cast out demons." There are three purpose statements here that make up a fully developed theology of the missional church. The first dimension of the disciples' calling was to be with Jesus. Those four words are a comprehensive theology of the purpose and action of the gathered church. We gather to be with Jesus, because he promises to be present when we gather in his name. We gather to celebrate and testify to the fact that he is present. This is the motivating power of our public worship. We encounter him present in the proclamation of the Word. With the Second Helvetic Confession, we are bold to claim, "The preaching of the word of God is the Word of God."[11] He is present to us in the exposition of the biblical Word. We meet him in his promised spiritual presence at the table, and we receive his gift of body and blood to nourish and cleanse us. And we are told, as we do so, that "as often as you eat this bread and drink the cup, you proclaim the Lord's death until he comes" (1 Cor. 11:26). The text itself reveals the essential linkage of the gathered dimension with the scattered and the sending dimension: going out from that table, we proclaim the salvation accomplished by our Lord's death and the assurance of our future with him, which he will seal in his promised return.

In the Marcan text, "to be with him" is followed immediately by "to be sent out to proclaim the message." The gathering leads immediately into the sending and the scattering. All through Scripture, the movement from gathering to scattering is basic. This is the fundamental missional movement of the people of God: from their called-together life, in which the priority of Word ministry and the collegiality of calling are practiced, to their sent and scattered life, in which they serve as Christ's witnesses. This is the basic thrust of our Lord's emphasis upon our calling to be light, and salt, and leaven. Where Christendom constantly divides the gathering from the scattering, the biblical testimony insists on their necessary interaction. At the climax of a major thematic argument in 2 Corinthians, Paul assures the Corinthian Christians, "Yes, everything is for your sake" (2 Cor. 4:15). Christendom reductionism will often put a period there. The gospel is about my savedness. Christianity is about what we gain as benefits and blessings. The gathered life of the church is to maintain my salvation and provide me assurance that it is valid. The light is to be put under a bushel. But the text does not stop there: "Yes, everything is for your sake, so that grace, as it extends to more and more people, may increase thanksgiving, to the glory of God." All that we receive, which is so very much, is aimed at the extension of grace to

11. "The Second Helvetic Confession," Presbyterian Church (U.S.A.), *The Book of Confessions* (Louisville: Office of the General Assembly, 1996), par. 5.004.

more and more people. Our gathered life around the table of thanksgiving, the Eucharist, is to be oriented to the global thanksgiving of those to whom grace has been extended. It's in that constant movement from gathered to scattered that God is truly glorified.

The test of our missional leadership lies here, at the junction between gathering and sending. We walk worthy of our calling in our gathered life so that we can learn how to walk worthy of our calling in our sent-out, scattered life, in our personal apostolates. We are not to focus upon how successfully we do our gathered life ∠ especially since most of the criteria for success in our culture are suspect anyway. We are to ask how our gathered life has truly prepared us for worthy walking where God is sending us. One of my colleagues in homiletics once put it very well in a discussion we had. She said that, in her work as a teacher of preachers, she is constantly asking, "What is the connection between what people hear, say, and do inside the sanctuary in Christian worship and the way they interpret and respond to the world outside the sanctuary?" This is the question that must energize missional leaders if their missional communities are to walk worthy of their calling. But let me point to a particularly important nuance of her question. She speaks of the scattered and sent life of the community in terms of how they "interpret and respond to the world outside the sanctuary." She is referring, I believe, to the myriad ways in which our post-Christian context challenges us with questions and dilemmas and seductions for which Christendom has not prepared us.

Among the great challenges with which our mission field confronts us are the confusion and distortion of the gospel that are the residual deposit of Christendom. As missional communities, we do not live in a neutral or an indifferent world as far as the claims of Christ are concerned. A missiological analysis of our particular context will reveal widely diverse attitudes about the Christian message and its organized expression in the church. The undeniably large numbers of committed and serious Christians are mixed in with many versions of cultural Christians, constituting a field that is truly made up of wheat and weeds. Cultural Christianity comes in all kinds of shapes and forms and expressions, but one thing is generally true of all its exponents, and that is the rigorous separation of the Christian religion from every other dimension of life, especially the public square and the workplace. For cultural Christians, the idea that Christian identity is centered on the calling to witness is particularly repugnant. Then there are the inoculated former Christians, the intentional rejecters of the gospel, or rather, of the particular distortion or corruption of it against which they are reacting. Their numbers are legion. There are the convinced modernists who are certain that at some point in the eighteenth or nineteenth century, a new human race was born, the enlightened and rational European who has moved beyond the intellectual immaturity of the Christendom that preceded him or her. That component of our cultural chemistry dominates the university world. There are also the religious pluralists and individualists, the various versions of Sheila-ists described by Bellah and his colleagues in *Habits of the Heart*,[12] who craft their own religiosity from the resources of the world religions, New Age spiritualities, and a broad range of repopularized paganisms. Their cultural power is evidenced in the large sections of bookstores devoted to spirituality and religion, which in quantity and diversity far outpace the offerings in the general area of Christianity — as a visit to any large bookstore will make clear. There is also a growing contingent in North American society that is so shaped by the end of Christendom that they are effectively pre-Christian. They have never had any contact with an organizational expression of the Christian faith. They don't know why so much jewelry is shaped as a cross. They are in some ways the most open to Christian witness because it is all new to them. Their numbers are particularly great on the West Coast.

It is into this diverse mission field that we are sent when we disperse into the world as the gathered church now entering into its apostolates. To equip the saints for the work of service must mean to equip Christian witnesses for this challenging mission field. In its times of gathering, the missional community needs to learn how to translate the gospel into these various contexts. Our discipling must, very concretely and practically, take account of the challenges that we meet in our apostolates. How shall the Christian teacher in the public school system carry out her apostolate in a context where conversation about the faith is virtually prohibited? How shall the Christian businessperson carry out his or her apostolic vocation when the neighbor you are to love is your competitor? How shall the Christian accountant advise his or her clients with integrity when the normative conduct of the prevailing culture is to manipulate the financial data for personal gain and reduced taxes? The missional leadership that can engage in this kind of formation for personal apostolates will have to practice a collegiality of shared experience and expertise. There are likely to be more qualified equippers of the saints among the ruling elders who live in that Monday-to-Saturday world than among the teaching elders.

---

12. Robert N. Bellah et al., *Habits of the Heart: Individualism and Commitment in American Life* (Berkeley: University of California Press, 1985), pp. 221, 235.

The challenge of personal apostolates, of faithful witness practiced by all those sent out by the gathered community, takes us to the third component of that concise Marcan theology of the missional church. This statement gives all late-modern Western Christians pause. Together with our being with him and our being sent out by him, we are granted "the authority to cast out demons." I think that most Presbyterian congregations assume that one of the most important reasons to have a learned clergy is so that someone can explain why passages like this do not apply to them. But it may be one of the most important aspects of the equipping done by missional leadership for the conduct of personal apostolates in our post-Christendom world. Together, we need to face fearlessly what Visser 't Hooft prophesied about the Western world over thirty years ago.[13] We are living in a context of neo-paganism that is becoming ever stronger and more diverse. We need to accustom ourselves to the fact that the demonic, the idolatrous, and the seductive are pervasive aspects of our cultures. We are talking about the both obvious and subtle ways in which people are held captive by forces that are demonic precisely because they are so well camouflaged. In biblical terms, these are those "principalities and powers" in rebellion against God that shape our attitudes and values and expectations so effectively that we do not see how contrary to God's good will our lives and our societies are becoming. One can talk about the temptations of consumerism, the captivity to consumer credit, the obsessive preoccupation with youthfulness and fitness, the accumulation of things, the dictatorship of wealth, the manipulative power of advertising, the justification of violence in our entertainment, the rationalization of recreational sex — each of us can add more examples to this list. To walk worthy of our calling over against these tempting forces is, in Mark's text, to demonstrate that in Christ we have the power to cast out such demonic forces. In Christ, there is the liberation of our vision to see the idolatries and demons that hold people captive and the empowering of the will to opt to live alternatively. The formation of the missional community by Scripture will inexorably force these challenges onto our agenda. Missional leadership is called upon to risk engaging these realities, as threatening and unsettling as they are. They are for us the "meat offered to idols" realities, which test our missionary vocation and afford the opportunity to walk worthily in a new and different direction.

13. Willem Visser 't Hooft, "Evangelism in the Neo-Pagan Situation," *International Review of Mission* 63 (January 1974): 81-86; "Evangelism Among Europe's Neo-Pagans," *International Review of Mission* 66 (October 1977): 349-60.

The formation of the missional congregation to walk worthy of its call-ing, and the responsibility of its missional leadership to guide its equipping for the work of service, are clearly themes that call for a large conversation. Just as our book, *Missional Church,* was intended as an invitation to a con-versation about what a missionally centered ecclesiology might look like, my intention in these chapters dealing with missional leadership has been to describe the agenda and frame at least some of the questions that we, in all our diversity, need to engage as Christendom fades from the scene. Because there is much at stake, because there are many contending visions that come together around the theme and practice of leadership, it is my hope that the conversations themselves will be so guided by God's Spirit that they will be examples of worthy walking.

CHAPTER 10

Missio Dei: Integrating Theological Formation for Apostolic Vocation

John Flett's proposal for a Trinitarian understanding of the *missio Dei* that is rooted in the undivided being and act of God requires, as its totally integrated corollary, a theology of the church that cannot separate God's mission from the church's existence and purpose.[1] We have in a diversity of approaches already begun to explore the fascinating and sometimes daunting implications of this comprehensively Trinitarian understanding of mission. I would like to pursue this discussion further by exploring yet another implication of this challenge: What does a thoroughly Trinitarian definition and explication of the *missio Dei* mean for the task of theological formation of missional servant leaders of the church? How do our theological disciplines, as they have evolved over the centuries of Christendom, come together around the central task of missional equipping? How does apostolic vocation define and integrate theological formation?

This question relates directly to the task given to me as the first professor of missional and ecumenical theology at Princeton Theological Seminary. That task was to develop a curriculum in missional and ecumenical theol-

---

1. John Flett, *The Witness of God.*

This chapter originated as my presidential address at the annual meeting of the American Society of Missiology, which took place in Techny, Illinois, June 20-22, 2008. That conference was based on the research work of Dr. John Flett, since published under the title *The Witness of God: The Trinity, Missio Dei, Karl Barth, and the Nature of Christian Community* (Grand Rapids: Eerdmans, 2010). After Dr. Flett surveyed his project, several scholars responded from the perspectives of biblical scholarship, church history, and practical theology. My concluding address examined the implications of an appropriately Trinitarian theology of the missional church for the task of theological education. All of the papers presented at the conference subsequently appeared in the journal *Missiology,* in January 2011.

ogy that contributed relevantly to the Seminary's educational vision and commitments. To do this, I needed to revisit the question of the definition of "missional theology," which was the theme of my inaugural address at Princeton and of the first chapter of this book. What has the ensuing conversation taught me about how "missional theology" might relate to the classical disciplines of the theological curriculum? How, in particular, does it relate to its location in Princeton's Theology Department, with a linkage to the History Department, where Ecumenics continues to be taught? As a discipline or cluster of disciplines that requires that I relate to two academic departments, my task is by definition interdisciplinary. My concern is that this enterprise should also be integrative as we discover what might be the particular contribution of missional and ecumenical theology both to ministerial formation and theological scholarship.

We started with the claim that the time had come to move from "theology and mission" to "missional theology."[2] Since then, I have had the opportunity to test that proposal with courses engaging substantive numbers of master's students and a small group of doctoral students. They have substantively guided and often questioned my attempts to make that transition to missional theology. In a great variety of ways, our work is constantly placed in jeopardy by the fundamental neglect of mission as a major theological theme in Western Christian thought, a theme which has been frequently explored thus far. John Flett succinctly describes the problem in the second sentence of his book: "One of the key questions raised by this work concerns the widespread omission of mission from Western dogmatic imagination."[3] The term "missional" has been our conceptual tool with which we are attempting to address this omission as it evidently and fundamentally shapes the diverse theological disciplines that constitute the typical master's of divinity curriculum today.

We could have opted to take up Mackay's initiative and focus our efforts on his proposal of the field of ecumenics. He described this undertaking in the textbook he wrote for the discipline: "The field of discourse of the Science of Ecumenics embraces everything that concerns the nature, functions, relations and strategy of the Church Universal, when the latter is conceived as a world missionary community. Questions pertaining to the Church's essence, its mission, its unity, and its relations in the world, which have hitherto been

2. Darrell Guder, "From Mission and Theology to Missional Theology," *The Princeton Seminary Bulletin*, new series, 24, no. 1 (2003): 36-54.
3. John Flett, *The Witness of God*, p. 1.

dealt with separately, and have been discussed under diverse designations, will be treated together as constitutive phases of a single discipline."[4] There are many ways in which that approach is necessary and constructive as it contributes both to theological scholarship and ministerial formation. But our intention with the term "missional" moves beyond merely clustering the themes that relate to the church understood in terms of its mission.

This terminological experimentation is, to be sure, driven by all that we have learned in the twentieth century as we became aware that the Christian movement was in fact a global reality, a "world missionary community" (Mackay). Understanding that "great new fact of our time" has encouraged the gradual shift away from ecclesial thinking that centers on the church, especially the Western church, as an end in itself toward understanding the identity and purpose of the church within God's mission, subordinate to and focused upon God's purposes. The term "missional" was introduced in order to foster this more radical way of thinking about the church, and more generally, of doing theology. It was, as we stated in the Gospel and Our Culture Network's research project published in 1998, an attempt to unpack the operative assumption that "the church is missionary by its very nature."[5] That language anticipates the Trinitarian interpretation anticipated by Newbigin and now proposed by John Flett, which insists that the nature and mission of the church cannot be separated because of its participation in the mission of the indivisible God.

The term "missional church" and the project were intended to stimulate a conversation, which is certainly what happened. But in the process, the word "missional" became a cliché, a buzzword, a catch-all phrase that could mean everything and nothing. It has suffered the same fate that Stephen Neill addressed with regard to the term "mission" many years ago: "If everything is mission, then nothing is mission."[6] The same kind of problem has arisen around the term *"missio Dei,"* as Flett has explained. Definition of terms has become the necessary prolegomenon to any missiological conversation about the church. In my various encounters with the missional discussion today, I always have to clarify what the terms mean, be it *"missio Dei,"* or "missional," or even "mission" that is under discussion.

4. John Mackay, *Ecumenics: The Science of the Church Universal* (Englewood Cliffs, NJ: Prentice-Hall, 1964), p. viii.

5. Darrell L. Guder, ed., *Missional Church: A Vision for the Sending of the Church in North America* (Grand Rapids: Eerdmans, 1998) — the language of Vatican II, especially *Ad Gentes,* has become the common parlance of the missiological discussion globally.

6. Stephen Neill, *Creative Tension* (London: Edinburgh House Press, 1959), p. 81.

We have emphasized that there is an admittedly polemic character to the term "missional," as we are using it. We discuss "missional theology" as an attempt to deal with the problematic neglect of mission as the fundamental and centering theological theme of Christian thought and practice — that "omission of mission in Western theological imagination." It has to do with the fundamental rightness of Kähler's dictum, uttered now over a century ago, that "mission is the mother of theology."[7] One of my graduates, discussing the challenge of missional theology and ministry in his congregation, aptly described our use of the term "missional" as a kind of "permanent scaffolding" surrounding and holding up our theological disciplines. We would not need that scaffolding if our theological work were shaped by the *missio Dei*, if the entire doctrinal enterprise were, in diverse ways, truly focused upon the formation and equipping of the church for its apostolate. If mission were truly the mother of our theology, if our theological disciplines were intentionally conceived and developed as components of the formation of the church for its biblical vocation, we would never need to use the term "missional." What might that look like in our theological guilds?

Let me begin with some comments about the relevance of our theme for the biblical disciplines. This brings us back to the issue discussed above (especially in chapters 6 and 7) under the theme "missional hermeneutics." The numbers of those involved in the exploration of biblical interpretation as a discipline of "missional hermeneutics" is growing. We are testing the idea that the scriptural documents are witnesses to missional calling and formation. They are written and intended for communities that understood themselves as called and sent to be witnesses to the gospel. Their apostolic vocation constitutes the lenses through which they receive and engage these writings. As George Hunsberger put it back in 1994, the scriptural testimony constitutes the "warrant" for the assumed evangelistic task of every apostolic community.[8] What the apostolic missionaries were doing in these communities when they were evangelized and formed for mission now continues in the apostolic scriptures. One of the oldest and most frequently emphasized claims of the Reformation is that the church is the creation of the Word of God, as empowered by the Holy Spirit. That authority becomes concrete as the community is equipped for its witness through its encounter with the

7. Martin Kähler, *Schriften zur Christologie und Mission* (München: Christian Kaiser Verlag, [1908] 1971), p. 190; see David Bosch, *Transforming Mission: Paradigm Shifts in Theology of Mission* (Maryknoll, NY: Orbis, 2011), p. 16.

8. George Hunsberger, "Is There Biblical Warrant for Evangelism?" *Interpretation* 48, no. 2 (1994): 131-44.

Word of God written. This is an enormously challenging and productive way to interrogate the Scriptures and to experience their formative power. It appears to many of us to be so obvious as to obviate any apology for this approach. The term and practice of "hermeneutics" should be missional by its very nature. But it clearly is not, and so we must speak of "missional hermeneutics," propping up the enterprise with this conceptual scaffolding.

How does this theme fare in the encounter with the field of church history? I recall a reaction I received just after I delivered my inaugural lecture as Princeton's Henry Winters Luce Professor of Missional and Ecumenical Theology. One of my colleagues in church history came up to me and said, "I really think that all church history needs to be taught as mission history." He was advocating, I think, "missional church history" as an essential dimension of the theological formation for apostolic vocation. David Bosch, in the second third of his magisterial textbook, *Transforming Mission,* shows us one way to investigate the church's missional faithfulness as she moves from one paradigm to another over the course of time. Dale Irwin and Scott Sunquist have moved us further along the way toward "missional church history" with their remarkable reworking of the story as "the History of the World Christian Movement." Of course, Kenneth Scott Latourette started us into this exploration with his still profoundly challenging volumes laying out *A History of the Expansion of Christianity.* The growing numbers of monographs on the history and development of the Christian movement in other parts of the world are contributing today to our ability to interpret Christian history missionally. I think here especially of the provocative work of the late Kwame Bediako. Perhaps it is the historians who least need to rely upon the missional scaffolding today.[9]

In the classic discipline of doctrinal and systematic theology, the missional scaffolding is clearly still needed. I can speak here as a missional theologian who seeks to function in a classical Theology Department. It is still possible, and, in fact, usual to think the faith systematically and to rehearse the great doctrines without any attention at all to the fundamental and centering importance of the *missio Dei.* A "missional theologian" may not really be welcome in the circles of systematic theologians, not because of some kind of theological apartheid but because the theme is simply not present — it

---

9. Bosch, *Transforming Mission;* Dale Irwin and Scott Sunquist, eds., *History of the World Christian Movement* (Maryknoll, NY: Orbis, 2001); Kenneth Scott Latourette, *History of the Expansion of Christianity,* 7 vols. (New York: Harper, 1937-1945); Kwame Bediako, *Theology and Identity: The Impact of Culture upon Christian Thought in the Second Century and in Modern Africa* (London: Regnum, 1992).

is lacking from the "theological imagination." Obviously John Flett's Trinitarian recasting of the *missio Dei* calls for the engagement of systematic and doctrinal theologians. It is important to note that, next to me, his other two doctoral supervisors at Princeton were systematic theologians, Bruce McCormack and Daniel Migliore. It remains to be seen, however, whether that guild will recognize and accept the challenge posed by missional theology as we are dealing with it here.

Let me explore this absence of mission from the dogmatic imagination further, beginning with some thoughts about the doctrine of ecclesiology. The thesis I have been defending in this book is that we only understand the calling and purpose of the church correctly when we do so in terms of the triune God's missional purpose expressed in and through the calling, forming, equipping, and sending of the witnessing church. Missional ecclesiology is, I suggest, the necessary way to do ecclesiology, the only way to avoid separating the church's being from its act. I am here echoing the insistently missional character of Karl Barth's ecclesiology, for which one quotation will stand as representative of countless such statements in the *Church Dogmatics:* "The gathering and upbuilding of the *community* of those who acknowledge Jesus Christ is depicted [in the New Testament] as a *necessity* grounded in Himself," and "this community is sent out and entrusted with the task of mission in the world, again with a *necessity* grounded in Himself. Jesus Christ would not be who He is if He lacked His community, and if this community lacked, or was even capable of lacking, a missionary character."[10]

Now, if theology is about "faith seeking understanding," then, it seems to me, its dominant topic must be that apostolic faith that is to be expressed in faithful witness. The gospel is about news that is so urgently good that it must be shared. To receive the gift of faith is to be called into a relationship of discipleship with Christ that results in apostolate — in his sending out his witnesses. Thus, to be granted gospel faith is to be drawn into the gospel's commission, to be mobilized as servants of its mandate. Following Paul in Romans 12, that understanding entails the "transformation by the renewing of our minds," a process of profound conversion that enables us to recognize and to practice the "good, and acceptable and perfect will of God" (Rom. 12:2). That good, acceptable, and perfect will of the triune God is the healing of the nations, the reconciliation of all things, the new creation made

---

10. Karl Barth, *Kirchliche Dogmatik* IV/2 (Zollikon-Zürich: Evangelischer Verlag 1955), p. 305; ET: *Church Dogmatics* IV/2, trans. G. W. Bromiley (Edinburgh: T. & T. Clark, 1958), p. 275.

possible in Christ, the inauguration and consummation of the kingdom of God. God's missional purpose is summarized in John: "For God sent the Son into the world, not to condemn the world, but that the world might be saved through him" (John 3:17). To understand the Trinity rightly is to participate in the enabled action of witness, which carries out the mission of God the Father, the Son, and the Holy Spirit. Christology and Pneumatology must be explorations of the person and work of the Son and the Spirit that generate not just orthodox propositions of truth but ways of thinking and deciding by which the Spirit enables faithful witness to the Son who is the Lord and Savior of all humanity and history. The ecclesiology that emerges out of the New Testament documents is, I will contend, clearly a missional ecclesiology. "Mission is the mother of theology." In our exploration of missional ecclesiology in this book, we have argued that interpreting the Nicene marks in the reverse order, beginning with the fundamental dimension of apostolicity which reorients catholicity, holiness, and unity, is another complementary way to formulate such a doctrine and practice of the church.

We have, I hope, persuasively argued that, as heirs of the Western tradition, we can and do develop whole ecclesiologies that never mention the fundamental missional purpose of the church. Our theologies of the church can focus entirely upon the church's inward functions as though they were its exclusive purpose. We can define the church's worship as an end in itself with no regard for the ways in which Christ encounters his people in Word and Sacrament in order to equip and send them into the world for which he died. We can recite the Nicene Creed with regularity and yet never grasp the character and purpose of the apostolicity that defines who we are and what we are for. Are not the reductionistic ecclesiologies of contemporary consumer-oriented churches that specialize entirely in "meeting the religious needs of their members" the product of centuries of ecclesiological reflection that has been more individualistic than Kingdom-centered? So, we need to lean on that scaffolding and speak of "missional ecclesiology" because it is still, regrettably, possible to do ecclesiology without mission.

Similarly, we can do eschatology without mission, invariably ending up with distortions of the biblical vision of God's certain future. Missional eschatology interprets the future outcome of our faith journey in ways that equip us for faithful and patient witness now. Peter in his first epistle sets out a profoundly missional eschatology by establishing the foundation of the gospel in the fact that God the Father has raised Jesus Christ from the dead. The apostolic author links that certain past tense of faith with the living hope we share as we look forward to the certain inheritance awaiting us. In the passage from the past tense of the resurrection to the future tense of the consummation of that hope, we are protected by the gift of faith as we look forward to the completion of what God has begun. Though tested now by ordeals compared to the gold refined by the assayer's fire, we are enabled to know and respond to Jesus Christ, to love him without having seen him. "As the outcome of our faith we obtain the salvation of our souls" (1 Pet. 1:9).

Missional eschatology takes seriously our Lord's Ascension Day injunction that we are not to know the "times or the seasons," the "chronoi or kairoi," of God's consummating action. We are liberated from our human desire to speculate and to know the unknowable — a cultural captivity that ends up wasting a lot of trees and paper and diverting Christian witness from its true center. We are, instead, empowered to carry out the dominical mission to be Christ's witnesses in Jerusalem, Judea, Samaria, and to the ends of the earth.

In the studies in this volume, I have frequently linked the theological silence regarding mission with the problematic reductionism of the gospel that also characterizes Western Christianity. I don't need to restate that critical analysis. My hunch is that the Christian movement has always found ways to reduce, to domesticate, to deradicalize the gospel, by tolerating or even propounding dichotomies that subvert the gospel, making it more palatable and manageable. As I have constantly revisited this theme, I began to see similar patterns in the ecclesiological justifications of the clergy-lay distinction, in the separation of the kingdom of God from the message of personal salvation, in the recasting of the church as an institution that primarily administers salvation and preserves its members' savedness, and, in our modern context, in the polarity between evangelism and social justice that plagues most mainline denominations. My modest grappling with this challenge became a book on the theology of incarnational evangelism, published in the mid-1980s, in which I argued that the purpose of God's gift of salvation was that we should become witnesses for God's mission through everything that we are, that we say, and that we do.[11]

That little book was instrumental in the invitation to become a professor of mission and evangelism (it appears that there were not many Presbyterians willing to tackle evangelism as a theological theme!). Once there, and discovering that I was in fact a missiologist, I found in Bosch a discussion of evangelism that addressed my concerns about this false dichotomy in a compelling way. While acknowledging that "evangelism offers people sal-

---

11. Darrell Guder, *Be My Witnesses: The Church's Mission, Message, and Messengers* (Grand Rapids: Eerdmans, 1985).

vation as a present gift and with it assurance of eternal bliss," he goes on to emphasize that

> . . . if the offer of all this gets center-stage attention in our evangelism, the gospel is degraded to a consumer product. It has to be emphasized, there-fore, that the personal enjoyment of salvation never becomes the central theme in biblical conversion stories (cf Barth 1962: 561-614). Where Chris-tians perceive themselves as those enjoying an indescribably magnificent private good fortune (:567f), Christ is easily reduced to little more than the "Disposer and Distributer" of special blessings (:595f) and evangelism to an enterprise that fosters the pursuit of pious self-centeredness (:572). Not that the enjoyment of salvation is wrong, unimportant, or unbiblical; even so, it is almost incidental and secondary (:572, 593). It is not simply to *receive* life that people are called to become Christians, but rather to *give* life.[12]

Peppered throughout this paragraph are references to a section of vol-ume IV/3 (second half) of the *Church Dogmatics,* where the theme is "The Christian as Witness." It is part of paragraph 71, which is titled "The Vocation of Man." Three thematic subsections precede it: "Man in the Light of Life," "The Event of Vocation," and the "Goal of Vocation." It is precisely at this crucial juncture in Barth's argument that he demonstrates what Bosch meant when he said that "one theologian has developed his entire ecclesiology in terms of the [claim that the church is missionary by its very nature]: Karl Barth."[13] In corroboration, he cites Johannes Aagaard's description of Barth as "the decisive Protestant missiologist in this generation."[14] What Bosch and Aagaard saw, and which very few Barthians have recognized, is that Barth develops his theology of salvation as reconciliation in such a way that his missional ecclesiology is woven through the argument. In the same grand outline, he develops his Pneumatology as well as his doctrine of the human sinfulness that obstructs God's saving work. He is, in effect, demonstrating that problem of false dichotomies, of which the division between God's Being and Act is the prime and powerful cause. As John Flett argues, since "there is no breach in the being and act of God, so there should be no breach in the

---

12. Bosch, *Transforming Mission*, p. 424.

13. Bosch, *Transforming Mission*, p. 382.

14. Bosch, *Transforming Mission;* see Johannes Aagaard, "Some Main Trends in Modern Protestant Missiology," *Studia Theologica* 19 (1965): 238.

being and act of the community" (see footnote 4). The further implication of this Trinitarian principle is that there should be no false divisions in the theological explication of the gospel as it translates into the life and action of the church.

Bosch recognized in the grand outline of Barth's doctrine of reconciliation (a volume in three books!) just how profoundly missional the entire theological project really is. The doctrine of justification is expounded by the discussion of "The Holy Spirit and the Gathering of the Christian Community." The gospel of sanctification is expounded by the discussion of "The Holy Spirit and the Upbuilding of the Christian Community." The missional focus then erupts dramatically in Barth's insistence that our understanding of the gospel of reconciliation is truncated and unavoidably reductionistic if we stop with justification and sanctification. The biblical testimony requires that the justifying and sanctifying work of the Spirit must lead to and eventuate in the vocation of the Christian person and the sending of the Christian community. Paragraph 71 deals, as I said, with the "Vocation of Man," and it is followed in paragraph 72 with the discussion of the "Sending of the Community of the Holy Spirit." Embedded in this great exposition of the evangelical necessity of vocation is Barth's critique of what he calls the "classic definition of what it means to be a Christian."[15]

What I had, in rather naïvely instinctive ways, and many years before, begun to understand with my concern about the benefits-mission dichotomy, was developed here with a clarity and persuasiveness that still astonishes me. For Barth "the Holy Spirit and the Sending of the Christian Community" is the capstone theme, which draws all the theological strands of the reconciling gospel into the actual definition and task of the church. His strategy echoes Newbigin's missionary ecclesiology summarized in his discussion of the congregation as "the hermeneutic of the Gospel."[16] In this theological project, the reductionisms of our Western traditions are addressed if not corrected. An ecclesiology without mission is impossible. Instead, in Barth mission becomes the driving force and impact of the gospel of reconciliation, which by the work of the Holy Spirit, gathers, upbuilds, and sends the missional church. Whereas the classic definition of a Christian is one who lives out the enjoyment of the benefits of the gospel, a radically missional

15. See Darrell Guder, *The Continuing Conversion of the Church* (Grand Rapids: Eerdmans, 2000), pp. 97-119, 121-31.

16. Lesslie Newbigin, *The Gospel in a Pluralist Society* (Grand Rapids: Eerdmans, 1989), pp. 222-33.

redefinition is necessary: the Christian is called to be the witness to God's accomplished work of healing reconciliation in Jesus Christ and to be that witness in the called community. With this emphasis, Barth has drawn together the major biblical strands for missional ecclesiology: the discipleship for apostolate of the Gospels, the formation of the witnessing church of Luke-Acts, Paul's Body of Christ as earthen vessels and the frequent injunction to walk worthy of the calling, and Peter's chosen race, royal priesthood, holy nation, God's own people, all of whom exist to declare the wonderful deeds of him who calls us out of darkness into his marvelous light.

This is the understanding of vocation that I have in mind with the title of this chapter: "integrating theological formation for apostolic vocation." It is apostolic vocation that defines Christian purpose. "You shall be my witnesses." That vocation is implemented by the Holy Spirit through the gathering, upbuilding, and sending of the witnessing community. Baptism is ordination to apostolic vocation. The Lord encounters us at his table to restore us, to nourish us, to equip us, and to send us out as his Body bearing his love into the world. The Word is proclaimed apostolically, prophetically, evangelistically, pastorally, and instructively "to equip the saints for the work of ministry, for the building up of the body of Christ." This vocation is an essential dimension of Christian salvation, the witness to what God has done in justifying and sanctifying his people. And this vocation continues into the world as every member, bearing a flame of the Spirit, is sent into the mission field as light, leaven, and salt, to be Christ's apostolic community at work. The test of missional theological formation must necessarily be the faithfulness of the lay apostolate when the church is scattered in the world.

For such witnessing communities to be faithful to their vocation, they require missional formation. What the apostolic missionaries were doing when they remained in their newly formed communities to instruct and equip them to be witnesses must continue in faith communities today as the apostolic Scriptures do their Spirit-empowered work. As the Gospels invited the first communities for which they were written to join the disciples in following Jesus in order to be equipped and sent out by him, those Gospels carry forward that discipling for apostolate today. The challenge before the theologians and seminaries who serve the church by teaching and equipping their future servant leaders is to discover how such theological formation for apostolic vocation is to be done today. It can only happen as the theological disciplines reconceive themselves in terms of the missional vocation of the church and of each Christian person. It can only happen as the servant scholars of the church recognize that their disciplines are not ends in themselves but instruments for formation, for equipping, for that transformation that happens by the renewing of the mind. Our goal needs to be an understanding and practice of the theological disciplines we teach that does not need the scaffolding term "missional" because our work is focused on the vocation of witness to be practiced and taught by those whom we teach. Missional vocation is, I am persuaded, the divinely appointed center around which, or telos toward which, all our theological disciplines are to be integrated.

In the first two seminaries in which I served as a missiologist, my discipline was located with the Practical Theologians. I quickly discovered, as I worked with my colleagues in the various disciplines that make up a Practical Theology Department, that they struggled with a kind of theological inferiority complex. They saw themselves caricatured as people who work on methods and techniques, who were the "how-to" people whose job was to take the serious theology of their colleagues in the classical disciplines and "apply" it to the doing of ministry. They were not perceived as colleagues who did serious theology. Very rightly, they have protested and continue to do so. It is a very good thing that there is a groundswell of resistance to such caricatures and dilutions. It is time, however, to move from reaction to construction, and I am persuaded that there are resources in the missional theological exploration for that constructive theological process. The dichotomy between ecclesiology as the formal doctrinal discipline and practical theology as its so-called application is a further example of the fateful breach between being and act. The problem, I think, is not so much with the so-called practical theologians, as it is with the theoretical theologians who imagine that doctrine can exist without practice. It would be profoundly reductionistic to do, say, the theology of Paul, but to stop the enterprise at those powerful "therefores" at hinge points in the epistles, where what follows explicates what the truth of the gospel actually does and says as it is witnessed to. Missional theology seeks to think the faith in terms of its practice, and to practice the faith in terms of its meaning and purpose. We have much to learn from the catechetical disciplines of the church in the first centuries of our history. They shaped faith by shaping conduct, by doing good news in order to grasp good news. Doctrine was learned in relation both to liturgical worship and the practice of the love of one's neighbor. Theological work needed to be done so that emerging Christian communities could carry out their witness faithfully in oppressive and hostile contexts. They needed doctrine that did not divide between thinking and doing — doctrine as we experience it in Jesus' earthly ministry, following him as his disciples so that we can serve his mission as his apostles.

The task of missional theology is daunting. It requires much hard work, sorting out our Christendom legacy in terms both of its resources for faithful witness today and its reductions and dilutions of the gospel. There are deeply embedded patterns of cultural captivity present in every theological and ecclesial tradition. There are intellectual breaches and polarities that distort the mission of God. There are patterns of power and violence with which the Christian church has made its compromises, thus profoundly diminishing its faithfulness to its vocation. Congregations in our culture struggle with their missional vocation when the demands of institutional maintenance and the desire for organizational success assert themselves. I find more and more reasons to insist that the challenge before us is not one merely of renewal, or retooling, but of conversion — the conversion of the church to its radically simple missional vocation. Since conversion is a work of God's Spirit and not under our control, our theological formation for apostolic vocation must be done in a posture of patient and confident prayer. Paul gave us the quintessential prayer for our missional conversion in his epistle to the Philippians 1:9-11: "It is my prayer that your love may abound more and more, with knowledge and discernment, so that you may approve what is excellent, and may be pure and blameless for the day of Christ, filled with the fruits of righteousness which come through Jesus Christ, to the glory and praise of God."

CHAPTER 11

Missional Ecumenism: The Vision and the Challenge

Part One

When Kenneth Scott Latourette wrote his classic seven-volume *History of the Expansion of Christianity,* he devoted three volumes to the nineteenth century alone, which he called *The Great Century.*[1] He needed those three volumes to lay out the massive expansion of the Christian movement in the modern missionary movement during that dynamic century. The seventh and final volume only addressed the first half of the twentieth century, concluding with 1945. He titled it "Advance through Storm," and in it he grappled with the truly dialectical character of the Christian movement in its most recent history.[2] By the middle of the twentieth century, Christianity had become a global movement with growing churches across the southern hemisphere, while at the same time, its decline in the traditional so-called Christian cultures of the West was already unmistakably in process. That global character of Christianity was the great new fact of our time to which William Temple referred when he was consecrated Archbishop of Canterbury during World War II. The global character of Christianity was the outcome of the Western missionary movement. Its momentum in the

1. Kenneth Scott Latourette, *A History of the Expansion of Christianity,* vol. 4: *The Great Century: Europe and the United States;* vol. 5: *The Great Century: The Americas, Australasia and Africa;* vol. 6: *The Great Century: North Africa and Asia* (Grand Rapids: Zondervan, 1970; New York: Harper & Row, 1941-1943).

2. Kenneth Scott Latourette, *A History of the Expansion of Christianity: Advance Through Storm* (Grand Rapids: Zondervan, 1970; New York: Harper & Row, 1945).

This essay was presented at Trinity Lutheran Seminary, Columbus, Ohio, as the T. A. Kantonen Lectures, on September 26, 2013.

nineteenth century was truly impressive, but by the mid-twentieth century the problematic character of mission's many-faceted linkage with Western colonialism was also producing critique and even the disavowal of mission among some Christians in the North Atlantic societies.

As the twentieth century dawned, there was good reason for the optimism that was expressed by the watchword for world mission expounded by John Mott: "The evangelization of the world in this generation."[3] The Protestant mission world gathered in Edinburgh in 1910 to review in detail the amazing expansion of Christian mission and to address a great range of questions and challenges that required urgent attention if the Western commitment to share with the world "the benefits of the Gospel and western civilization" was to succeed. But within twenty years of Edinburgh, there were voices that questioned whether that success should be pursued further. When looking back upon that debate, which continues in diverse ways up to today, one cannot deny that the foreign mission movement actually worked. As we all know, the majority of world Christianity is located today outside the boundaries of traditional and declining Northern and Western Christendom, and it consists of the churches planted by the much-criticized modern missionary movement. Simply sorting out the many dimensions of this ironic situation has generated and continues to occupy the attention of many scholars who in diverse ways and from diverse assumptions pursue Latourette's analysis of the "expansion of Christianity" further.

So, when we look back upon the whole sweep of the twentieth century from the vantage point of the second decade of the twenty-first century, we might conjecture that it would have taken at least three of Latourette's volumes if not more to tell the increasingly complex story of the modern Christian movement. The complexity is especially evident when we consider the contemporary debates and initiatives related to what we have called the Ecumenical Movement since 1910. Of particular concern is how, in this movement, mission and unity relate to one another. To put it in other words, what is "missional" ecumenism?

It was out of the foreign mission fields that the urgent concern arose for the unity of Christian witness. Any historian of nineteenth-century Western missions will validate that.[4] All through the nineteenth century, there was a

3. John R. Mott, *The Evangelization of the World in This Generation* (London: Student Volunteer Movement, 1900).

4. See, e.g., William Richey Hogg, *Ecumenical Foundations: A History of the International Missionary Council and Its Nineteenth Century Background* (New York: Harper & Brothers, 1952; reissue: Eugene: Wipf & Stock, 2002).

growing sense that the divisions the Christian mission took with it "to the ends of the earth" were a growing obstacle to the envisioned Christianization of the world beyond the boundaries of Western Christendom. Western missionaries shared not only the benefits of the gospel and Western civilization with their converts and daughter churches: they exported the ancient and modern divisions of Christianity with which Western Christians had largely made their peace. The emerging geography of non-Western Christianity became, during the nineteenth century, a variegated tapestry of many European confessional traditions and polities, often in close proximity to each other and inevitably engaged in competition and even conflict. Thus, by 1910, there was a broad consensus among Protestant mission agencies and leaders that the divisions of Christianity needed to be confronted for the sake of credible witness. The connection of the church's ecumenicity and its fundamentally missionary nature began to emerge as a major theme that would, over time, generate a great range of diverse actions and projects. The Ecumenical Movement unfolded, both within Western Christendom and beyond its boundaries, as a dominant focus of the world Christian movement, taking on many institutional forms. The goal was to foster Christian unity for the sake of Christian witness, and the steps to that goal were a great spectrum of experiments and innovations that tended initially to emphasize cooperation, federation, and, ultimately institutional unification. Initially, as we shall explore further, the theological question of unity was not in the foreground.

The ecumenical idea, from 1910 on, was a catalyst for a truly remarkable diversity of actions to foster Christian unity. John Mott traveled around the world, encouraging the continuing expansion of mission efforts as they resulted in the formation of more and more so-called "daughter churches." His favored strategy in the first decades of the modern Ecumenical Movement was the foundation of national councils of churches or mission societies to foster cooperation among Christian communities within a cultural region. Among the many structural outcomes of these efforts to replace ecclesial competitiveness with cooperation were institutions such as the International Missionary Council, the Faith and Order Movement, and the Life and Work Movement. They were all understood as intentional continuations of the Edinburgh Conference's vision, and they prepared the way for the formation of the World Council of Churches, beginning in 1948 in Amsterdam.

Next to those efforts to bring about Christian unity at the global level, divided churches in particular contexts began formal explorations that became processes of negotiation to bring about actual church unions. The Church of South India is perhaps the best known and undoubtedly one of the most remarkable outcomes of the church union expression of the Ecumenical Movement. Both the solid theological work and the polity innovations that characterize the CSI may serve as a resource and an inspiration for efforts today to overcome the dividedness of the church. The history of the CSI since its inception, with its ups and downs, continues to contribute in important ways to the global ecumenical conversation.

Some expressions of ecumenicity have focused *within* ecclesial traditions: Reformed and Lutheran cousin communions found their way into structural union, recognizing that their divisions were more the result of differing waves of emigration that brought European ecclesial traditions to North America and the Antipodes. Their lack of unity was often more a historical accident than a doctrinal conflict. There have been other non-doctrinal causes of Christian division. The Civil War and the conflict over slavery split American Baptists, Methodists, and Presbyterians — and it took the Presbyterians a century to get over that division when the old southern and northern streams finally were reunified in 1983. The ecumenical vision led to the formation of a number of united or uniting churches, such as the United Church of Canada, the Uniting Church of Australia, and the merger of the Presbyterian and Congregational churches of England as the United Reformed Church.

The ecumenical vision was not limited, however, to the union of churches and organizational efforts at cooperation, as important as such undertakings were and are. Concerns for institutional unity began to trigger theological explorations in which profound and formative questions of the church's purpose, its place within the canon of Christian doctrine, began tentatively to find articulation. At Edinburgh, ecclesiological questions were scrupulously avoided, at the behest of the representatives of the Anglican Communion, who otherwise would not have been willing to participate. Within ten years of Edinburgh, the theological work of the Faith and Order Movement was initiated under the leadership of an American Episcopal bishop, Charles Brent. As the twentieth century rolled on, the ecumenical vision found expression in theologically significant initiatives that began to ask about the "why" of the church. As the purpose for the church was investigated in diverse ways by diverse traditions, the question of ecclesial unity became more and more a profoundly theological theme, and a consensus began to become apparent that the linkage of mission and unity was not merely a question of strategy, or process, or cooperation, but of the gospel itself. One can recognize, retrospectively, how these dialogues and consultations were steps on a pathway toward a unity that needed both theological and practical definition.

We can look back upon some remarkable steps along that pathway, while acknowledging that the exploration of mission and unity was, in fact, going on in a myriad of ways at every level from local to global. I think of the ecumenical hospitality practiced by Pope John XXIII and the leadership of the Second Vatican Council, as they invited Protestant observers to participate in their deliberations. That ecumenical hospitality finds expression at a number of places in the documents of the Council. And it is clearly linked to the centrality of mission, as summarized in the often-quoted statement, "The pilgrim church is missionary by its very nature."[5] A "missional ecumenism" was emerging.

In the 1960s, the European churches that arose out of the Protestant Reformation engaged in a process of consensus formation that resulted in the Leuenberg Agreement. This remarkable statement, also known as the Concordia, has been signed by around one hundred churches. It formulates commonly affirmed understandings of the central tenets of the Christian faith. That consensus has concrete implications, because the Agreement establishes mutual recognition among the signatory churches of each other's ordered ministries, sacraments, and membership. The argument laid out in the Leuenberg Concordia arrives at such a remarkable consensus by means of the acknowledgment that the reasons for division several centuries ago, although valid then, no longer need to divide these churches today.

I can illustrate the significance of the Leuenberg process with my own story. When I was ordained to that Lutheran call in northern Germany in 1964, I was asked by the Lutheran official to whom I reported to refrain from celebrating the Lord's Supper with the young people I served because I was not ordained on the basis of the Lutheran confessional documents. The exception to that practice would be if I were with my young people in a foreign setting in which no ordained Lutheran was available. Two years into that appointment, the supervisor changed and the entire issue was set aside, and I was told to do whatever I deemed best for the ministry I was called to carry out. When I returned to southern Germany several years later to serve as the theological teacher of men and women who were to be ordained as deacons, the issue did not even arise until I asked if there were any concerns about my presiding over the Lord's Table. I will never forget the comment

---

5. Vatican II, *Ad Gentes*, 9; see David Bosch, *Transforming Mission: Paradigm Shifts in Theology of Mission* (Maryknoll, NY: Orbis, 2011), pp. 380-81.

of the Consistory member who was responsible for my work: "You know, Herr Guder, here in Württemberg we've never taken our Lutheranism all that seriously!" By that time, Leuenberg was about to be signed.

From its inception in the 1920s, the Faith and Order Movement focused its theological efforts on the issues that continued to divide Christians and churches. Its most significant accomplishment was the working document titled *Baptism, Eucharist and Ministry*, published in 1982 and sent out to the global church for response. The impressive volume of responses from the church ecumenical made clear that the theological analysis and proposals of the document did, indeed, confront those ecclesial issues that most powerfully and consistently divided Christians and churches from one another: the theology and practice of the sacraments, and the ordering of ministry. If one interrogates BEM from the perspective of the growing ecumenical exploration of the church's mission, one finds formulations that stress witness and relate the internal practices of the church to her missionary mandate. "Baptized believers demonstrate that humanity can be regenerated and liberated. They have a common responsibility, here and now, to bear witness together to the Gospel of Christ, the Liberator of all human beings."[6] We even find a reference to God's mission: "The very celebration of the Eucharist is an instance of the Church's participation in God's mission to the world. This participation takes everyday form in the proclamation of the Gospel, service of the neighbor, and faithful presence in the world."[7] The discussion of "ministry" begins by turning to "The Calling of the Whole People of God." The ecclesiology that surfaces in the first six paragraphs of the Ministry discussion certainly takes the centrality of mission for the church seriously: "The Holy Spirit unites in a single body those who follow Jesus Christ and sends them as witnesses into the world."[8] But the subsequent discussion of ordered and ordained ministry not only results in what is for a Reformed theologian a problematic tendency towards sacerdotalization, but also seems to focus the church's purpose and mission upon the particular functions and responsibilities of the ordered ministers. Be that as it may, the Faith and Order process is an impressive demonstration of the way in which the ecumenical movement was confronting and engaging the doctrinal questions of the church's purpose, nature, and action.

---

6. World Council of Churches, *Baptism, Eucharist and Ministry* [Faith and Order Paper No. 111] (Geneva: World Council of Churches, 1982), ¶B III, 10, p. 3.

7. *Baptism, Eucharist and Ministry*, ¶E II, E, 25, p. 13.

8. *Baptism, Eucharist and Ministry*, ¶M I, 1, p. 16.

The many-faceted ecumenical vision has also found expression in nu-
merous bilateral conversations that have resulted in important acts of ecumenical cooperation and mutual recognition. Thus, we now have among our
various Protestant denominations agreements that allow for pastoral calls
across denominational lines. Perhaps one of the most notable expressions
of the ecumenical vision within our American context was the Consultation
on Church Union which was initiated by Bishop James Pike and Dr. Eugene
Carson Blake, Episcopal and Presbyterian leaders in the 1960s, and which
drew nine Protestant denominations into an intensive process of theological
consultation working towards a union — which was never accomplished. I
will return to that later.

The questions and issues that made up the discourse of the Ecumenical
Movement, in its many organized forms, gradually stimulated a theological
exploration, in diverse ways, which began to raise hard questions about the
relationship between mission and ecclesiology. There were many factors that
contributed energy to these discussions. As we look back, we can discern
how, gradually and often unintentionally, these discussions came to the fore.
The doctrine of the church was not a major focus of the emerging churches
of the non-Western mission field. Western missionaries brought their catechisms and books of order with them and formed new churches more or
less after the pattern of the various denominations they represented. Those
theological resources, whether rooted in the Reformation or in later forms of
Protestant innovation, were all characterized by a curious deficiency. Their
doctrinal or confessional discourse on the church, its purpose, and its activities, virtually never referred to the Christian mission. The relationship
between mission and church, however it is understood, does not find expression in our Western ecclesiological traditions. This is what led Wilbert
Shenk to define Western "Christendom" as "church without mission."[9] It is
perhaps more accurate to say "Christian theology without mission," since
the activity of mission has always found expression in some way or another
across the centuries of Western Christendom. But theological *reflection* on
the essential link between mission and church has not been a part of our
traditions. David Bosch points out that the so-called Great Commission at
the end of Matthew does not play a major role in biblical scholarship until
quite recently.[10] It is not a dominant theme in the theologies of the church

9. Wilbert Shenk, *Write the Vision: The Church Renewed* (Valley Forge, PA: Trinity Press
International, 1995), p. 35.
10. Bosch, *Transforming Mission*, pp. 57-58, 347-49.

across the centuries of Western Christendom. What would be the relevance of a missionary commission like Matthew's in a world that is already Christian and has been such for centuries? It is not until William Carey's "Enquiry into the Obligation of Christians to Use Means for the Conversion of the Heathen" in 1792 that the Great Commission again begins to challenge the church with its missionary mandate.

I make it a practice to ask Presbyterians when and how mission emerges as a theme in our Book of Confessions. The theme does not occur in any of the Reformed confessions of the sixteenth century and thereafter — until 1903. By the beginning of the twentieth century and after almost a century of intensive engagement in foreign mission, it had become problematic for the Presbyterian Church to be so profoundly engaged in world mission with no reference to it in our sole doctrinal standard at that time, the Westminster Confession of Faith with its two catechisms. So the old northern stream added paragraph 35 to the Westminster Confession, titled "Of the Gospel of the Love of God and Missions." It makes the case that the gospel is for all, that all are to be invited to respond to it, and that "Christ hath commissioned his Church to go into all the world and to make disciples of all nations." Therefore, missions are one of the things that the church should do, although, even here, mission does not so much define the church as it is one of the church's legitimate practices, next to worship, service, and fellowship.[11]

The Reformation did not correct that absence of mission in its theologies of the church. Its theological focus was upon a major and essential theological course-correction having to do with the doctrine of salvation. The character of Western established Christianity, the assumption that European Christendom is God's divinely ordained order for Western cultures, was not questioned. Of course the Reformation *solas* have a profound impact upon the doctrine and practice of the church. There are resources that inform our understanding of evangelization and mission in both Luther and Calvin, and they need to be engaged. But the theological process of the Reformation, seen as a whole, did not result in the centering of the church's purpose and action upon God's mission. The exception, of course, is the Radical Reformation, which does indeed couple its rejection of established Christendom with a reclamation of the church's missionary mandate — and with explicit reference to Matthew 28.

The Ecumenical Movement, starting from a deep concern for the integ-

---

11. See Presbyterian Church (U.S.A.), *The Constitution of the Presbyterian Church (U.S.A.); Part I: Book of Confessions* (Louisville: Office of the General Assembly, 1999), 6.187-90.

rity of Christian mission and the problem of Christian dividedness for that integrity, became the catalyst for a probing reexamination of Christendom's understandings of the church itself and its purpose within its own context. The searchlight moved from the so-called younger churches to the old, established churches of the West, whose ecclesial compromises within the context of Constantinian establishment and power became more and more a theological concern that urgently called for attention. One may summarize the movement as a shift from ecclesiocentricity to theocentricity. Was the church to understand itself theologically as an end in itself, or was its theological sense of itself to be shaped by its purpose and identity within God's healing purposes for creation?

There are many portents of this modern critique of Western ecclesiocentricity that we recognize when we look back at how the ecumenical vision emerged. Wilbert Shenk identifies several of them in his helpful little book, *Write the Vision:* John Wesley's revolutionary movement outside of parish churches to the fields where the working classes gathered to hear him proclaim the gospel; Sören Kierkegaard's *Attack upon Christendom;* Walter Hobhouse's contention in the Bampton Lectures of 1909 that the church must repent of its Constantinian compromise of its purpose as it recovers its original missionary nature; Karl Barth's dramatic conversion in his first pastorate in Safenwyl from the cultural Christianity of his day to the radical gospel of the Romans commentary; Cardinal Suhard's worker priests in Paris in the 1940s.[12] The theological and ecclesial ferment represented by these and many other persons was paralleled by the growing emphasis in the conversation of the International Missionary Council on the mission of God as definitive of the church. By the 1930s, the participants in the International Missionary Council were largely in agreement that the church is essentially and primarily defined as the agent and instrument of God's mission. Karl Hartenstein, the noted German Lutheran missiologist from the 1920s to the 1960s, summarized the discussion of the International Missionary Council's deliberations in Tambaram, India, in 1939 with the laconic statement: "Whoever says church says mission, and conversely, whoever says mission says church."[13] It was Hartenstein who first used the term *missio Dei* (not Karl Barth, as is often erroneously claimed), when he wrote in 1934, ". . . mission today is called to

12. Shenk, *Write the Vision, passim.*
13. Karl Hartenstein, "Was haben wir von Tambaram zu lernen?," *Das Wunder der Kirche unter den Völkern der Erde: Bericht über die Weltmissionskonferenz in Tambaram,* ed. Martin Schlunk (Stuttgart: Evangelischer Missionsverlag, 1939), p. 194.

examine itself in every way and always anew before God whether it is what it ought to be: missio Dei, the mission of God, yes, the sending Christ the Lord commands of the Apostles: "As the Father has sent me, so I send you."[14]

The theological understanding of mission that was finding articulation from the 1930s on was ultimately summarized with the term "the mission of God," the *missio Dei*. This term was used to interpret the heated conversations of the Willingen meeting of the International Missionary Council in 1952 and became thereafter a major thematic focus of the emerging ecumenical discourse. The theme of that meeting was "the missionary obligation of the church," illustrating what David Bosch would later describe as the merger of ecclesiology and missiology into one discipline. The purpose of the meeting was to examine the theological foundations of mission, especially in light of the rapidly changing global context. That change was powerfully expressed by the expulsion of all Western missionaries from China in the immediately preceding years. At the same time, the decline of Western Christianity was by now a widely observed and argued theme. To reorient the church's understanding of its calling around God's mission clearly meant to move away from the church as an end in itself. Karl Hartenstein again summarized the emerging ecumenical consensus in his "theological reflection" upon the Willingen outcomes: "Mission is not a matter of human activity or organization; its source is the triune God himself. The sending of the Son for the reconciliation of the universe through the power of the Spirit is the basis and goal of mission. From the 'missio Dei' alone comes the 'missio ecclesiae.' Thus mission is placed in the widest conceivable framework of salvation history and of God's plan of salvation."[15] The liminal character of the theological process going on at that time is well captured by the title of the book in which Hartenstein's "Theological Reflection" appeared in 1952: *Mission zwischen Gestern und Morgen* [Mission between yesterday and today].[16]

Those discussions and investigations of the ecumenical movement that began out of a concern for the unity of the church for the sake of its mission were now involved in a process of theological reorientation that was fundamentally redefining the church in terms of God's mission and its calling to serve that mission. Many voices joined this conversation and contributed substantially to this theological exploration. The great diversity of inter-

14. Karl Hartenstein, "Wozu nötigt die Finanzlage der Mission," *Evangelisches Missions-Magazin* 79 (1934): 217.

15. Karl Hartenstein, "Theologische Besinnung," in *Mission zwischen Gestern und Morgen*, ed. Walter Freytag (Stuttgart: Evangelischer Missionsverlag, 1952), p. 62.

16. Freytag, ed., *Mission zwischen Gestern und Morgen*.

preters and approaches that characterizes this theological journey in the latter decades of the twentieth century is itself emblematic of the comprehensive ecumenicity of the undertaking. In 1936, John Mackay, as the new president of Princeton Seminary, appointed himself Professor of Ecumenics and therewith invented the discipline. A few years later, he would write the first textbook in the field: *Ecumenics: The Science of the Church Universal.*[17] German missiologists such as Karl Hartenstein, Walter Freytag, Wilhelm Andersen, and a little later, Hans-Werner Gensichen, contributed substantially from a Lutheran perspective to the theological reorientation of ecclesiology as the doctrine of God's mission and its implementation in the world through God's called people. The American Lutheran missiologist James Scherer continued that tradition in English. Dutch Reformed mission theologians developed a comprehensive theology of mission that related to all of the theological disciplines and actually shaped the curriculum of at least two seminaries founded in the twentieth century solely for the research and teaching of mission for the equipping of Dutch Reformed missionaries. That legacy continues to shape the discussion in the work of missiologists such as Johannes Verkuyl and the South African David Bosch, whose textbook, *Transforming Mission,* defines the discipline of mission theology today internationally.[18] One can and should understand Karl Barth's dogmatic project as the theological formation of a church in the post-Christendom West that understands itself in terms of its vocation to be Christ's witness in the world. Lesslie Newbigin went out to India as a Scottish missionary in the 1930s, and returned in retirement to Britain in the 1970s to become the premier missiologist of the West, probing the challenges of the secularized context now recognized as an especially difficult mission field. He was the catalyst for what came to be known as the Gospel and Culture discussion, which in the 1980s began to spread to America. Here it became the Gospel and Our Culture Network, which published the research project *Missional Church* in 1998 as an appeal for a wide-ranging theological discussion of Newbigin's challenging question: If Western cultures have become post-Christian and post-Christendom mission fields, how do the churches located in these cultures become missionary churches?[19] The term "missional" was intended to

17. John A. Mackay, *Ecumenics: The Science of the Church Universal* (Englewood Cliffs, NJ: Prentice-Hall, 1964).

18. J. Verkuyl, *Contemporary Missiology: An Introduction* (Grand Rapids: Eerdmans, 1978); Bosch, *Transforming Mission.*

19. Darrell L. Guder, ed., *Missional Church: A Vision for the Sending of the Church in North America* (Grand Rapids: Eerdmans, 1998).

center the discussion on the fundamental purpose of the church as the agent, instrument, and sign of God's mission at work in the world.

This missional theological journey has been enriched by the recent publication of Cheryl Peterson's excellent proposal for an "ecclesiology for the twenty-first century." She moves the discussion ahead as she pointedly centers the debate around the question, "*Who* is the Church?"[20] The disintegration of Christendom has advanced to the point that it must now be clear that we are involved in a profoundly threatening theological identity crisis. To quote her: "It is not simply that the church is culturally irrelevant or inauthentic: these are symptoms of the underlying issue, which is that we don't know who we are as church" (p. 4). Her trenchant analysis of the current ecclesiological crisis, especially in North American Protestantism, is coupled with a thoughtful survey of major recent responses, which she addresses under three rubrics, "Church as World Event," "Church as Communion," and "The Missional Church." For someone who has some investment in the "missional church initiative" since the 1998 publication of the book with that title, I am grateful for the careful and balanced way in which she engages and appreciates the work that we have done. She is one of those who understands why the neologism "missional" was imposed upon the discussion, and who is contributing to the constructive advance of the discussion.

Lest, however, this very brief survey of the emergence of ecumenical theology out of the profound concern for the integrity and unity of Christian witness should be understood triumphalistically, it must be conceded, I think, that at every step of the way there has been resistance to the challenges to the ecclesial status quo. The problematic patterns of Constantinian establishment have proven to be deeply etched into the thinking and attitudes of Western Christianity. I have proposed that we investigate the ways in which established Western Christendom has proven to be reductionistic at crucial points. The two *key* expressions of that reductionism have to do with a gospel that is reduced to the savedness of the individual Christian, and a church that is reduced to the role of managing that savedness. It is reductionistic because it reduces the fullness and wonder of the apostolic gospel and its resulting vocation.

That gospel is about individual salvation, of course, but that salvation is defined by God's healing purposes for the created cosmos. The church is, to be sure, the community gathered by God to celebrate his grace revealed in

---

20. Cheryl Peterson, *Who Is the Church?: An Ecclesiology for the Twenty-First Century* (Minneapolis: Fortress Press, 2013).

Jesus Christ. But it is gathered not solely for its own sake but to serve God's healing purposes as witnesses and firstfruits of the work of salvation completed in Christ. That witness must always point to the salvation, the healing, which are both God's purpose and God's accomplishment at the cross and Easter. But the new creation that results from God's salvific action is good news for all the world, from Jerusalem, to Judea, to Samaria, to the ends of the earth. Its central and comprehensive creed is the ancient confession that Jesus Christ is Lord. The church's witness is to the inbreaking reign of God in Christ, the risen Lord, and the good news of life under God's rule.

The ecclesiocentricity that becomes more and more the target of missiological critique continues to shape the attitudes and practices of Christians and their congregations in late modernity. The actual theological shape of that ecclesiocentricity was described by Cardinal Avery Dulles whose classic theological treatise, *Models of the Church,* originally published in 1976, reviewed and analyzed the ecclesiological traditions of the West.[21] I suspect that many of you will have read his wonderful little book. He suggested that there were five basic models by which the church is defined and understood in the Western tradition (in a later edition, he added one more model to make it six). They are the church as institution, as mystical communion, as sacrament, as herald, and as servant. He defined each model by interrogating it with questions like these: What are the "bonds that unify the church"? Who are the "beneficiaries that are served by the church"? What is the "nature of the benefits bestowed by the church"?[22] He emphasizes that no single model exists in isolation from aspects of the others; ecclesial reality can be described as mixed church economies (to use Rowan Williams's phrase), in which aspects of all the models are present but certain emphases dominate. The first three models are largely represented by and summarize the ecclesiology of the Roman Catholic tradition. In all three of them, the beneficiaries of the church's existence are its members, and the benefit they receive is their own salvation and all that contributes to it. Only with the herald model, which is for Dulles the Protestant variant, does the focus shift from the members as beneficiaries to the world to which the church is sent as herald of good news. The servant model carries that forward with its emphasis upon the church's calling to serve the world in the imitation of Christ, the healer.

21. Avery Dulles, S.J., *Models of the Church* (Garden City, NY: Image Books, 1978, rev. 1987).

22. Dulles, *Models,* p. 45.

The discussion of the models and their various interpretive categories calls the pattern of ecclesiocentricity into question. Is the church an end in itself? Is its primary focus the spiritual welfare of its members? Is the purpose of the gospel the institution of the church? Or, to put it in the terms of a consumerist society like ours, is the primary purpose of the church to meet the religious needs of its members? Is it, in fact, the case that the actual mission of the church is its own maintenance? While there was growing agreement within the missiological discussion that the church was "missionary by its very nature," as Vatican II summarized the consensus, it has proven to be very difficult to move that profoundly missiological way of thinking into the life and practice of local congregations. Among the theologians and missiologists grappling with the challenges of global Christianity, the end of Western Christendom, and the multifaceted process called "secularization," the issues were recognized to be fundamentally biblical and theological. The collapse of the Constantinian project was increasingly recognized as a dangerous but crucial opportunity for the Christian movement to confront its compromises and captivities and to rediscover its missionary vocation.

But at the same time, the organizational challenges of denominational survival and success have called for a different expertise, an approach that focuses upon strategy, growth, innovation, efficiency, and success. A virtual cottage industry of church program consultants has emerged that borrows from the insights of secular organizational development and popular religious psychology to come up with effective ways to fight the decline and rebuild thriving churches. As it turns out, there are many who really continue to believe that the church exists primarily for its members, and its calling is to meet their religious needs. It is ironic that this very Protestant and often Evangelical focus upon members' needs has much in common with the benefits and beneficiaries of Dulles's first three models.

So, while the missional church discussion does resonate with many who are alert to the meaning of the end of Christendom and concerned about faithful Christian witness in a changing cultural context, it also evokes criticism from those who find it much too theological and not sufficiently focused upon strategies and methods to guarantee the church's institutional survival and ultimately its success. While the missional church initiative assumes that the end of Christendom is both a challenge and an opportunity, there is a strong and vocal movement, at least in the United States, that is energetically seeking ways to restore Christendom and to reclaim the cultural hegemony we once had but have now lost. That is the agenda of much of the conservative right wing in America.

We have surveyed the modern ecumenical movement in terms of its rootedness in the passionate desire for the unity of Christian witness. We have seen how that energy from the so-called non-Western churches spurred a theological exploration that ultimately led Western ecclesiologists to enter into a profoundly unsettling and threatening investigation of the church's purpose, its calling, and its cultural captivities and reductionisms. The ecumenical vision, as we have seen, has fostered an impressive spectrum of initiatives, experiments, and innovations, and there is much there for which we can only praise God and express our gratitude. But there is a widespread sense today that the ecumenical movement is in the doldrums. The visionary passion that inspired a Church of South India seems to have abated. What has happened to the ecumenical idea? Could it be the case that this century-old movement is now engaged in its own identity crisis, to borrow Cheryl Peterson's theme? It is to this question that we turn in part two.

Part Two

What might be the evidence that backs up my claim that the ecumenical movement appears to be in the doldrums? It is certainly not meant as a disavowal of the many impressive accomplishments in the movement's first century. Global Christianity is clearly in a very different place today, compared to its situation at the time of the Edinburgh Conference. My survey was intended only to illustrate the complex and enormously diverse ways in which ecumenism has developed and continues to flourish. But, at the same time, we cannot ignore the ways in which the ecumenical vision appears to be faltering. Without going into great detail, I point to factors like these:

The organizational weakening of major ecumenical institutions, which can partially be understood as the ripple effect of the decline of ecumenically engaged denominations primarily on both sides of the North Atlantic, and the resulting loss of financial resources. The financial struggles of the ecumenical agencies located in Geneva are well known. For a long time the question has been raised as to whether it represents the best stewardship to continue maintaining these agencies in one of the most expensive cities in the world. The World Communion of Reformed Churches, after being part of the Ecumenical Center in Geneva since the mid-twentieth century, has just moved its headquarters to Hannover, Germany, where it is being hosted by the Reformed Church there. We can point to similar fiscal struggles with national, state, and local councils of churches — many in the United States have quietly folded their tents. As we all know, the denominational resources to support such organizations have been dwindling now for a long time.

The debate within united or uniting churches about the impact of their own unions. Not a few voices within various union churches are looking back on their history thus far and asking if their union efforts have resulted in increased vitality in their communities. There does not appear to be much evidence that the general decline of Western Christendom has been in any way forestalled by these efforts. I have heard more than one colleague from a united church comment about the excellent theological work that was done in the process of uniting, and the subsequent loss of engagement with that theological legacy as they struggle with elemental institutional survival. Even the Church of South India is now challenged to ask hard questions about its ongoing historical development. Speaking as one of its own, Joseph Gnanaseelan Muthuraj asked his colleagues in 2010: "Does the modern CSI preserve, maintain and re-kindle the glow of faith, hope, courage that were demonstrated in the words and actions of those who were responsible for the birth of the united church in South India?"[23] The question is raised after a searching analysis of internal problems, especially with the role and function of the episcopacy in the CSI, which was one of its most distinctive and innovative contributions to the ecumenical process.

The proliferation of diverse forms of ecumenical networks in the decades since the formation of the World Council of Churches. There are many examples of international and ecumenical networks that, in one way or another, take up the Edinburgh legacy of cooperation for the sake of witness. The ecumenical movement has become organizationally pluralistic. Although one can and should see in the emergence of, say, the Lausanne Committee for World Evangelization from 1974 onwards an expression of that ecumenical vision, it is clearly also a reaction to aspects of the institutional Ecumenical Movement that is critical and unavoidably also competitive. The reactionary and competitive character of this ecumenical proliferation is, of course, directly related to the way in which the Ecumenical Movement has developed under the aegis of its primary institutional agency the World Council of Churches. This leads us to the next factor contributing to the doldrums of the movement.

The decades of controversy within the World Council about the basic understanding of mission and its practice. This factor requires a bit of

23. Joseph Gnanaseelan Muthuraj, *We Began at Tranquebar* (Delhi: Indian Society for the Promotion of Christian Knowledge, 2010), p. 296.

background. In 1959, Lesslie Newbigin interrupted his missionary service as Bishop of the Church of South India and returned to London to lead the International Missionary Council as it prepared to be merged with the World Council of Churches. That merger famously took place at the New Delhi Assembly of the World Council in 1961. Newbigin, speaking on behalf of the IMC constituency and celebrating this merger, saw it as the public affirmation that the church and its mission were inseparably linked. The essentially "missional" character of the church's purpose and practices were to shape the ecumenical process from New Delhi onward. In his new role as the Director of the Commission on World Mission and Evangelism, which was the continuation of the IMC legacy within the WCC, Newbigin set about the task of ensuring that "when we say mission we say church, and when we say church we say mission." Within a few years, he returned to a bishopric in the CSI. In the years that followed, it became progressively clear that the ecumenical vision was now being interpreted in diverse and sometimes contradictory ways. Much of the evangelical mission world refused to join the Geneva process. One could qualify that by saying that they could not join the Geneva process, because the World Council was an organization of churches with no membership option for mission societies and agencies. For decades there was intense debate about the Ecumenical Movement's basic understanding of mission. We already referred to the critique of the modern mission movement as one ongoing dimension of the ecumenical process worldwide. These debates tended more and more to polarize into the theologically questionable distinction between evangelism and social justice. It is a very complicated story that defies quick and easy summaries. The conflicts continue to simmer, which is certainly a problem for the theologically and ecclesially constructive advance of the Ecumenical Movement today. It must be emphasized, however, that on both sides of this controversy, there have always been persons and groupings who were committed to a more holistic understanding of unity and mission and who have sought ways to advance that synthesis. As evidence of concrete contributions in that spirit I refer to the remarkable CWME document of 1982, *Mission and Evangelism: An Ecumenical Affirmation.*[24] This is the outcome of an ecumenical drafting process that drew together a great diversity of representatives of global Christianity and arrived at a consensus on the theology of mission and evangelism that was truly ecumenical, unapologetically gospel centered, and concretely

---

24. *Mission and Evangelism: An Ecumenical Affirmation* (Geneva: World Council of Churches, 1982).

relevant to the challenges facing the member churches in their myriad of contexts. Its widespread grateful reception was proof that the ecumenical theological process was functioning productively. Most recently, the Commission on World Mission and Evangelism has developed a document that does not replace but leads on from and builds upon the 1982 statement. It is titled *Together Toward Life: Mission and Evangelism in Changing Landscapes,* and it was presented and adopted by the General Assembly of the World Council at Busan in 2013. It should be welcomed and will, I trust, receive the same kind of constructive reception given to the 1982 document. I earnestly hope that it will serve to bridge the tensions and draw together the energies of ecumenists all along the theological spectrum so that the "unity we seek" may begin to take concrete shape.

The Curious Journey of the Consultation on Church Union (COCU) in the United States. I have already referred to this forty-year project, initiated by Blake and Pike in the 1960s, as an example of the ecumenical vision's taking on concrete shape. Its decades of work generated some remarkably constructive theological resources for the quest for unity. Like the documentation that accompanied the negotiation of the Church of South India, the COCU documentary history is a wonderful resource for serious theological engagement of the church's vocation as both missional and united. The history of its proposals for a church that would unite all nine of its member denominations, and possibly more, is less edifying. They evoked virtually no support from COCU's constituencies. The process finally ended in 2002 with the formation of an organization called Churches Uniting in Christ (CUIC). With all respect for this attempt to advance the ecumenical vision, it is not resulting in any concrete steps toward visible unity. At least in the Presbyterian Church U.S.A. there is virtually no awareness of its existence. This brings us to perhaps the most discouraging aspect of our ecumenical journey:

The abandonment of any serious concern for the unity of the church as mainline denominations grapple with both their decline and the virulent theological and ethical controversies that are contributing to it. I need not explain to you the realities of our present-day decline. Every denominational tradition that, on this side of the North Atlantic, continues an expression of Western Christendom in Europe (that is how I define "mainline") is threatened today with disintegration. None of us knows what our various denominations will actually look like twenty years from now. We are struggling with deeply painful splits and divisions that are consuming our energies and polluting our witness. It is a perplexing and hurtful irony that denominations that have long been characterized by ecumenical commitment, that have themselves gone through processes of church union, and that have provided leadership to the ecumenical level at the international level, are today experiencing and fostering divisions that, to put it bluntly, are a massive renunciation of those ecumenical convictions and commitments. Given all that has happened under the large symbol of the ecumenical movement, it is a truly sad passage that jeopardizes missional ecumenism.

This crisis constitutes, I think, the major challenge confronting the ecumenical movement in the West today. However, it is not easy to explain just why it is happening in denominations with long and well-documented commitments to the ecumenical vision. One might consider the possibility that the ecumenical commitment has always been more focused at the level of church administrations and hierarchies. Local congregations, in America's voluntarist and entrepreneurial polities, have generally been less enthusiastic about ecumenical cooperation beyond joint Good Friday worship services and shared efforts to address social problems such as homelessness and hunger. Our incredibly pluralistic mosaic of local churches makes the United States unique among virtually all the nations of the world. It is only in America that one can encounter a crossroads with a different church on each corner. And it continues to be likely that these churches have relatively little contact with each other. As the financial problems grow, and congregations become less viable, new forms of cooperation and even partnership are beginning to surface. But it would be fair to say that the ecumenical vision has never had as strong a base of support in congregations as did, say, the foreign mission movement until the latter third of the twentieth century.

My hunch is that the primary reasons for this ironic tolerance of divisiveness on the part of ecumenically committed churches are more complicated than those sociological and demographic factors. I suspect that the issues are, at bottom, deeply theological, and that they are related to the questions of the church's purpose, vocation, practices, and identity that have emerged in the twentieth century and that constitute the agenda of what many call "ecumenical theology." The intention of the term "missional church" is to address precisely such questions. As Christendom ends, we encounter more and more evidences of the difficult legacy we have inherited from its long history. We can only understand who we are today by investigating how we got here. This calls for a carefully calibrated study and interpretation of the Christendom history of Western Christianity, an engagement that requires dialectical sensitivity. The Constantinian project from the fourth century onward continues to shape us profoundly: as I said, its attitudes and assumptions are deeply embedded in our culture and shape our context, even as the project is disintegrating. May I add a cautionary note with regard to how we deal with our Christendom legacy? We should learn from the Leuenberg approach that it is arrogant to stand in judgment over the generations of Christians who precede us in the West. It is an unallowable judgmentalism to dismiss the faith and testimony of earlier generations of Christians because of our alleged clearer vision of our call. God has been present and faithful through all the generations of Christendom, regardless of how reductionist and even heretical its message and practices might have been. So, while we must practice fearless criticism and deal with inherited distortions and problems, we do so with a sense of gratitude for God's faithfulness over the centuries. It is helpful to bear in mind Karl Barth's characterization of the course of human history as a process defined by the providence of God and, at the same time, human confusion.

When it comes to the unity of the church, and especially to the essential bond between unity and mission, I would contend that our formation as citizens of Christendom has left us completely unable either to define or to envision what Christian unity might look like when the unity established by Christendom begins to disappear. To explain what I mean, I would like to turn to an interpretation of the Nicene marks of the church, which, since the publication of the study *Missional Church* in 1998, has become more and more persuasive for me. I note with appreciation that Cheryl Peterson has also discovered the missional resource represented by the Nicene marks, so that our interpretations are complementary. Our investigation is framed by the question: How did the New Testament communities and the apostolic mission that founded them understand the unity of the church? It was clearly a very major concern, as evidenced by biblical discourses like the high priestly prayer of Jesus in John 17, the entire argument of Ephesians, Paul's challenging of divisiveness in the Corinthian church, and his exposition of imitation and mentoring in Philippians. The character of that unity is not defined in institutional terms, however. There is clearly evidence that congregations were organized. But there is very little detail about how that was done. There was no centralized headquarters of the Christian movement, neither in Jerusalem nor in Antioch nor in Rome. In the salutation of his epistle to the Philippians Paul mentioned the overseers and deacons, never to mention them again in the entire book. Following the *textus classicus* in John, the emphasis is clearly upon the apostolic witness, which can only take place in communities that are unified under and shaped by the Trinitarian mission: "As thou didst send me into the world, so I have sent them into the world. . . . I do not pray for these only, but also for those who believe in me through their word, that they may all be one; even as thou, Father, art in me, and I in thee, that they may also be in us, so that the world may believe that thou hast sent me" (John 17:18, 20-21).

This unity is far more than forms and practices of cooperation and partnership, as we have interpreted it since Edinburgh. It is a unity that is given with the call to follow Christ and that is true and active in every community that is seeking to carry out that vocation. Thus Paul admonishes the Ephesians to be "eager to *maintain* the unity of the Spirit in the bond of peace" (Eph. 4:3). To understand what the "unity of the Spirit in the bond of peace" looks like, we must make our way to a theological understanding of unity that emerges out of the apostolicity, the catholicity, and the holiness of the called, gathered, equipped, and sent community. We need to interpret the Nicene marks in the reverse order.[25]

Apostolicity is the foundational and definitive characteristic of the missional church. The church is defined by its sentness. The apostolic generation initiated the church's mission, beginning in Jerusalem, moving out into Judea, crossing over to the other side of the tracks in Samaria, and spreading outward to the ends of the earth. The purpose of that apostolic mission was not simply the saving of souls, as Christendom's reductionism would have it, but the formation of communities that were to continue that witness to the inbreaking reign of Jesus Christ as Savior and Lord. The purpose of each apostolic church was its continuing mission, its translation of its apostolic mandate into the particular context in which God had placed it. Thus, apostolicity is fundamentally missional, and not just genealogical. We are not only building upon the foundation laid by the apostles, we are incorporated into their history as it continues from one sent community to the next. Everything that the community is, does, and says is defined by this apostolic identity and purpose. The Nicene marks read backwards define the true church in terms of its vocation. Karl Barth makes the same point when he insists, in his exposition of the gospel of reconciliation, that justification and sanctification must lead into and take concrete shape in vocation. That vocation is to be Christ's witness, as is made plain by our Lord's statement in Acts 1:8: "You shall be my witnesses." If our Christian identity is not drawn into and shaped by our vocation, if God's mission does not reorient the church from itself to the world in which it is sent, then we are reducing the church to a *Heilanstalt,* the salvation institution of reductionist Christendom.

---

25. The argument here revisits the question of the missional interpretation of the Nicene marks discussed in chapter 6, and represents my continuing work on this theme.

That foundational and formative apostolicity of the church takes concrete form in the catholicity of the church. Rather than interpreting this Nicene mark with the term "universal," Justo González and Nicholas Lossky, among others, suggest that we should understand it in terms of the word picture in the Greek term: *kat' holon* — in accordance with the whole. The *holon*, they suggest, is the historical gospel, the life, death, resurrection, and reign of Jesus Christ. That event continues to shape human history in the necessary translation of the gospel from one culture to the next. While the *kat'* part takes the context seriously, the *holon* ensures that it is the same central and unique event that is being translated and thus expanding the witness to the ends of the earth. The apostolic vocation is and, since Pentecost, has always been multicultural, multilingual, and multi-organizational. Contextual diversity, not institutional uniformity, is essential to the unity we seek. It is the demonstration of the Spirit actively at work that the translation happens, that new witnessing communities are constantly being formed, and that the reign of Jesus Christ, the one and only Lord, continues to be acknowledged and witnessed to. It is especially relevant today, as we learn what it means to be part of a global movement, that our witness to the world is always centered in and defined by Jesus the Christ and yet is culturally as diverse as the cultural families of humanity. This is the missional significance of catholicity, which Lamin Sanneh defines in terms of the infinite translatability of the gospel.[26]

This apostolic and catholic witness is then to be holy. It is to be shaped and equipped by God's Spirit for God's service. The obedience to which the Christian community is called is an enabled obedience: God's Spirit is at work in the community to make it a faithful witness, corporately and personally. In the language of Paul in 2 Corinthians 3, the Holy Spirit is at work in the community to write the Christians gathered as Christ's letter to the world. The holiness of the church has to do with all of those imperatives in the New Testament, directed to witnessing communities not as the steps they must take to be saved, but as their formation as recipients of the grace of salvation so that they can witness to it. Almost one hundred of those imperatives are formed with the reflexive pronoun *allelon*, "one another." The holiness, the "set-apartness" of the Christian community, focuses first of all on its corporate witness in its place. And that focus is very much upon all the ways that the community demonstrates the gospel not only in its speech but in its actions.

---

26. Lamin Sanneh, *Translating the Message: The Missionary Impact on Culture* (Maryknoll, NY: Orbis, 1991).

In preparation for the 1989 World Council Conference on Mission and Evangelism in San Antonio, Lesslie Newbigin was asked to provide a Bible study on the theme "Mission in Christ's Way."[27] This study in effect engages the meaning and practice of the holiness of the apostolic community. The concern is for the congruence of the community's message with its publicly lived life. That is the purpose of the biblical formation of holy communities: that they should be credible evidence of the healing power of the gospel. "Mission in Christ's Way" has become an important and formative theme in ecumenical theology. It must, of course, deal contritely with those problematic episodes of mission history in which that necessary congruence was absent. The holiness of the church was denied when the gospel of peace was proclaimed hatefully, the gospel of grace was announced judgmentally, and the gospel of healing was expressed in ways that wound. For the formation of the missional community, the holiness of the church entails joining the disciples in the four Gospels to experience Jesus as the teacher who is equipping his students to become his "sent ones." If they are to be able to do that, they must learn to see the world through the eyes of Jesus, who embodies God's love for the world in who he is, what he says, and all he does. As they learn to do mission in Christ's way, they are enabled by God's sanctifying Spirit to serve God as Christ's ambassadors, as light, as leaven, as salt.

Out of apostolicity, catholicity, and holiness, unity emerges as the shape of Christian witness in the world. This must result in a definition and practices of unity that are radically different from the organizational approaches that see unity as a structural issue. The legacy of Christendom with the establishment of the church in a privileged relationship with state and society has created an entirely different way of imagining unity. The unity of the church is inextricably involved in issues of power, wealth, property, influence, and organization. Oneness has been for centuries defined in terms of submission to the church's hierarchy. Going back to Constantine, it has been a sensitive issue in the relationship of church and state. An established church that is divided constitutes a major problem for an authoritarian state, which needs to have its major religious agency well aligned with its institutional priorities. The religious wars that followed upon the Reformation were all about the political necessity of the unity of state churches under their worldly governors.

Even after the introduction of the separation of church and state, the unity of the Western church, or better, churches, continues to be under-

27. Lesslie Newbigin, *Mission in Christ's Way: A Gift, a Command, an Assurance* (New York: Friendship Press, 1988).

stood in institutional ways that focus upon power, constitutional process, and methods of decision-making. Realism about institutional realities continues to influence the ecumenical process in most of Western Christendom, so that there is very little tangible engagement in endeavors to bring about the visible, concrete unity of a church that radically rejects the theological justification of its denominational pluralism. The goal of visible and concrete unity, which was Newbigin's unabashed vision and commitment, is modified in most of our ecclesial contexts by the focus upon cooperation, federation, association, mutual recognition.

The challenge for the ecumenical movement is to allow this Nicene process of formation to transform our understanding and expectations of unity. The unity that characterizes the apostolic church is a crucial form of witness exercised by the gathered community in the world into which God is sending it. Its unity is not, therefore, an internal matter, but has to do with the public character of the local congregation. It is essential to its mission. The crux for missional witness is our Lord's instruction of the disciples in what he calls his new commandment: ". . . that you love one another; even as I have loved you, that you also love another. By this all people will know that you are my disciples, if you have love for one another" (John 13:34-35). Paul is carrying out the same kind of missional formation with the Philippian community when he prays for them "that your love may abound more and more, with all knowledge and discernment, that you may approve what is excellent . . ." (Phil. 1:9).

Understanding the unity of the church as its witness shaped by apostolicity, expressed in its catholicity, equipped by its holiness, will require a major reorientation for Christian communities shaped by Christendom. Newbigin argued that the goal should be understood as "reunion," as the reclamation of what is fundamentally true of the church in that it is called into being by God's Spirit, empowered to believe and to witness by the Spirit, and serves God's healing purposes in the world. That is, as I said, why Paul appeals to the Ephesians "to *maintain* the unity of the Spirit in the bond of peace." Such unity, as witness, emerges out of repentance. Newbigin puts it plainly: "All disunity among Christians is a contradiction of that upon which their being Christians rests. It has the character of sin, being a repudiation of the God-given nature of the Church. The quest for unity must therefore be regarded not as an enterprise of men aimed at constructing something new, but as a penitent return to that which was originally given but subsequently denied."[28]

---

28. Lesslie Newbigin, "The Nature of the Unity We Seek," *Religion in Life* 26, no. 2 (1957): 182.

The missional witness of the unified church requires that this unity be visible. This is the basic conviction of "missional ecumenism" as I understand it. To cite Newbigin again: "The unity we seek is a visible unity . . . visible to the world, a sign by which the world may be brought to faith in Christ as the Apostle of God and the Mediator of his love."[29] But, Newbigin hastens to add, this does not necessarily mean that the visible church will be a "large ecclesiastical organization." If apostolicity and catholicity are to define unity, then the emphasis upon public witness will mean that every gathered community, in its cultural and organizational distinctiveness, is constantly demonstrating to a watching world that it is but one expression of a global community of infinitely diverse communities that all serve the same Lord, proclaim the same message, and support one another as the brothers and sisters they are because they are God's children.

Obviously, as heirs of Christendom with its politicized approaches to the structuring of church institutions, we cannot imagine what that unity might look like. If we could, then we would be dealing with the current controversies that are splitting our churches in very different ways. We would be asking about the ways in which New Testament communities are challenged to deal with their conflicts as a tangible witness to the watching world that the reign of Christ does, in fact, radically alter corporate conduct to make it "worthy of the calling with which we have been called." We would be asking ourselves about the apostolic passion for unity demonstrated in the way the New Testament church dealt with the Jewish/Gentile controversy. We would read 1 Corinthians as a primer for the witness of unity in a context of intense debate and outright disagreement. We would recognize that, from Pentecost onwards, the Christian community has struggled with issues of profound importance about which there was no consensus. Dealing with such debates in a way that demonstrated God's healing love at the center of the community was the practice of unity defined by apostolicity, catholicity, and holiness.

The unity we seek is a given, a gift, a struggle, and a promise. Newbigin emphasizes that the unity we seek is "one into which we have to be perfected."[30] It will proceed out of corporate repentance and testify to our dependence upon God's healing and forgiving grace. The church knows itself to live and act as a community that is *simul justus et peccator* (simultaneously justified and sinner). Expressing our apostolic vocation through catholic diversity, our unity will serve and incarnate our mission as we form com-

29. Newbigin, "The Nature of the Unity We Seek," p. 186.
30. Newbigin, "The Nature of the Unity We Seek," p. 187.

munities whose public life, quoting Newbigin, "ensures that wherever and whenever Christians meet together they . . . know themselves to be, and should be known to be, one family with the whole family of Christ from the day of Pentecost till today, and that this knowledge of unity should be a matter not only of inner experiences but also of recognizable outward signs."[31]

This is the vision and the challenge of "missional ecumenism": the centered and multicultural confession that the church is apostolic, catholic, holy, and therefore one. The challenge entails the church's risking the enabled obedience that translates our calling into public corporate conduct that is worthy of the calling with which we have been called.

31. Newbigin, "The Nature of the Unity We Seek," p. 187.,